REMINISCENCES OF A
19TH CENTURY GLADIATOR

The Autobiography of John L. Sullivan

JOHN L. SULLIVAN

Heavyweight Champion of the World

Edited
by
JAMES BISHOP

Promethean Press

Reminiscences of a 19th Century Gladiator

Promethean Press
PO Box 5572
Frisco, TX 75035
www.promethean-press.com

Manufactured in the United States of America

ISBN 978-0-9810202-3-5

TABLE OF CONTENTS

Foreword   **3**

Introduction   **7**

Chapter One: Boyhood and Boxing Beginnings   **11**

Chapter Two: Rounds of the Pugilistic Ladder   **21**

Chapter Three: The Championship Reached   **35**

Chapter Four: Two "Artful Dodgers" from England   **53**

Chapter Five: Victories With The Gloves   **61**

Chapter Six: Greatest "Knock-Out" Tour On Record   **73**

Chapter Seven: Big Glove Engagements   **81**

Chapter Eight: From New England to Old England   **97**

Chapter Nine: Battles Both Sides of the Atlantic   **109**

Chapter Ten: Pacific Ocean Voyage   **123**

Chapter Eleven: Rules of the Ring   **145**

Chapter Twelve: Training and Diverse Topics   **153**

Chapter Thirteen: From New England to Old England   **163**

ADDENDUM

The Fall of John L. Sullivan   **181**

Sullivan's Sorrowful Return   **186**

Sullivan Benefit in New York   **187**

Sullivan Talks Out   **190**

A Pupil of Ananias   **193**

John L. Sullivan's Word   **194**

John L. Sullivan "Broke"   **195**

John L. Sullivan's Busy Day   **196**

John L. Sullivan Bankrupt   **197**

Sullivan Spent a Fortune   **198**

John L. Sullivan Sees Roosevelt   **200**

John L. Sullivan's Nephew Pardoned   **201**

John L. Sullivan's Views On the Big Fight   **202**

Corbett's Unpleasant Remarks to Former Champion Now Forgotten   **204**

The Boston Strong Boy   **207**

John L. Sullivan to Retire   **212**

John L. Sullivan Farming   **213**

John L. Sullivan Opens Campaign Against Drink 214
John L. Sullivan, 59, Dies Suddenly 217
Roosevelt Lauds Sullivan 219
Memorial Service for Dead Gladiator 116
Corbett at Sullivan Bier 116
John L. Sullivan Buried 116
Physical Examination of John L. Sullivan 116

FOREWORD

Old John L. has been a greater power for good in this country than many a highly respectable person who would scorn to meet him on terms of equality. He has been my friend many years, and I am proud to be his.

Old John has many excellent qualities including a high degree of self-respect. He also has a large measure of native ability. I know that his former profession is not a very exalted one, but he was a fair fighter, he never threw a fight, and, in his way, he did his best to uphold American supremacy. Do you remember his little speech when Corbett defeated him - gratification that it was an American who whipped him?

John's best fight, however, was made after he lost to Corbett. I mean his whipping John Barleycorn. That was a real victory, and I am proud of him for having made it. Since then I believe he has been the most effective temperance lecturer I have known of. He has been effective because he could appeal to classes of men and boys others, however gifted, could never hope to reach. His hold on the public has been longer maintained than any other champion I ever heard of. Men and boys would go to hear him, and the old fellow's honesty was convincing. I like John for this contribution to good citizenship.

I admired him in his prime. He was a good fighter and clean. I liked his willingness to meet all comers as fast as they came. This marked the real champion and explains why, in defeat, he is still a popular idol.

John is an old friend. He used to call at the White House occasionally just as he sometimes calls at Sagamore Hill. Once he called at the White House on a personal matter - he told my secretary it was personal and I saw him at once. After we had shaken hands, he laid a heavy black cigar on the desk.

"Have a cigar, Mr. President," he said.

I told him I did not smoke.

"Have another - give 'em to a friend," he replied, laying another on the desk.

The social amenities having been attended to, I asked what I could do for him.

"I come to see you about a nephew," said he, "my favorite nephew. He is in the navy and in trouble."

John explained that he had enlisted in the Marines, got into trouble of some sort, and deserted, for which he was sentenced to a dishonorable discharge.

"Now, Colonel," said he, "that's something we can't have. We don't

3

want anything like that in our family. He's a good boy, Colonel, just a trifle wild. I wish you could have him in hand a little while. You'd fix him.

"It's a tough case, too, Colonel," he went on. "Here's this boy, my favorite nephew; I've done everything for him, but he doesn't do anything for himself. Why, he even went and took up music."

John did not explain whether he had taken up violin or barrel-organ, but he left no doubt that he felt this was beneath the Sullivan dignity.

The boy was all right. I was glad to do what I could for John. Since then he's told me the boy has done well. I failed to ask, however, if he persisted in music.

I [once] had two visitors [at the Harvard Club], Archbishop John Ireland and John L. Sullivan, both old friends. And would you believe it, the young barbarians, fresh from the refining influences of my venerable Alma Mater, paid more attention to the pugilist than they did to the prelate! Had they known that John Ireland had a record as a first-class fighting man in the army and since, it might have been different. As it was, to talk straight New York, they fell for the fighter, but couldn't see the man of the Church.

It might interest you to know that old John and the Archbishop are rather good friends. Their common interest is temperance, and they had a real good chat. John thinks the Archbishop is all right, and the Archbishop respects John's good qualities. Under other conditions the Archbishop thinks John might have made a splendid churchman. I don't.

John was intended for a prizefighter, and it would have been too bad to spoil the best fighter of them all and make, perhaps, a second-rate clergyman, with, probably, less real power for good than old John has exercised. I told His Grace this, but of course he could not be expected to concede as much as that. He does, however, think well of John.

Of course it may be said that Sullivan was better than his profession. This, in large measure, is true. I liked old Bob Fitzsimmons, but as a man he was not to be compared to Sullivan - he had the fighting instinct all right, but he lacked Sullivan's brain. Sullivan has had little more schooling than Fitz, but he has profited more by his travels and he is better informed on most matters than most men who have had no better opportunity in school work than he has had.

That, however, is not the secret of his holding his own with the public. That's to be explained by his rugged honesty and the fact that he was a champion who was always willing to fight.

After all, there is a lot of the primal man in most of us.

Theodore Roosevelt

Adapted from the book, Talks With TR, *by John J. Leary*
Houghton Mifflin Company, 1920

INTRODUCTION

"Are you going to stay caged up here all day?"

"Yes; rather than run the gauntlet of the gang laying for me in front of your hotel. Do you know if I ventured out there now I would be grabbed by the arms and legs and almost pulled to pieces by fellows that want to feel my muscle?"

The scene was in a Western city, and was one of many encountered by the speaker.

"That's him sure."

"No."

"I tell you he went up that way."

"Big?"

"You bet. Hold on till he comes down," - were some of the ejaculations heard from the crowd that swayed in the office and surged in the street."

"Why, I am not safe even in this private room. Only a little while ago the door was opened with a bang and a chap with a tragic stride and stagy voice" -

"Is it him?" was the interruption just at that moment from a gawky looking Paul Pry, who peered through the door. "Is it him?"

The bent of his curiosity seemed to have turned his nose into a corkscrew and his neck into an interrogation mark.

"It is him - now go."

In spite of this assurance he continued in a kind of litany, with "Is it him?" until, in a moment when he had just reached "Is it" - the "him" rose with the rage of Hercules crushing the hydra and hurled the animated question from the room.

"It is him!" was heard in the hallway, and between the sounds of halting steps, and as he stumbled down the stairs his words arose like the "Excelsior" of the Alpine youth, "It *is* him!"

This is the style in which they tell of the curiosity to see the champion out West, and it may be taken as a sample of what has met him during his career with all degrees of dignity, from that of the Prince in England to the native in Samoa.

The author, now that he has decided to round out the career which gave rise to it, does not desire to remain any longer "caged up," but to present himself as far as he may be of interest on the printed page.

"Oh, that my adversary would write a book," was the saying of one who believed that an author always makes himself a mark for attack. In spite of this I am willing for once to drop my guard, ceasing to lead off, to feint, to fib, to duck or ward, allowing my head to be held in chancery between the covers of a book, and yet looking for lively cross-counter dealings.

Yours Truly,

John L. Sullivan

REMINISCENCES

OF A

19TH CENTURY

GLADIATOR

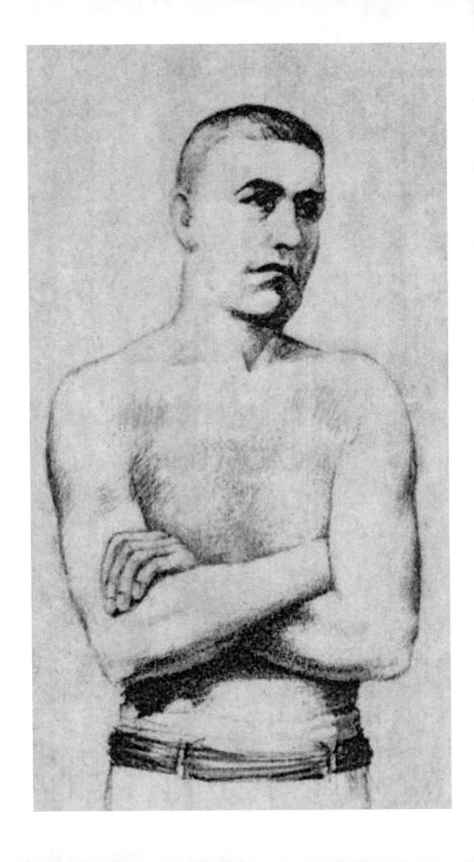

CHAPTER ONE
BOYHOOD AND BOXING BEGINNINGS

I was born on the 15th of October, 1858, in Boston, my parents then occupying a house on Harrison Avenue, nearly opposite Boston College, the location being about that of the new Homoeopathic Dispensary. Here we lived until I was ten years of age, when we moved, successively, to Parnell and Lenox streets and Boston Highlands.

My father was a native of the town of Tralee, in County Kerry, Ireland, and my mother of Athlone, in County Roscommon. Both are now dead. The remainder of the family are a sister and a younger brother.

As I am the only one who has been noticed for size or strength, people have sometimes been curious to know from whom mine came, particularly as my father was a small man, being only five feet three and one half inches, and never weighing more than one hundred and thirty pounds. My mother was of fair size, weighing about one hundred and eighty pounds, and some have given the credit to her. One writer, after I had grown in reputation as an athlete, said: "Sullivan derived all his great physical strength from his mother, who in her youth was considered a woman of remarkable physical and mental powers." Whatever there may be in this, it should be borne in mind that my uncles and the other relatives of my father in Ireland were all large men, and were known in their section of the county by a Celtic word which might be translated as "the big Sullivans".

Here it may not be improper to mention the great family of Sullivans known in American history, as their father came from the same spot as mine, to settle in the same part of this country, and as they were remarkable for size and muscular strength, in addition to their powers as governors, generals and judges. John Sullivan was in 1774 a member of the first General Congress. In December of that year he took a leading part in the daring achievement of a party of American patriots who rowed by moonlight to the British fort, William and Mary, near Portsmouth, overpowered the force, and captured a hundred barrels of powder that were afterwards used at Bunker Hill. In this way a Sullivan has received the honor of striking the very first blow of the Revolution.

During the Revolution he was regarded as one of the most trustworthy officers in the service of Washington and was by his side on the Christmas Eve of 1776 when he crossed the Delaware and routed the British. After the success had been gained he was made Governor of

New Hampshire.

Governor James Sullivan of Massachusetts, his brother, was one of the commissioners appointed by Washington to settle the boundary lines between the United States and the British Provinces. His son of the same name was a man of physical as well as mental strength, and won reputation as a judge.

John L. Sullivan, another son of the governor of Massachusetts, possessed high ability, especially in science and engineering. He constructed the great Middlesex canal, which was the connection between Massachusetts and New Hampshire before railroads; and he also invented the first steam towboat, for which he was awarded a patent in preference to the famous Fulton.

The mother of the two Governor Sullivans, as might be expected, was a woman of much spirit. There is a story told of a visit which she paid to the governor of Massachusetts when he had as his guest his brother, John, of New Hampshire. The servant, not knowing her, informed her coldly that she could not see the governor - he was engaged.

"But I must see him," exclaimed the old lady.

"Then, madam, you will please wait in the anteroom."

"Tell your master," said she, sweeping out of the hall, "that the mother of two of the greatest men in America will not wait in anybody's anteroom."

The Governor having called his servant, on hearing the report said to his brother, "Let us run after her; it's mother for certain." Accordingly the two governors sallied out, and soon made amends for her offended dignity.

Like almost all Boston boys I was given good opportunities for education. I was first sent to the Primary School on Concord Street. My teacher there was Miss Blanchard, a lady that stood no nonsense from any of the boys. But she was good hearted and had as much interest in the poorer class of children as she had in the upper ten. After going through the primary school I went to the Dwight Grammar School on Springfield Street and graduated. I attended night school at the old Bath House, Cabot Street, which was afterwards turned into a voting place election house. I never had much trouble with the teachers in any of my school experience.

Miss Jones, of the grammar school, sent me one day for my medicine which I received at the hands of my old friend, Jimmy Page, who was principal or headmaster of the school. That was the only time that I ever had to take the rattan, which I did like a little man. It was commonly taken for granted that if a boy cried he was a weak one. I guess I wanted to cry but I couldn't, although he gave me what I deserved; and I was quite a hero after that among the other boys. During my school years in spare time and after school I played ball, marbles, spun tops, and did everything of the kind that boys do. I had no occupation to take up my attention after school hours, and of course went through all the sports that boys go through at that time of life.

As to my studies, I took better to mathematics than I did to anything else, and I was always on the lookout to avoid geography when it was geography day. My traveling experience has since given me more real facts about geography than I could have learned in a book in 10 years. In school days I had many a fracas with the other fellows, and I always came out on top. After leaving the public school I went to Comer's Commercial College, and attended about one year. From that I went to Boston College, Harrison Avenue, where I studied about 16 months. It was the desire of my parents to have me study for the priesthood, but it was not mine.

My first work was in the plumbing trade with the firm of Moffat & Perry. In those days it was the custom with boys, generally, when they wanted to become apprentices, to be bound to a trade by their father; in other words, a man signed a written contract to teach the trade so that the boy would become a master mechanic after learning the business. I had gone for a situation, and as I thought I would like plumbing, I got a position for myself. I worked at the plumbing trade for six months. When the water pipes in the old Williams Market, which had an armory overhead, at the corner of Dover and Washington streets, were frozen, a journeymen and myself were sent there. We went with all the necessary appliances which were used for thawing out pipes in the plumbing business, including a lighted torch and hot water, and after a half day's work at that, the journeyman and myself had some words, in which I told him that I thought I had carried water enough and that he could have a few hours at that work himself. This caused some feeling between us and resulted in our having a scrap over the affair, and he made his escape to the shop, which was only a few doors from where we were working. I was paid $4.00 a week for being an apprentice. The journeymen at that time were paid all the way from three to six dollars a day.

Naturally, after I left school, I joined baseball nines, among which were the Tremonts, Etnas, Our Boys, and several other clubs. As I was considered a pretty good baseball player, I had been offered $1,300 if I would play ball for the Cincinnati Club in the years 1879 and 1880.

I left the plumbing to learn the trade of a tinsmith with James Galvin, corner of Warren and Dudley streets, for whom I worked eighteen months, and quit on account of disagreement with a man who worked on the same bench, who had just become a journeyman as I became an apprentice. Then I went to playing baseball again with different amateur clubs.

The first time I ever put a boxing glove on was at a variety entertainment at Dudley Street Opera House, Boston Highlands, and when I went to the entertainment I did not expect to be called upon to do that; but at that entertainment there was a strong young fellow named Scannell, who stated to the audience that he was anxious to meet me or any one in the audience. I had the reputation of being able to hold my own with any young man, and, after considerable talking one way and the other, they asked me to put on the gloves with Scannell. I did not want to do so, but finally consented.

I was working at tinsmithing then, and had no tights nor had made any arrangements for boxing, but simply took off my coat, rolled up my shirt sleeves, and put on the gloves. When we put up our hands, he hit me a crack on the back of the head, and the first thing I did was to punch him as hard as I could, knocking him clean over the piano which was on the stage. This was the first actual experience of mine at boxing, and I will never forget this experience, nor do I think he will.

I quit my trade as a tinsmith because I could not agree with the journeyman who worked on the same bench with me. We argued a great many different subjects; about dogs, game cocks, baseball, and anything and everything in sporting circles, and a great many other things. We never could agree on anything, because he claimed he always had something better than anybody else. His dogs were better than any I had ever seen, his gamecock was better than any I had; in fact, anything I had was no account, and his was number one. Our quarrels and arguments kept up quite a while until finally he said one day something about proving to me that I was wrong, and wanted to fight it out to prove it, and when I said, "Alright; come out into the yard," he quit, and would not go. If ever I wanted to lick a man in the world, he was that one, and I would have given a good deal if he only would have come out. From that I went to the mason's trade, at which I worked about two years and learned that on account of having a better opportunity, as my father used to work at the business.

I played amateur baseball with a great many teams before I took to boxing. I was paid $25 a game for playing with the Eglestons, of which they would play two games a week - Wednesdays and Saturdays. For them I played principally first base and left field, although I could play in any position.

At the age of 19, I drifted into the occupation of a boxer. I went to meet all comers, fighting all styles and all manner of builds of men, until the present day. I never was taught to box; I have learned from observation and watching other boxers, and outside of that my style of fighting is perfectly original with me. Someone has said that old Professor Bailey claimed the credit of teaching me, but he was wrong in the assertion, as

I never took a boxing lesson in my life, having a natural ambition for the business.

I was always a big fellow, weighing 200 pounds at the age of 17, and I had the reputation for more than my proportionate share of strength.

I remember one time of a horse car getting off the track on Washington Street, and six to eight men trying to lift it on. They didn't succeed, and so I astonished the crowd by lifting it on myself. I used to practice such feats as lifting full barrels of flour and beer, or kegs of nails above my head, but I gave up those things as I found that men who did feats of strength made themselves too stiff for any good boxing. I could lift a dumbbell with the best, but I do not use more than a two-pounder, as it is nimbleness and skill that a boxer needs.

It was on account of these feats that I first got the name of "Strong Boy." There was a light boxer named Fairbanks that I called "Billy-go-lightly," and he replied by calling me "John, the Strong Boy."

Now that I have touched on the subject of nicknames, I may as well give a little list of titles that have been given to me after various victories in the ring, not with the idea that I endorse them myself, but that:

"A little nonsense, now and then,
Is relished by the wisest men."

"The Boston Hercules." "Knight of the Fives." "The hard-hitting Sullivan." "The Boston Miracle of huge muscles, terrific chest and marvelous strength." "The king of the ring." "The youthful prince of pugilists." "The magnificent Sullivan." "Boston's philanthropic prize-fighter." "Young Boston giant." "The finest specimen of physical development in the world." "The terrific Boston pugilist." "Trip-hammer Jack." "Spartacus Sullivan." "The king of pugilists." "Monarch of the prize ring." "The scientific American." "Hurricane hitter." "Mighty hero of biceps." "His fistic Highness." "Champion of champions." "Boston's pet." "Boston's pride and joy." "The cultured slugger." "Sullivan the Great." "The Napoleon Bonaparte of sluggers." "King of fistiana." "Sullivan the wonder." "The champion pounder." "Professor of bicepital forces." "Prize-fighting Caesar." "The Hercules of the ring." "The Goliath of the prize ring." "America's invincible champion." "A champion who never knew defeat."

Whatever I have attempted to do, I have always looked on the bright side, that is to say, that there is nothing I have undertaken to do, since I have reached the age of understanding, in which I have not made it a point to be successful. When going into a ring, I have always had it in my mind that I would be the conqueror. That has been my disposition particularly as to my fighting propensities.

The first time I ever started to spar in public with any noted man of reputation was with Johnny Woods, better known as "Cockey Woods," in Cockerill Hall, Hanover Street, Boston, in 1878. He was a resident of Boston, and was a big man who once was matched to fight Heenan, "The Benecia Boy." I soon disposed of him.

The following year, 1879, I sparred with Dan Dwyer, in Revere Hall, corner of Green and Chardon streets. He was considered a strong boxer. I had the best of the encounter, and surprised a great many of the wise ones who thought I would not be in it, as he was called "the champion of Massachusetts."

Another victory gained by me in those days was over Tommy Chandler, one of the "old timers," but not the "Tom" of Pacific coast fame. I sparred with Professor Mike Donovan at the Howard Athenaeum at his benefit, given him by his management and friends, in Boston, in which I wound up with him in three rounds and endeavored to knock him out, when the master of ceremonies made us shake hands and we departed to our dressing rooms.

In a conversation which took place while we were upstairs, he said to me, "You tried to knock me out."

I replied, "No, I did not try very hard."

He said, " Well, I will be honest, I tried to knock you out."

I then told him "I tried to knock him out and if I had landed it would have been all day with him."

When he went back to New York he said to Joe Goss, George Rooke, and all the knowing ones, that there was a fellow up in Boston by the name of Sullivan, who, in his estimation, was going to be the boss of them all.

Jack Hogan, of Providence, was another candidate who shared the fate of those mentioned.

The following year, 1880, on the sixth day of April, I demonstrated to the wise ones that I was to become to the world one of the greatest exponents of the manly art, by disposing of one of England's greatest champions, Joe Goss, at a testimonial given to him by his numerous friends at Music Hall, Boston, in which we sparred three rounds. In the second round I dealt him a blow which virtually ended the contest. Goss was given time to recover, and through the advice of Tom Denney and Billy Edwards, I sparred the last round without trying to knock him out, which I could have done. After this he was heard to remark that my blows were like " the kicks of a mule."

A writer describing the affair at the time said:

"Sullivan's terrific hitting on this occasion created quite a sensation."

Now one word about old Joe Goss. As a pugilist and a boxer, he was a gentleman in every respect, being of a kind-hearted, social, and of a genial disposition, and beloved by every one who knew him. I have seen Goss put his hand in his pocket to assist the needy, and one of his great hobbies was always to fondle and caress the little ones, of whom he was a great lover. From the first time we became acquainted, which was on the occasion of our boxing together, at his benefit, we became warm and personal friends, and continued so until the hour of his death.

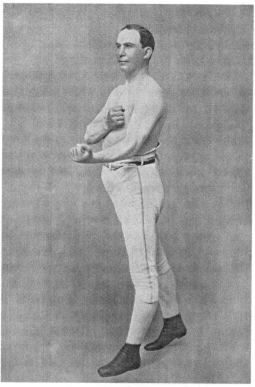

Joe Goss

As Goss had fought some of the best men in England and America, and this encounter naturally leads up to my battling for the championship of the world, I find it a fitting occasion to bring up here the records of the English champions from the time of Tom Figg, when the science of boxing was coming into shape, down to the present. The names of the fighters and the dates of great events are as follows:

1719 - Tom Figg
1734 - George Taylor
1740 - Jack Broughton
1750 - Jack Slack
1760 - Bill Stevens
1761 - George Meggs
1764 - Bill Darts
1769 - Tom Lyons
1777 - Harry Sellers
1780 - Harris
1785 - Tom Jackling (alias Johnson)
1790 - Ryan (Big Ben)
1792 - Mendoza

1795 - Jackson (retired)

1803 - Jem Belcher

1805 - Pearce (the Game Chicken)

1808 - Gulley (declined the office)

1809 - Tom Cribb (received a belt, not transferable, and cup)

1824 - Tom Spring (received four cups, and resigned office)

1825 - Jem Ward (received a belt, not transferable)

1833 - Deaf Burke (claimed the office)

1839 - Bendigo (W. Thompson), (beat Deaf Burke, claimed champi-onship, and received a belt from Jem Ward)

1841 - Caunt (beat Nick Ward, and received belt by subscription; this belt was transferable)

1845 - Bendigo (beat Caunt and got the belt, but declined to fight again)

1850 - Perry (the Tipton Slasher), after his fight with Paddock, claimed the office, as Bendigo declined fighting again)

1851 - Harry Broome (beat Perry, and succeeded to the office).

1853 - Perry again claimed the office (Harry Broome, having forfeited to him in a match, and retired from the ring).

1856 - Tom Paddock (beat H. Broome for £200 a side and the title).

1857 - Tom Sayers (beat Perry for £200 a side, and the new belt).

1860 - Tom Sayers retired after his fight with Heenan, leaving the old belt open for competition.

1860 - Tom Hurst (the Staleybridge Infant), beat Paddock. Both claimed the office of champion. The belt was handed to Hurst.

1861 - Jem Mace (beat Hurst).

1863 - Tom King beat Mace and claimed the belt, which he subsequent-ly gave up, declining again to meet Mace Mace again claimed the belt.

1865 - Joe Worwald beat Marsden, £200 a side and the belt, both hav-ing claimed the championship. Belt handed to Worwald. Forfeited £120 to Mace, who again claimed.

1866 - Jem Mace and Joe Goss (a draw, £200 a side and the belt).

1867 - Joe Worwald received forfeit from O'Baldwin, £200 a side and the championship. Baldwin was absent at the starting place. Worwald claimed the belt.

1867 - Jem Mace and O'Baldwin (a draw, £200 a side and the champi-onship; the belt in abeyance).

1868 - Joe Worwald and O'Baldwin (a draw, £200 a side, and the title in America).

1869 - McCoole (beat T. Allen, in America, for championship of the world).

1870 - Jem Mace (beat T. Allen, in America, for championship of the world).

1872 - Jem Mace (draw with J. Coburn, in America, for championship of the world).

1879 - Mace still holds the champion belt of England

1885 - Jem Smith beat Jack Davis

Subsequent events in connection with the English and American championships are told in later chapters.

CHAPTER TWO
ROUNDS OF THE PUGILISTIC LADDER

The unbroken line of victories in boxing, on which I entered at this time, served to increase the feeling of interest which I had felt from boyhood in the champions of England and America, and the ambition to write my name among their records with my own hand. Two years before I entered the ring of life the famous "Yankee Sullivan," who had encountered America's first champion, Tom Hyer, and had fairly outfought Morrissey, was murdered by the Vigilance Committee at San Francisco; yet his deeds were still rated by many as those of "one of the pluckiest fighters that ever stood in a ring."

But the pugilistic subject that was freshest in the public mind in my early boyhood was the battle between the champions of America and England, Heenan and Sayers. I was only two years old when it took place, the remembrance of it was so well kept up by the pictures, songs, and controversies about it in the years following, that it was still a matter of common talk when I became old enough to understand such things.

Speaking of this battle I am reminded of an odd incident told by one who saw it, which has an interest here, as it connects the event with the popular traditions of "Yankee Sullivan," who has just been referred to, and serves to show the prevailing fancies in regard to him.

The account says:

"It was a curious sight to witness the meeting between Heenan and Sayers. Neither had ever seen the other until they confronted between the ropes, and they cordially shook hands. They scrutinized each other closely and passed some remarks on the beauty of the morning. Then Sayers asked John if he wanted to bet anything on the result and was told that all the American's money was already wagered, after which each coolly sauntered over to his corner amid the wildest cheers. At this moment a spectator from America pressed against the ropes and put into Heenan's hand the heel of an old shoe with the observation: 'This is the heel of Yankee Sullivan's shoe, Jack; he swore he never lost a fight while it was in the ring. Leave it there and go in and lick England.'"

This anecdote would seem to be an inversion of the old Greek tradition about Achilles, whose heel instead of being a protection was his only weak point.

Although the heel did not prove strong enough to get for Heenan the English championship belt, to which Americans believed him entitled, it must have discouraged poor Sayers, for he left the belt open for competition. This was the time when Jem Mace won it by conquering the giant, Sam Hurst, known as the "Staleybridge Infant." Mace, in 1866, fought a draw for it with Joe Goss. He held the honors of the belt at the time that the latter was overcome by myself. As for Mace, his acknowledgment of my superiority over him was complete, as will be seen later on in the account of his refusal to spar with me unless I would promise not to knock him out.

After showing supremacy over Joe Goss my next victim was George Rooke, a brother of Jack Rooke, of Manchester, England, with whom I sparred on the 28th of June, 1880, at the Howard Athenaeum, in Boston. I knocked him out in the space of two rounds, having felled him to the stage seven times, when the curtain was rung down and the show brought to a close. After that event I gave several exhibitions with Dan Dwyer.

Within the same year I ascended two rounds of the pugilistic ladder towards the championship, by what should be considered the double defeat of John Donaldson, the "Champion of the West." It is proper first to tell how the matter came about. When Joe Goss and Paddy Ryan were to have fought at Erie, Pennsylvania, for the championship of America, I went to be a witness of the battle, and while at Buffalo, I learned that Donaldson, who arrived the same time as I did, was willing to fight anybody for a purse. I decided on the impulse of the occasion to meet his challenge. As soon as this response became known to the public, much interest was aroused in that section to size up the "Strong Boy." When Donaldson had done his sizing up he refused to have anything to do with me.

About this time it was announced everywhere through the papers, that I was willing to fight any one in America with gloves. The sporting men, therefore, sought to bring about a match with the "mittens" between myself and this man, whom they considered the strongest to be found in that line.

John McCormick, who was then with the *Cincinnati Inquirer*, and who has written under the nom de plume of "Macon," came to Boston and offered me $150 and expenses to go to Cincinnati and spar with Donaldson in Robinson's Opera House.

We met for the first time in December, 1880. An account by an eye-witness says:

"Sullivan's extraordinary strength and wonderful quickness were made apparent at the start, and Donaldson wisely kept out of his way as much as possible. Once Sullivan caught him as he was getting away, and over went Donaldson on his beam ends, to the intense delight of the boys. After three rounds Donaldson wanted to quit, and pulled off his gloves despite the cries of the audience, who, like Oliver Twist, wanted 'more.' He said he was sick and not in condition to spar, but he was finally induced to go on just once more. Sullivan went at him again like a flash, and had it all his own way to the end."

The account continues:

"The bout created great excitement, and Donaldson, not satisfied, challenged Sullivan to fight with hard gloves for $500. Sullivan accepted, and a match was arranged."

In order to appreciate the character of the contest which was entered upon, the following sketch, written about that time, of the man who was my contestant, will be useful:

"Professor John Donaldson, of Cleveland, Ohio, stands five feet ten and one half inches in height, and weighs in condition 160 pounds. He is well known throughout the United States and Canada as a clever boxer. He is a well formed, athletic-looking Hercules, possessed of great muscular development, and in numerous contests in the ring he has proved that he is a pugilist of note. He has figured five times in the ring.

"Donaldson's first battle was a glove fight with Dan Carr, in Cleveland, Ohio, seven rounds in 23 minutes. He next beat Bryan Campbell in Bradford, Pennsylvania, winning in three rounds in eleven minutes. He then beat Bluett Boyd at Buffalo, New York on May 26, 1880, the fight lasting but two minutes and 45 seconds, Boyd being knocked out in the first round. He fought Jim Taylor at Mt. Clemens, Michigan, in August, 1880. They fought five rounds, occupying six minutes. Taylor was knocked down in every round, and out of time in the last. In this battle Donaldson proved he was a terrible hitter, but his experience with Sullivan proved that the new light was a far greater than he."

We fought (with gloves) for a purse on December 24, 1880. Dan Crutchley and Abe Smith, of New York, seconded Donaldson, while Jack Moran and Tom Ryan seconded myself. Patrick Murphy was referee. The account is as follows:

"The battle was a one-sided affair. Donaldson was whipped from the word 'Go.' Nevertheless he managed to make the battle last by running all over the ring to avoid Sullivan's terrific blows. The fight lasted through 10 rounds when Donaldson was knocked out of time. This may be said to have been Sullivan's first regular battle but it was nothing to be compared with some of the off-hand breakaways he had engaged in at Boston. This victory gained him quite a reputation. He had proved to his own satisfaction as well as to that of all observers that he could fight, and he also found out that he could strike a blow hard enough to knock down a mule which was something only a few of his friends knew."

Professor John Donaldson

I defeated him in 10 rounds, 21 minutes, in which he hugged the floor the greater part of the time. The next day, Christmas, he was arrested, about an hour before I was. Bob Linn, a friend of mine, went bonds for both of us. We were tried the following Wednesday and discharged, as there was no bill found against us. The evidence of some of the witnesses for the government side was very amusing, particularly in the case in which Johnny Moran, a brother-in-law of Peter Morris, the well-known English featherweight, champion of England at one time, gave his testimony to the prosecuting attorney. When he asked him if he had seen a fight, he said, "No; I've seen a foot race."

The district attorney asked him: "Who was ahead?"

He said, "Donaldson, and Mr. Sullivan was running after him but could not catch him."

At this the spectators had a very enjoyable laugh. No bill having been found against the principals, the judge, the prosecuting attorney, and my lawyer, who offered his services, Judge Fitzgerald and several other spectators and witnesses, adjourned to a neighboring saloon and partook of some sparkling refreshments.

The *Cincinnati Enquirer* said at this time, in referring to the visit to Cincinnati in connection with the Donaldson affair, "Mr. Sullivan's modest and unassuming manner at once gained him friends. That he is not averse to trying conclusions with any man living will be seen from the following challenge:

CINCINNATI, December 9, 1880

To the Editor of the *Enquirer:*

I am prepared to make a match to fight any man breathing, for any sum from $1,000 to $10,000 at catch weights. This challenge is especially directed to Paddy Ryan and will remain open for a month if he should not see fit to accept it.

Respectfully Yours,

JOHN L. SULLIVAN

Paddy Ryan refused to spar with me at Springfield, Massachusetts, and on the plea that I was not worthy of his standing, said, "Go and get a reputation."

I did "go and get a reputation," as the records for a short time after this show, and I finished it, more effectually than Mr. Ryan could have foreseen, at the expense of his own reputation.

After bidding adieu to Cincinnati, I took a train to my home, in Boston, and then on Monday, the third day of January, 1881, Joe Goss and myself gave a joint exhibition, in which I sparred with Jack Stewart, called "Champion of Canada." I made him run off the stage in the space of two rounds, and gave him a kick behind as he was running into his dressing room, because it made me mad to see a big fellow like him running away after being paraded around, and saying what he was going to do at this exhibition.

At the close of the performance, Joe Goss and I wound up the exhibition in which we split $1,300 between us. With his part, he opened a sporting house on La Grange Street, Boston. I went to New York with Billy Madden. There I was tendered a testimonial benefit at Harry Hill's, on the 31st of March. It was at this time that the New York sporting men found a lively sensation in the novelty of an offer posted by me to give $50 to any pugilist in the world who would stand before me during four rounds, Marquis of Queensbury rules, ordinary gloves being used. This was the first time that anything of this kind had been offered.

When at the close of my benefit entertainment this offer was announced to the audience, it was accepted by the clever heavy weight, Steve Taylor.

John Mahan, who was better known by the name of Steve Taylor, was a native of Ireland, and during a portion of his career was a politician under the Tweed regime, and was also coroner of Jersey City. When Jem Mace first came to this country he was regarded as almost the only American who could make any stand against him. He was described as a six footer, of very powerful build, and as agile as a cat. In 1876, he won reputation as a game and scientific boxer in a draw which he fought in the Lyceum Theatre, New York, with Dwyer, the Brooklyn champion. Among his other experiences were those of training Paddy Ryan for the fight with Joe Goss, and sparring over the country with Mace. Subsequently he made a similar tour with my own combination.

On the occasion of which I now write, the referee was Matt Grace, the well-known collar and elbow wrestler, Dick Hollywood standing up for Taylor and Billy Madden for myself. After I had got in a few hard knocks in two rounds, Taylor acknowledged defeat. I made him a present of half the prize which he had failed to win with the gloves.

After this time the rating of Taylor was expressed in the saying, "Taylor takes off his hat only to Sully."

In April, 1881, a match was arranged for a fight, under the London prize-ring rules, with gloves, between John Flood, a New York heavy-weight, called the "Bull's Head Terror," and myself. A purse of $1,000 was raised, of which the winner was to get $750. Flood was a native of Ireland, and when a boy came to America. At the time of the fight he weighed 180 pounds.

During my time of training the *Boston Globe* said:

> "A Globe reporter visited Sullivan yesterday at the Sherman House in Natick, where he is the guest of Mr. Dan Sheehan. Sullivan looks the picture of health, and is training himself into fine condition. He said, 'Tell the Boston people that I will bring back the championship to the Hub, where it belongs. I would like much to meet Paddy Ryan in the ring, and then give up and settle in some business.'"

The fight with Flood, which took place May 16th, was under the management of William H. Borst, who arranged, in order to avoid the police, that it should take place on a barge on the Hudson River, nearly opposite Yonkers. Flood was seconded by Barney Aaron and Dooney Harris, and I by Joe Goss and Billy Madden. I appeared there with only a few friends, and a job was put up by the New York people that the Boston man should not win under any circumstances. I knocked my man out before they had realized what had happened, and there was no chance for them to carry out their job. The referee was Al Smith, a reliable and straightforward man in all pertaining to sporting matters, and old Joe Elliot, who for years was the sporting editor of the *New York Herald*, being holder of the stake money.

An account of the battle written at that time says:

"Upon stripping it was seen that, although a powerful-looking man, Flood's physique was decidedly inferior to that of his antagonist, and the odds in betting, which all along had been in favor of Sullivan, were increased.

"As usual, after shaking hands, Sullivan lost no time in getting to work, dashing instantly at Flood and using both hands with such effect that the round was finished in a trice, with Flood down, having received several severe blows, the effect of which he failed to shake off during the brief time the contest lasted. The rounds which followed were counterparts of the first, Sullivan having his man completely at his mercy from first to last, and administering severe punishment while receiving scarcely any himself.

"In every round, Flood was either knocked down, fought down or thrown. Finally, at the conclusion of the eighth round, when they had been fighting 16 minutes, and when Flood had been downed with a jawbreaker, the New Yorker's backer himself threw up a towel as a signal of defeat, saying that he did not wish to see a good man, who was willing to fight on, punished longer, when he plainly had no show to win. His action was approved of by the spectators, who saw that Flood was beaten, and that it was folly for him to continue. The display made by Sullivan convinced old pugilists and ring-goers who witnessed the mill that he is the most promising Knight of the Fives in America. Had his hands been bare, the contest must have ended much sooner than it did. Flood was willing enough, and did all he could to stem the tide of battle, but he was completely outclassed. The fight being finished, Sullivan crossed over to Flood's corner, cordially shook his hand, saying, 'We met as friends, and we part as friends,' and then started a subscription for his beaten antagonist."

Paddy Ryan, on witnessing the fight, said, "Sullivan is a clever young fellow."

On the 13th of the following month, I had a wind-up bout with Flood, in a sparring exhibition at Clarendon Hall, New York. A daily paper of that city has the following:

"Excited discussion was indulged in previous to the opening, relative to the proposed prize fight between Sullivan and Paddy Ryan, of Troy, as it was generally believed that Sullivan would issue a challenge from the stage, Sullivan being the winner. Sullivan was loudly cheered on his appearance. He stepped to the ropes, and said:

"'I am ready at any time to meet Paddy Ryan in a glove fight.'

"'A glove 'fight decides nothing!' shouted James MacGowan,

of the *Police Gazette*. 'I have a blank check signed by Richard Fox; if you want to make a match, I will fill it up for $5,000 or $10,000.'

"'I will fight with bare fists for $1,000,' replied Sullivan. 'I can't say any more than that now, until I see my backers.'

"'$1,000 don't amount to anything,' said MacGowan.

"'Better men than Ryan or I have fought for $1,000. There's Jem Mace, Tom Allen, and others,' retorted Sullivan. 'I'll fight Ryan a fist fight if I can get the money.'

"The dialogue between Sullivan and MacGowan caused no little excitement in the audience. One of Sullivan's friends, jumping to his feet, exclaimed:

"'If Ryan wants to fight for $1,000, a match can be made right away.'

"'Ryan won't fight for $1,000. It wouldn't be worth fighting for,' remarked Mr. MacGowan. "Sullivan retired to the rear of the stage, and the wind-up with Flood proceeded."

The sparring with Flood is described in another account as follows:

"Harry Hijl was master of ceremonies. The principal set-to was between Sullivan and Flood. At half past 10 o'clock they appeared on the stage, in ring costume, to spar three rounds according to the Marquis of Queensbury rules. Sullivan looked as strong as an ox, and pretty confident of getting the better of his opponent again. Flood was nervous and eager to begin and opened the first round with a left-hander which was neatly stopped. Some hard hitting ensued, Sullivan delivering blows rapidly on Flood's face and staggering him. The men had clinched when 'Time ' was called. In the second round Sullivan attacked, and Flood could not successfully defend himself. When time was up Harry Hill separated the men. The third round was full of hard and skilful hitting."

From New York I went to Philadelphia, where I renewed my offer of $50 to any one whom I could not knock out in four rounds with the gloves. I gave an exhibition in Arthur Chamber's Hall, where Fred Crossly, a stout and ambitious boxer, was made to quit, after I had boxed with him for a few minutes.

The next week I put in at John Clark's Olympic Theatre as a boxer; my income being $150 for the week. I allowed John Clark, the proprietor, to use my name on one night, the performance being given out as a benefit to me, though in reality it was a benefit to himself. Having offered $50 to anybody that I could not stop in four rounds, Marquis of Queensbury rules, an aspirant named Dan McCarty, came to win glory. I put him in the land of dreams in 30 seconds.

The following account is from a Philadelphia paper:

> "'As there are three men in the hall,' said Mr. Clark, 'who, it is understood, would like to try Mr. Sullivan, I hope they will come to the front.'
> "In a short time a man was seen making his way through the crowd. It proved to be Dan McCarty, of Baltimore.
> "Sullivan went to work at once. He drove McCarty to the side of the dressing room, and with a left-hander full in the face brought the man on his knees. Hardly had the prostrate foe arisen, before Sullivan with a tremendous right-hander on the neck sent him sprawling on his back, and the fellow lay almost lifeless. It had taken just 40 seconds to give McCarty enough.
> For a few minutes there were grave doubts about resuscitating the defeated pugilist. As Sullivan was returning to the dressing room a gentleman was heard to say:
> "'Well, I have seen all from Hyer down to the present day, but none could have beaten that young fellow, Sullivan.'"

Leaving Philadelphia, we went to Chicago, where Madden and myself gave an exhibition at McCormick's Hall, on the North Side, on Clark Street. We made the same offer of $50 as elsewhere. Parson Davies was interested in the exhibition, he receiving 25% for his services, and Captain James Dalton, a tug man, was an aspirant for the $50. A Chicago report says:

> "Dalton stood up like a log before Sullivan. Excitement ran at white heat. Cheers and applause rang through the building. Sullivan smashed him viciously a few times, and considerably disfigured the ambitious tugman's countenance. He was a trifle groggy when time was called for the fourth round, and after a few passes, Sullivan knocked him so stiff that when the allotted 10 seconds had passed he was unable to put in an appearance, consequently forfeiting all claim to the $50. Sullivan gave him $25, however, and after this fact had been announced, the crowd dispersed. Sullivan created quite a sensation, and Chicago sports offer to match him to fight anybody for $1,000 to $10,000. Dalton had successfully downed John Dwyer, Ryan, Donaldson, Chandler, and others. Dwyer was heard to remark of him, 'There is one of the most dangerous young men with his hands, in America.'"

From Chicago I went to Mt. Clements, Michigan, a summer resort, about 20 miles from Detroit. While there a bully attempted to jostle me off a raised sidewalk, one evening. I asked him what he meant by doing that. He used a vile lot of epithets to me, and said, "I will show you." I tried to use diplomacy to avoid him, but he was bent on trouble, and attempted to strike me. I was under the necessity of putting him to sleep in less than two minutes. When the citizens heard about it the next day, they sent a prominent druggist of the town named Crane, to reward me with the sum of two hundred and $50 for teaching this bully a lesson, as he had been abusing and browbeating everybody in the town. The money I refused.

I then went back to Chicago, where I gave another exhibition in McCormick's Hall, making the same offer of $50. A man named Jack Burns, "the Michigan giant," six foot six and a half, came to accept and win fame. When I saw him, I said, "How will I get at that fellow; he is so tall that I think it would be a good scheme to get a step ladder, so to be on equal height with him." But when we got our hands up and set to work, I soon brought him down to my size by hitting him a punch in the pit of the stomach and one on the point of the jaw which settled further hostilities. He landed in the second row of orchestra seats. When he got up he was heard to remark, "I suppose when Sullivan tells about this they will say he is a windy duck!"

I returned to Boston a few days after. The efforts which had been made in Chicago for securing a match with Paddy Ryan being continued after my arrival home. A good deal of delay and disappointment had been caused by the disagreements as to the amount to be fought for.

On the fifth day of October, 1881, the first $500 was put up on my behalf as a forfeit in Harry Hill's hands for a match for $2,500 a side with Ryan. The next deposit went on November 9th, consisting of $1,000 a side, and the last deposit of $1,000 was sent on the 7th of December, making the total stakes $5,000. Harry Hill was agreed upon as final stake-holder.

During the interval between the making of the match and the preparations for my battle with Ryan, I gave exhibitions in various places on the way to New Orleans, in company with Billy Madden, Pete McCoy, and Bob Farrell.

In October, 1881, Mike Donovan published an offer to meet me with the gloves at his benefit at Madison Square Garden, on the 24th of that month. The upshot was the following scene, as described in a New York daily paper:

> "'How about this Sullivan match?' cried a man near the plat-form when the wrestlers had withdrawn.
> "'Hi don't know,' replied Mr. Hill. A chorus of howls followed this brief colloquy, which increased, when somebody suggested that the mention of Mr. Sullivan's name was a sell as he was away on a sparring tour. While the rumpus was at its height, a stalwart young man mounted the platform. His presence was the signal for cheers. It was Sullivan.

"'Gentlemen,' said he, 'I have come here tonight to spar this man, Mike Donovan. He has published his willingness to give me $50 to spar with him four rounds according to the Marquis of Queensbury rules and I have come all the way from Philadelphia to do it. I don't care for the money, but I have been snapped at so by this man, who has been dragging my name through the newspapers, that I want to spar him anyhow.'

"This defiance was greeted with loud applause, during which Donovan climbed to the platform beside Sullivan and expressed the desire to be heard.

"'I ain't got no show against this man,' he began.

"'Then what did you challenge him for?' someone asked.

"'Yes,' shouted the spectators, 'what did you challenge him for?'

"'Because,' said Donovan, 'he has said I was a cur. I want him to understand that I ain't a cur, for I've fought eleven battles in the ring, and no man that does that is a cur. [Cheers.] Now, I want to do the right thing, and I'll box Mr. Sullivan four rounds according to the rules of the prize ring.'

"'Gentlemen,' said Mr. Sullivan, 'this is anything but fair, but it is, nevertheless, just what I expected from this man. Governed by prize-ring rules, he can run away or lay down on the stage and I can't get at him. However, for the sake of meeting him, I waive all objections and will box him as he desires.'

"The applause which greeted this manly declaration had scarcely subsided when Donovan threw a wet blanket on the matter by objecting that Sullivan had not given him the use of his name for the entertainment and that therefore he ought not to accommodate him. This backdown was rewarded by the spectators with jeers and hisses, to quiet which Harry Hill volunteered the statement that Captain Williams, who was present, objected to the men meeting each other for the reason that the bad blood engendered might lead to serious consequences."

The *News*, commenting on this, said: "The Queensbury rules are the accepted rules for glove contests, and the London rules for the naked fists. Donovan knew this when he made the subterfuge, in order to avoid meeting Sullivan. The whole thing reduces itself to this: Donovan challenged Sullivan and backed out."

When I arrived at New Orleans I gave an exhibition, after which, I went to Bay St. Louis, Missouri, where I made my training quarters in preparing for my fight to wrest from Ryan the championship of America.

As this subject leads me up to the records of the championship which I was about to capture, it is proper to give here the list that I have prepared of dates and events, showing the rise and succession of the

American champions from the first famous claimant down to my own predecessor. This will prove a fitting supplement to the list of English champions with which I closed the last chapter.

February 7, 1849 - Tom Hyer, the first champion of America, fought with Yankee Sullivan for $10,000, and the championship at Still Pond Creek, Maryland. Hyer defeated Sullivan and then retired from the ring. Yankee Sullivan succeeded him.

October 12, 1853 - Sullivan fought John Morrissey for $2,000, and the championship at Long Point, Canada. Sullivan had defeated his opponent when a quarrel ensued and the crowd broke into the ring, Morrissey held his corner, but Sullivan left the ring, thus losing the fight.

May 20, 1857 - John Morrissey beat John C. Heenan for $2,000 a side and the championship. Morrissey then retired from the ring, though again challenged by Heenan.

August 1, 1857 - Dominick Bradley fought S. S. Rankin, for $1,000 a side and the title at Point Albino, Canada. The men, who were both giants fought at catch weights according to London prize-ring rules. Bradley won.

April 17, 1860 - John Heenan fought Tom Sayers in England and won, but he did not receive the honors to which he was entitled. The battle was for four hundred pounds and the championship of England and America. Sayers's friends seeing that the champion was defeated cut the ropes and the battle ended in a wrangle. The stakes were drawn, and each pugilist was presented with a champion belt. The belt given to Heenan had not been paid for and he was obliged to return it.

May 17, 1863 - Joe Coburn and Mike McCoole fought for the title at Charlestown, Maryland. Coburn won.

December 10, 1863 - Heenan fought King and was defeated. He then retired from the ring and Joe Coburn was the next champion.

October 4, 1864 - Coburn went to Ireland to fight Jem Mace for the title and $5,000, but the battle did not take place, Mace being afraid of Coburn's regulations. After this Coburn retired for the first time from the ring.

May 16, 1865 - Bill Davis, who then claimed the championship, fought with James Dunn for $2,000 and the title, in Pike County, Missouri, and was defeated. Dunn retired and Davis claimed the championship.

September 19, 1866 - McCoole, who disputed Davis's right to the title, fought with him for $2,000 and the championship, at Rhodes Point, Missouri. McCoole won.

August 31, 1867 - McCoole fought Aaron Jones at Busenbark Station, Ohio, for $2,000 and the championship, and again won.

May 27, 1868 - McCoole, who had held the title undisturbed up to this time, met Joe Coburn, who had again decided to enter the arena, at Cold Spring Station, Indiana, to fight for $5,000. McCoole entered the ring, but Coburn was arrested before he reached it. McCoole was arrested later, and both were sentenced to serve 40 days' imprisonment at Lansingburg, Maryland.

October 29, 1868 - Ned O'Baldwin, the Irish giant, and Joe Worwald, who had both claimed the championship of England, came to this country and offered to fight any American for the title. As no one accepted the challenge, O'Baldwin was matched to fight Worwald for $2,000 and the championship of the world. The pugilists met on the above date at Lynnfield, Massachusetts, and after having fought one round, were both arrested.

January 12, 1869 - Tom Allen, the English pugilist, fought Bill Davis at Foster's Island, St. Louis, Missouri, for the title and $2,000. Allen won. June 15, 1869 - Tom Allen fought McCoole at Foster's Island, near St. Louis, for $1,000 and the championship. Allen beat McCoole's face to a jelly, and won the fight, but McCoole was declared the winner on an alleged foul.

May 10, 1870 - Jem Mace and Tom Allen fought for the title and $5,000at Kennerville, New Orleans. Mace won.

May 11, 1871 - Mace and Joe Coburn met at Port Dover, Canada, to fight for the championship. The pugilists were in the ring one hour and sixteen minutes without striking a blow.

November 31, 1871 - Mace and Coburn fought for the championship at Bay St. Louis, Mississippi. The battle ended in a draw.

September 23, 1873 - Tom Allen beat McCoole at Chateau Island, near St. Louis.

November 18, 1873 - Ben Hogan fought with Tom Allen for $2,000 and the championship at Pacific City, Iowa. The contest ended in a wrangle, although Allen was in a fair way to win.

September 7, 1876 - Joe Goss, who had been brought over from England by Jem Mace, fought Allen for $2,000 and the championship, in Kentucky. Goss was declared the winner by a foul.

May 9, 1879 - Jimmy Elliott and Johnny Dwyer fought for $1,000 a side and the title in Canada. Dwyer won and retired.

May 30, 1880 - Joe Goss fought Paddy Ryan for $1,000 and the championship of America, at Collier Station, West Virginia. The battle, which lasted one hour and 27 minutes, was won by Ryan.

CHAPTER THREE
THE CHAMPIONSHIP REACHED

The line of succession in the American championship, from the time of Tom Hyer's victory over Yankee Sullivan, to my own over Ryan, is marked by a series of battles royal that make lively reading now that I get into a position where I am entitled to look along the list of my predecessors. "The greatest pugilist that ever stood in a ring" is the title that has been given to Hyer by one authority. Hyer's reputation must certainly have grown more out of the style and quality of his fighting, than the number of those he fought, for the only victories of which there is any record are those over George McChester, better known as Country McCloskey, and over that "tough importation from the land of blackthorns," Yankee Sullivan. The fight with the former occurred at Caldwell's Landing, New York, September 9, 1841. For a hundred rounds Country McCloskey refused to give up, though receiving terrible blows from the gigantic Hyer. Irritated by his obstinacy, Hyer was heard to mutter, "Oh, let him come, let him come on; I'll kill him this time!"

This plucky opponent persisted in coming on, although his second, Yankee Sullivan, urged him to stop; and, after one hundred and one rounds had been fought in two hours and 55 minutes, Sullivan threw up the sponge, seeing that it was useless for McCloskey to stand any more punishment.

With rare audacity, Yankee Sullivan, a much smaller man, then challenged Hyer, whose tremendous executions he had witnessed. The battle that resulted January 10, 1849, at Rock Point, Maryland, for stakes of $5,000a side, was the most remarkable in the early history of the ring, on account of the stakes which were greater than any that had ever been fought for before, and especially because of the desperate manner in which so unequal an encounter was waged. Yankee Sullivan, whose real name was Frank Ambrose Murray, had before this time won fame for science and endurance by his victories in England over Hammer Lane, Oliver Hammond, Tom Secor, Professor Bell, and Bob Caunt. An idea of the unequal character of the contest with Hyer can be got from the account of the first round.

Sullivan darted toward Hyer, who stood resolutely awaiting him with his body well forward and in formidable readiness, and coming up to him with a sort of run, Sully let fly with his left at the head, but did not get it in. He then got away from a short attempt to counter with his left, but Hyer followed the effort with an instant discharge of his right in Sullivan's fore-head, which made a long abrasion of the scalp, but which, notwithstand-ing the power of the blow, showed neither blood nor discoloration at the time. Gathering himself for a return, Sullivan then rushed in at the body, and, after two or three ineffectual exchanges, clinched his antagonist with the underhold and struggled for the throw.

This was the great point on which was to depend the result of the fight. Sullivan relied mainly for success upon his superior wrestling, and it was calculated by his friends and backers that a few of his favorite cross buttocks would break his young antagonist in his lithe and graceful waist, and not only render him limpsy with weakness, but stun him with the falls. The most terrible anxiety, therefore, existed, as to the result of this endeavor. In the fierce agitations the spectators who stood in an outer ring of plank laid over the snow some feet distant from the ropes of the arena, involuntarily rushed forward and swarmed against the ropes. Two or three times did Sullivan knot his muscles with an almost superhuman effort, but all served only to postpone his overthrow, for, when he had spent his power by these terrible impulsions, his iron adversary wrenched him to the ground with the upperhold, and fell heavily prone upon his body. This decided the largest part of the outside betting in favor of the upper man, and shouts of joy went up for Hyer.

When the 16th round was reached, after Sullivan had astonished the spectators with his skill and determination, it became clear that his fight-ing star was set, at least for that day, and McCloskey took him from the ring without waiting for time to be called. Although the battle lasted only 17 minutes and 18 seconds, it was rarely equaled for the amount of pun-ishment administered. Sullivan went to the Mount Sinai Hospital, Baltimore. It has been claimed that Sullivan would have fought more cool-ly, and therefore with more effect, but for the animosity then existing between him and Hyer. This suggests the remark that the spirit which car-ried on the early events of the American prize ring was rather of war than scientific sport. Much ill-feeling existed in those years on account of the native American movement, of which Hyer was taken as the physical rep-resentative.

Another example of an encounter in which the same spirit entered was that between the noted Bill Poole and John Morrissey, which took place at Amos Street dock, June 27, 1854. Morrissey fought at great dis-advantage, as it was in the neighborhood where Poole and his partisans held sway, and he was defeated after severe punishment.

Morrissey, not being able to get a battle with Hyer because $10,000 a side was demanded, fought with Yankee Sullivan at Boston Corners, October 12, 1853. After 37 rounds in 55 minutes, the umpires and sec-onds got into a fight, and Sullivan felt fresh enough to "take a hand in the outside music." During the confusion, "time" was called. Sullivan not being able to get back into the ring, although he had the better of the encounter, was declared the loser.

Morrissey won the title of "Champion of America" in the fight with John C. Heenan, "the Benecia Boy," October 20, 1858, and he retired from the ring. It is a curious fact that, notwithstanding the determined spirit with which they encountered each other, both Morrissey and Heenan hailed from Troy, New York, and their fathers were friends in Ireland.

John C. Heenan then succeeded to the championship. A Southern writer has called him "the John L. Sullivan of his day." His name brings up the records of one of the most remarkable contests known in the ring - that which he fought with the English champion, Tom Sayers, at Farnborough, England, April 17, 1860. Only the regular championship stake of $1,000 was fought for, but the fact that the men were considered the best that England and America could send against each other, gave the affair a sort of international interest.

An article in the *Clipper Annual* on this subject says:

> "The stakes that have been won and lost on prize-ring encounters within the last decade have been much heavier, but in nearly every instance it was the consuming desire to secure immediate wealth rather than a praiseworthy attempt to show individual superiority, that actuated the high contracting parties, while in all the engagements in which the illustrious John L. Sullivan has participated, he has been so pronounced a favorite that, while the attention of the pugilistic world was naturally attracted by his battles, the fact that the element of uncertainty was lacking, detracted from the interest that would otherwise have been invested in the result.
>
> "The fight between Heenan and Sayers, too, furnished one of the very few instances in which the odds in betting were on the smaller man when they faced each other in the ring, for in struggles in which the weapons provided by nature form the chief factors, size, weight, and muscular power must receive due consideration."

An eye witness of the fight writes:

> "I found that my fellow voyagers were to be noblemen led by Lord Palmerston, lawyers, physicians, bankers, literary and society men, and the better class of those known in the sporting world on both continents.
>
> "Sayers showed great generalship in prolonging the battle for two hours and six minutes, although he was no match for Heenan, and in nearly every round he went down or was

thrown down. In the 37th round the referee left his post, so that he was not at hand to declare the result of the seven rounds that were fought after that. The fight was called a draw by the English, although at the end Sayers was pulled away insensible while Heenan had strength enough left to punish Sayer's seconds for refusing to throw up the sponge. He then bounded over the ropes and proclaimed himself champion of the world.

"After the fight, the English champion was ranked by many with the heroes of the Crimea and of Lucknow; hundreds of pounds were subscribed for him by persons of all conditions of life, and he was feted by merchants on the London and Liverpool 'Changes. His opponent received equally flattering and substantial testimonials in America."

The last battle in the series up to the time in which I won the championship from Ryan was that in which he gained the title by defeating Joe Goss at Collier Station, West Virginia, in 87 rounds, lasting one hour and 27 minutes.

The fact that I took the lead of Ryan in performing the feat through which he gained the championship is rather pointedly put by an article in the *Kansas City Times*, which says:

"Sullivan knocked Joe Goss out in four and a half minutes before Ryan won the championship from that pugilist. It took Ryan an hour and 27 minutes to do what Sullivan, as a boy, did in less than five minutes."

The public concern about my prospective contest with Ryan gave rise to a great deal of gossip and speculation in the newspapers for months previous, some being interesting and some rather funny.

A reporter in a Louisville paper describing an interview with me, says:

"Sullivan is a handsome man, and if he were not there is no one around this office that would say anything to the contrary. He is known as the hardest hitter in this country, and in all of his contests, none of which have been without gloves, he has knocked his opponent out of time in less than 20 minutes.

"'Do you go into training at once?' inquired the reporter.

"'Yes,' said the fighter; 'my fighting weight will be 175 pounds, and I will have to take a training of about six weeks to reduce myself into condition.'

"'Do you think you will win the fight?'

"'Oh, yes,' answered Sullivan, 'I never yet failed to knock my man out of time, and I don't think I will now.'

"'Besides having great strength a prize-fighter has to be very scientific, don't he?' asked the interviewer.

"'He has got to be clever,' said the deep bass voice, 'but fighters are born. A fighter can't be made out of a stiff. Some fellows will stand up and fight 10 or 15 minutes and then run away, and you can't catch them. But a man that can stick four hours and be half pounded to death has to be born.'

"'I'll tell you what it is,' spoke up the west-end reporter, 'we 've got in this town a lot of hoodlums who imagine that they can mash anybody up they choose. Now, if you would get several of those on the stage and spat them about one lick each, you would receive a vote of thanks from the citizens, and would be given the freedom of the city by the mayor.'

"'I wouldn't hit those fellows, but we've got two or three little men in our crowd that might knock them out of time for you.'

"'Your contests have been hotly contested, have they?' was the next question.

"'I've had 'em pretty hot, but when I hit 'em once or twice they usually weaken at once. The longest fight I ever had was about 20 minutes, and that fellow was on the floor the most of the time.'

"'Suppose Ryan gives you a long fight. Do you still think that you can beat him?'

"'Certainly I do. Most people imagine that because all my fights have been short that I can't whip a man unless I do it in 15 or 20 minutes. But that 's where they are mistaken, for I know that I can fight just as well after an hour's slugging as I can at the beginning.'

"'What will Ryan fight at?'

"'About two hundred, I guess.'

"'That's a big difference in weight, isn't it?'

"'Yes, but I don't care, for I am in my best condition at 175 pounds.'

"'Why don't you fight in Kentucky? The law here wouldn't take any notice of it until you were all safely out of the State,' suggested the scribe.

"'I want to fight where I am certain there will be no interference. I picked out New Orleans, and did so because I wanted the fight to come off. They might run me in here in Kentucky, as they did poor Joe Goss when he and Allen fought.'"

A sporting writer, in referring to myself, said: "He is the phenomenon of the modern ring as Gus Hickman was of his day, and if he is only true to himself and to his record, even if he should meet a Bill Neat, he will not be disgraced."

Speaking of Bill Neat, in connection with remarks in the papers previous to my fight with Ryan, I give the following curious comparison published by a friend of the latter, simply because it tells a bright little episode from the annals of the British ring:

"The battle between Ryan and Sullivan may turn out similar to the battle between Bill Neat and Tom Spring, fought years ago in England. At the time the nobility of England patronized fighting there arose a phenomenon in the shape of a giant Bristol butcher, named Bill Neat. He had knocked half a dozen provincials out of time, and had actually, on one occasion, knocked down an ox. Finally, in 1823, Lord Hayne, a young sprig of nobility, brought Neat down to London, and took him in disguise to the house of Tom Spring, the champion at that time. There Neat kicked up a row with Spring and they had a clinch. They were parted, and then Spring made a match with him for £500 a side. Soon it was whispered about that the unknown was Bill Neat. Spring's hands had been used up in previous fights and he had been retired for three years. His friend and backer, Captain Kelley, came to him and said:

"'Tom, your hands are gone and you can't win. This is Bill Neat. He is a murderer and he'll kill you.'

"'That's all right,' says Spring. 'I 'm going to whip that man, anyway. I don't care whether he can knock down an ox or not. There's just one fight left in me and I'll whip that man easy.' But in spite of that talk Spring's friends were afraid to back him. The shops of all London were shut up and 30,000 people looked at the fight. That was in Andover in 1823. Spring was of a handsome shape and his skin was as white as a woman's.

"'Come here, my pretty waiting-maid,' said Neat, as they stood stripped in the ring.

"'If I'm going to be a waiting-maid to you today,' said Spring, 'I'll prove a faithful servant.'

"And so he did. He walked around Neat as a cooper round a cask, and every time that the man who could knock down an ox struck out to kill him he hit only nothing. Spring was away every time but he was always back again in time to get in a good one, and after fighting eight rounds in 37 minutes, Neat fell all bleeding and battered out of all semblance to humanity. The coming battle between Ryan and Sullivan will probably result in the same manner as the Neat and Spring battle. Sullivan is no doubt a hard hitter, and maybe turn out a wonder and a surprise, and whip Ryan in the coming battle, but the chances, judging by the performances of both pugilists, are against him."

It is too bad to have to spoil so ingenious a comparison by remarking in passing that Ryan was taller and heavier than I, and was also the loser of the fight in this case, so that facts would make *him* out to be the "Bill Neat," and *me* the "Tom Spring," of the affair.

The opponents of prize fighting also had their utterances through the papers about this time. A correspondent signed "Scranton" in the *Times-*

Democrat in a rather sarcastic note says:

> "'Conge' suggests that Sullivan and Ryan meet in the Fair Grounds. His ideas are correct, and if his plan is carried out you can immortalize yourself by sending an invitation to the Mississippi Legislature; and on their arrival they should be presented with a pocket Bible, with the story of David and Goliath marked."

How far the Mississippi Legislature was from availing itself of his kindly suggestion, was shown by the fact that on January 17, 1882, after four weeks of my training, a bill was taken up there, holding out such soft inducements as $1,000' fine and five years in prison for us to engage in such contests.

A paper of the 19th, in referring to this, said:

> "When the purport of the special telegram from Jackson, Mississippi, became known to the admirers of both men located in the Crescent City, all hands felt at once that their reputation for good-fellowship and square play was at stake, and before many moments the wires had conveyed the intelligence to both of the famous sluggers that 'there was danger ahead.' A well-known Chicago gentleman who stood chatting with a group of sporting men at the corner of St. Charles and Common streets, when the private telegram informing them of the nature of the bill was first shown by one of the party, said:
>
> "'It's a snap game on the part of some legislator, and I'll give $200 toward getting both men out of the State by means of a special train right now.'
>
> "'I'll give $100,' said a sporting man standing near. 'And I another,' chimed in a third. Then a council of war was held, and after a thorough canvass of the situation, it was resolved that there was at least time enough to spare before the bill could become a law, in which the men could be removed from the quarters that they occupied in Bay St. Louis and Mississippi City, respectively. It was evident to all hands, however, that no time could be lost in the matter, and accordingly the early train, which left here yesterday morning, conveyed to the training quarters of both men representatives of the better class of the sporting element of the Crescent City, who had consented to take charge of the interests of the rival pugilists, and who had determined upon seeing fair play, and seeking no underhand favors for either man. The representative of the Boston boy was the first to arrive at the headquarters of his protégé, and, stating the nature of his errand, he caused a surprise party.
>
> "A look of dismay and disappointment came over both the face of Sullivan and his trainer that can be better imagined than

described. Arrangements for getting away were soon completed, and within a half an hour after the warning had been given the Boston boy and his friends, with all of their traps and fixtures, were aboard of the incoming train, bound for New Orleans; and Madden, after seeing him comfortably quartered, started out to look for a training place. Sullivan expressed himself as feeling first-rate, but regretted that he had been forced to leave Bay St. Louis, where he was well situated, and where he had had every reason to feel well satisfied with his treatment and surroundings. He looks in the best of condition, and is as confident as ever, saying that there will be a fight sure, even if he has to go to Texas or the island of Cuba to do battle for the championship. Madden returned to the hotel, and announced that he had secured training quarters at Carrollton, and that he was ready to move there right away. Sullivan's quarters are at Schroeder's Summer Garden, in Carrollton, where every facility for getting into perfect condition for the great mill will be accorded to him.

"The walking is good, and the roads for a distance of 10 miles, even in the rainy weather, passable. When Ryan's representative reached Mississippi City yesterday morning, and handed him the *Times-Democrat* containing the dispatch, the Troy pugilist looked it over and said:

"'That's rough, ain't it?' and then turning to his trainer, he asked: 'Can I fight him tomorrow, John? We can find a place and fight right away. I feel just like fighting.'

"'No, sir, you can't,' was the reply. 'The day has been named, and when it comes I will have you there.'

"'Alright,' replied the Troy man, turning away.

"Later in the day Ryan was visited by several prominent citizens of Harrison County, who assured him that there was no danger there at present, and promised that they would give him timely warning should any danger occur. The Trojan appeared cool and confident, and said:

"'This will in no wise interfere with the fight. I am ready and willing to do battle at my time, and when the occasion presents itself I will be found on deck.'

"Ryan was escorted to the St. James Hotel, where parlor No. 5 had been reserved for him, and here he was soon surrounded by a group of his friends and well-wishers. A few moments afterwards, during the general conversation that followed, he turned to his representative and said:

"'Just find a place where we can fight, that is all I ask; a fair field and no favors, and don't you ignore the other side in the matter. Let them be satisfied, too.'

"'You have the naming of the ground yourself, Paddy,' interrupted Roche, 'and I don't think they would consult you in the matter.'

"'Oh, well, Roche,' replied the good-natured Troy man, 'let 's be decent about the matter, and have a place that suits them as well as me. We don't want to be mean about it, I'm sure.' Then turning to his representative, he continued, 'See to it, please.' A short time afterwards he said with a smile, 'Sullivan says he will go to Cuba or Texas to fight. Don't be so - well, I - I'll go anywhere in the world; it's my last fight, and I am anxious to get out of the business, so that the sooner it is decided the better.'"

That my new training place was not without its humorous incidents may be judged from this odd little one, narrated by the New York Herald correspondent soon after my arrival there:

"There was to be a little exhibition of skill, which a few only were allowed to witness. With a very select party your correspondent was invited to attend. A rapid trip of 35 minutes over the New Orleans and Carrollton Railroad brought the party to Schroeder's Garden. There was a crowd of loungers, white and black, standing at the corner opposite the hotel, with eyes and mouths distended, as if watching for the greatest show on earth to appear. When the party came up, a colored school had just been dismissed.

"There was a dispute between two of the young viragoes, and a regular set-to immediately followed. A ring was made by their dusky sisters around the combatants, and one was at once dubbed Sullivan and the other Ryan. After a regular rough-and-tumble, Sullivan won, and a shout from the whole school proclaimed his popularity.

"In the principal public room at the hotel quite a number of the Boston boy's friends and admirers were found assembled, laughing over the incident given above."

Among the newspaper drolleries that preceded the fight was the following:

"Mr. Sullivan was invited to take a chair and wisely declined one of the reporter's imported Connecticuts.

"'No, sir,' said Mr. Sullivan, 'I know when I meet anything stronger than I am, and I cave.'

"This proof of perspicacity on the part of the visitor struck the reporter with as much force as would a blow from the same source. Recalling the wrecked condition of the fighting editor he hid behind an exchange (delicately choosing a sporting paper out of deference to his visitor) and, in that *dégagé, negligé, quantum suf* manner for which he is noted, said:

"'John, - I call you John because I want to be friendly - it has just occurred to me that a position is vacant on our staff which, in the language of the poker table, you are just the card to fill. In conducting with enterprise a great daily newspaper, one of that class of publications to which the world in its thirst for...'

"Noticing a bored look settling over the speaking countenance of the visitor, the reporter coughed and resumed -

"'Our fighting editor is now so much occupied in attending to his hospital duties that he will not be able to give us his services for some days. I would be glad to offer you his place - not temporarily, but permanently. Your duties may be onerous, they probably will be. For instance, a man near the river says he is going to use the editor as a mop to wipe up his floor, simply because our Western reporter stated that when this man's daughter was in San Francisco, her hair was so red it stopped a Chinese funeral. Again, our political editor (who is now absent from the city) remarked about one of our toney young men the other day that "Leander and his pants are both so tight that he can neither stand up nor sit down." This gentleman will probably feel it necessary to vindicate himself. Another item has just been called to my attention, which will probably attract notice; it is this: "The Robinson County whisky sampler and Councilman from the Fifteenth Ward might as well learn now as later that he cannot open a coal hole with a night key." I mention these little items that you may see towards what direction your duties will tend. You will be expected to attend strictly to any calls from injured citizens, will be furnished with surgeons in case of your being injured, and will receive $100 a week and your expenses. What do you say? Is it a go?'

"'Put it there,' said Mr. Sullivan, shaking the reporter's hand and squeezing it until the bones cracked like ice on a frosty day, 'you hold the position for me until I polish off Patsy Ryan and I'm your man.'"

The feeling in Boston on the morning of the battle is facetiously given by a correspondent of the *New York World* in the following:

"'You can just bet your sweet life, young feller, that our Johnny is goin' to salivate the Troy man today. Sullivan left here with that end in view, and the devil in him bigger 'n a tobacco factory.'

"A well-known local bruiser stood in Tom Early's place, on Lagrange Street this morning, his hands crossed behind his back, and his back in close proximity to a much-heated stove. The position and the heat of the stove seemed to make the pugilistic gentleman feel in a very comfortable and communicative condition. The room was filled with 'hitters' of all degrees of proficiency, from the South Cove youth, who spars at testimonial benefits, and generally gets knocked out of time, to the terror of the West End, whose reputation is established.

"'Say, young cove,' remarked a young man with pants spreading very much at the bottoms, 'I've bet all my money on our Johnny, and I'm just at this particular time as dry as a fish. If you want points on the mill, you've got to "shout "; do you understand that?'

"The reporter at once took the hint and the little matter spoken of by the 'amatoor,' as he styled himself, was at once attended to.

"'You gentlemen do not have any doubts that the fight will take place, do you?'

"'That mill's agoin' on just as sure as shootin'. The men that's took the trouble to go all the way down to Orleans ain't goin' to stand any guff; and don't yer forgit it!'

"'Has much "talent" left Boston to witness the fight?' the reporter man queried.

"'You can bet there has; why all of our pets is there, and the only reason we didn't go was because we bet all our "sugar" on our Johnny.'

"'What good men are still in the city?'

"'Well,' answered the young man, 'I think there's Tim McCarty, Jerry Murphy, "Fish" Kennedy, Sammy Blake, Uncle Bill Busby, Marcellus Baker, Professor Bailey, Ned Kelley and a few other good men left in this deserted village; but the pride of the town is down there, mebbe at this very minute on the battle ground.'

"'What will be the result should there be no fight - that is if the backers and trainers of one of the men should object at the last moment?'

"' Well, then, there'll be blood on the moon. If such a thing should happen, there'd be the bloodiest fight ever heard of at a "mill" in this country.'

"'Upon what do you base these conclusions?'

"'Why, when the Sullivan men left here they went with the idee that this fight must take place. They won't back down, you bet, and if the Ryan men try any "shenanigan" there'll be pistols out and blood will flow. You see all the men are away down South, a long ways from their homes, and in a country where shootin' irons are common instruments. They have a freer feelin', you see, than they would have North or even West.'"

Shortly before noon, on the 7th of February, 1882, the grounds in front of Barnes' Hotel, Mississippi City, were thronged with the thousands that had come by special trains from New Orleans and other parts to witness our battle for the championship. The gathering although animated was of an orderly character, and, as one spectator remarked, "A conference of clergymen could not have been more staid." The seats on the piazza of the hotel sold for high prices, and many ladies occupied them.

One of the interesting things to be noted previous to the fight was the lively sale of the colors of each combatant. It is always the fashion when there is going to be an important meeting between pugilists, for them to issue colors. The colors of a successful pugilist are highly prized by sporting men, and in many sporting houses of New York today the colors of John C. Heenan, Tom Sayers, Denny Harrington, and Tom King can be seen framed.

My colors on this occasion consisted of a white silk handkerchief with a green border; in the left-hand upper corner was an American flag, in the right-hand upper corner an Irish flag, in the lower left-hand corner an American flag, and in the lower right-hand corner an Irish flag. In the center was an American eagle.

Ryan's colors were also attractive. As an example of the interest in such things I may remark that a facsimile of the colors worn by me at this time was taken to China, where the Chinese workers in silk reproduced it in elegant style. They were subsequently brought to this country and presented to me.

About an hour's wait was caused by the delay in ring arrangements. A correspondent describing the scene at this time, as I looked out on Mississippi Sound, says:

> "Sullivan stood on the extreme western extension of the hotel, chatting with his friends. Your correspondent was near him when he turned to the view of the sea which lay before him. The water was as smooth as a fond. Far out a white sail gleamed in the morning sun, and a few fishermen were rowing out to their ground. I saw Sullivan's face change, and for a second the hard, determined mouth softened.
>
> "'What are you thinking of, Sullivan?' asked your correspondent.
>
> "'I was only thinking that I had never seen so beautiful a sea,' he replied, after a moment.
>
> "'Your ring is ready,' called Joe Goss just then, and the soft look faded away, and again Sullivan, the gladiator, stood where one second before was Sullivan, the sentimental.
>
> "'There's the boy who'll fight today in a way that you never thought he could do,' said Pete McCoy."

John Roche, of New York, and Tom Kelly, of St. Louis, were announced as Ryan's seconds, and James Shannon, of New York, his umpire, and Billy Madden and Joe Goss were mine, the umpire being John Moran, of Cincinnati.

Before the fight some excitement was caused by the fears of those who had heard of the proclamation of Governor Lowrey, calling on citizens to prevent it, but no posse appeared. An idea of the betting can be gained from the fact that just before we fought there was a bet of $1,000 to $800 in my favor.

At 11:40 I shied my castor into the ring, and hearty applause followed. Then there was over a quarter of an hour's wait for Ryan.

Joe Goss seemed impatient for the appearance of Ryan and cried out:

"How long will you be there, old man?"

"He'll be there soon enough for your conscience," replied someone in the crowd, and Joe Goss justly commented on the bad grace of the remark, asking those present to show no partiality and allow the best man to win.

After the crowd were entertained for several bets, at 12:02 the cries for Ryan were very loud and a minute later Ryan, in a suit of white drawers and undershirt, flesh-colored stockings and fighting shoes, threw an old hat into the enclosure, and came in at the northeast corner, accompanied by Johnny Roche, Tom Kelly, James Shannon, Joe Connick and others. Ryan was dressed in an overcoat and looked very pale, his old, good-natured smile seeming to have deserted him.

> "Sullivan sat in his corner watching Ryan's seconds preparing him, with a defiant and fearless expression on his countenance, which boded no good for his adversary, and showed that he was determined to make a hard fight.
>
> "Kelly and Goss tossed for corners and Ryan won, placing his adversary with his face towards the sun. The men here took their seats in their respective corners, Ryan going to the southwest and Sullivan to the northeast.
>
> "'Sullivan has lost the toss for the ground and the toss for the corner, and he will lose the battle,' observed one of Ryan's friends.
>
> "'Sullivan has lost twice, but I guarantee he will not lose a third time,' answered a Sullivan sympathizer.
>
> "When it was announced that a referee was about to be selected, the names of 'Brewster!' 'Hardy!' 'Bush!' were vociferously suggested by the crowd. Arthur Chambers, umpire for Sullivan, and James Shannon, Ryan's umpire, set themselves to the task of selecting a suitable person, with the advice of all their fellow-sympathizers.
>
> "'Give us a Louisiana man and a square fight,' was the cry. The claims of Mr. Jack Hardy, of Vicksburg, were pressed with some earnestness, and that gentleman stated that he knew neither of the men, and would do his best, if selected, to see that the best man won. The Sullivan party were shy about consenting to Mr. Hardy as they were not acquainted with him, and Joe Goss suggested that Harry Hill act. The latter being stake-

holder it was thought he could not act, and Charlie Bush was called far. Mr. Bush declined to act and the choice narrowed down to Mr. Alex. Brewster and Mr. Hardy. Mr. Brewster was unwilling to serve, but the requests of the Sullivan party were so earnest that he finally agreed to come down. The Ryan party, however, still demanded Hardy. The dispute was stubborn for some time, but Joe Goss finally suggested a compromise, "Let's get up this fight, let both men act as referees." His plan was agreed upon, and the referees and umpires took their places in the ring, which the seconds were also allowed to do.

The opening of the fight has been told in this manner by a spectator:

"After shaking hands, the men toed the scratch and there was a bit of sparring which was soon cut short by a lion-like movement on the part of Sullivan. Ryan had led out with a short one with his right, which did no damage except drawing a stinger from Sullivan's left on his face, which surprised him. Both closed to hi-fighting, with half-arm blows, which were quicker and stronger from Sullivan, although this was said to be Ryan's favorite mode of fighting. The dash forward of Sullivan disconcerted his adversary, as it was totally unexpected. After these exchanges Sullivan let go his terrific right hand, and Ryan went to grass like a shot, face downward, from a blow on his left jaw. First knockdown for Sullivan. Time, 30 seconds."

I think it timely to mention here that Ryan, subsequently describing his feelings, said: "When Sullivan struck me I thought that a telegraph pole had been shoved against me endways."

This was a sample of the style of fighting for succeeding rounds.

Bob Farrell, cousin of Joe Coburn's, said in describing that portion of the fight: "I have been in the business 25 years, and I never saw such work as Sullivan did. He went at Ryan as you would to chop a log of wood, and he broke him all up from the start."

"At the end of the third round," said Billy Madden, "Sullivan just pushed Ryan over; he did not want to kill him."

The reason I did not punish Ryan more toward the latter end of the fight was because my seconds spoke to me after the fifth round and told me not to go at him so viciously as I had him done and might kill him. I only wanted to win and had no desire to beat him unnecessarily. For that reason I did not strike him in the stomach, though I had opportunity after opportunity to do so.

The fight lasted nine rounds, making in all 11 minutes, or 10 and one half, as some watches showed, when Ryan was so disabled that the best care of physicians was required. Immediately after the fight I jumped over

Paddy Ryan

the ropes and ran a hundred-yard dash to my quarters, taking off my fighting clothes and shoes and putting on my street dress.

Much disappointment was manifested by the friends of Ryan at his loss of the championship, and it is claimed that from $100,000 to $200,000 changed hands in the result.

In regard to some newspaper controversy that followed, an editorial in the *New Orleans Democrat* said, under the heading "Let us have Fair Play":

> "It is amusing to observe the style in which the newspapers now speak of the Sullivan-Ryan fight. They describe it contemptuously as a mere brutal hammering of Ryan by Sullivan. They allude to Ryan's rupture and his truss and, barring all the past, one would suppose that Ryan was a helpless, old imbecile who had been inhumanly beaten by a cruel and callous giant. The fact is, however, that previous to the battle, nine tenths of the sporting men in the country looked upon Sullivan's pretensions with open derision. He was alluded to as a green and gawky boy, a chap who had never fought without gloves and who would give up at the first good blow. Ryan was lauded as a Hercules and a hero; a man who could endure any amount of punishment; who was a magnificent boxer and invincible wrestler, - in a word, a winner. It was the same up to the morning of the battle, - nay, up to the moment time was called. Experienced sports had examined both men and knowing all the facts bet their money on Ryan. Learned physicians explained on scientific grounds the conspicuous inferiority of Sullivan. They descanted on Ryan's elastic "snake-like" muscle, and Sullivan's over-trained attenuation, until listening to them, provided you did it with proper awe, you must have thought the backers of Sullivan the most besotted fools upon the globe.
>
> "Sullivan sat in the ring for half an hour waiting for Ryan. A heavy blanket enveloped him so that only his face could be seen. He was the subject of a vast deal of disparaging comment, and of little or no enthusiasm. He endured those depressing 30 minutes, feeling that popular sympathy was against him, knowing that 90 of every 100 present were anxious for his defeat; having, finally, to listen to the deafening ovation which greeted Ryan as he entered, and to contrast it with the cold welcome of his own appearance.
>
> "All this he had to bear, in addition to the trial of meeting a man of conspicuous powers, a man with the prestige of victory and a full knowledge of his own ability. If ever one's courage and self-reliance were put to a severe test, Sullivan's were during that trying half hour while he sat in the ring waiting for his adversary, uncheered by friendly encouragement and seeing

as plainly as he saw the day that not one in ten believed in him. That he defeated Ryan was due, not only to his magnificent, physical strength and skill, but to his imperturbable and intrepid spirit. It is silly and ungracious in Ryan or his friends to allude to their man's condition or his rupture.

"The latter was no worse than when Ryan fought with and conquered Joe Goss, and, as for his condition, they had every means of estimating that up to the very last moment. If Ryan was sick and feeble, as is claimed, how could he bring himself to bet $1,000 at the last moment and permit his friends to bet theirs?

"But, of course, this is all baby talk. Ryan was as good a man on the 7th as when he beat Goss; either that or he shamefully and treacherously sold out all who trusted him. Sullivan won the fight by virtue of superior science and irresistible strength."

An evidence of the completeness of the victory as it impressed the spectators was had in a remark of one of them:

"Mr. Sullivan has probably put an end to heavyweight prize fighting. It is altogether improbable that for many years a man will be found who would dare to face him in a prize ring. He cared nothing for Ryan's blows, and his own hitting is so tremendous that it seems beyond the power of man to recover from the shock of one of his hands let out from the shoulder."

CHAPTER FOUR
A SERIES OF PICNICS

"Sing a song of 'Science' fighters in the ring,
Less than 'leven minutes crystallized the thing;
When the fight was opened, Ryan, "mid applause,
Acted like a Trojan, which indeed he was;
Soon the Boston laddie with his fists and looks,
Caused a deep commotion "mid the pocketbooks.
Troy was very plucky, and with all his pain,
Wouldn't cry "Peccavi," but would try again.
Sports grew pale with anguish when they saw their means
Filling up the wallets from the land of beans."

They say that public interest in any affair has not reached its height until the rhymers have taken hold of it. Judged by this standard, my little affair with Ryan must have hit the popular fancy, as it drew out a mass of rhymes of which the above is a fair sample.

On the evening of the day when the fight took place, Ryan, having had his injuries cared for, reached New Orleans and went to the St. James Hotel, where I was stopping. Being in my room with a party of friends, I sent for him, and he partook of our festivities. Ryan being a good fellow had lost none of his many warm admirers.

He was asked a numerous number of questions as to how he felt during the fight. He said that he "never was in it " after the first blow, and there and then, before numerous people, stated that I was the wonder of the age.

"How does Sullivan's hitting compare with that of other fighters whom you have faced?" asked a veteran sport sitting in a seat opposite Ryan.

"I never faced a man who could begin to hit as hard, and I don't believe there is another man like him in the country. One thing is certain, any man that Sullivan can hit he can whip. Before he is downed he must either be met by a man who is as hard at hitting as he is, or by some wonderfully clever boxer. Such a man as Mace, if younger, might defeat Sullivan, but no slouch can do it."

"Why did you think you could defeat Sullivan? "

"Well, in the first place, I thought that I had an advantage in the way of experience. Then I knew that I was a pretty fair wrestler. Some people have very wild notions concerning Sullivan, I have heard it said dozens of times that he can't box. It is true that he is not what could be fairly called a brilliant boxer, but on the whole he spars about as well as the general run of pugilists. And he's not half as clumsy as some people say. Hasn't he knocked our best sparrers out with the gloves?"

"What do you consider Sullivan's strong points?"

"It may seem a strange way of answering the question," replied Paddy, with a smile, "but he is strongest in his strength. He is a wonderful man, physically, and seems to have been built for a fighter, and he can hit hard enough to break down any man's guard that I know of."

"He has a wonderfully large pair of hands," remarked the veteran opposite Ryan.

"Well, I should say he had," remarked Ryan with a grim smile. "Speaking of hands reminds me of that saying which old sporting men frequently repeat - that natural fighters always have small hands. I believe it is true that Sayers, Heenan, Yankee Sullivan and some of the best fighters all had comparatively small hands, but you know there is an exception to every rule; I shouldn't be surprised if Sullivan proved to be one of the exceptions. I see, by the way, that some of the papers call Sullivan 'Yankee' after the old-time hero."

"Yes, but the Boston boy's way of fighting is not like Yankee's at all," broke in the old veteran. "Yankee was a tricky fighter. I remember when he fought Bell on Hart's Island in 1842. Bell was a professor of boxing from Brooklyn. In the early part of the fight, Bell got Sullivan in a tight place across the ropes, 'Let me go, Bell, I'm done,' says Yankee. Bell started to go back to his corner, and while his back was turned, Yankee gave him a terrible blow behind the ear. When Yankee fought Tom Secor, he kept going down nearly every round. Oh, no; John Sullivan is not Jim Sullivan by any means."

"What have you to say of your treatment by the sporting people of the South? "

"I was well treated by every one, barring the thief who stole $300 out of my clothes when I was getting fixed up just after the fight. But I guess that fellow wasn't from the South," said Paddy.

"You had better treatment than old Deaf Burke had when he fought near New Orleans in 1837," exclaimed the veteran. "The old man was fighting Sam O'Rourke and getting the best of the fight, when a gang started in to lay him out. Old Burke succeeded in getting a bowie knife with which he kept the gang away until he reached a horse. He was glad enough to mount the horse and gallop away. The deaf 'un thought he was a goner, sure."

"You have said that you are through with prize fighting, Paddy?"

"Yes, I am through; I don't care to continue in the business unless at the top of the heap. What benefit would it be to me to whip any but the best man on the turf? Well, I know two persons who will be glad I am through," remarked Paddy.

"And they are...?"

"My wife and mother. And there is one thing would please me, too."

"What?"

"I'd like to see some of these men who think that Sullivan can't fight, get in the ring and test him."

Captain Jack Slote, an old New Yorker, and authority on sporting matters, was led to describe a fighting resemblance between the first American champion and myself. In speaking of the encounter between him and Yankee Sullivan, he said:

> "When the men faced each other they made a pretty sight. Talk about muscles - they were muscled! Well, it is no use to say much about the fight; it has been published a thousand times. Hyer seemed out of place at first, and Sullivan walked up to him and knocked him down. The blow and fall seemed to wake Tom up, and he went to work in earnest and whipped the 'Yankee.' After the second round Yankee Sullivan cried out: 'The brute has got all my dodges, and a lot of new ones that I can't touch!' John Sullivan," the captain concluded, "is a second edition of Tom Hyer. He is not one bit like Yankee Sullivan, - he is too good a man to be talked about the same time."

Having given Ryan's remarks, it may be proper to repeat a portion of a little dialogue which occurred about the same time, the answerer to the questions being myself:

"Did the fight last longer or shorter than you expected?"

"I believe in giving every man his just due. Ryan is a game man; but I was sure of downing him from the start. When the first round was over I knew I had him."

"Didn't you feel a trifle nervous on the send off?"

"You may think it strange but I didn't. I had perfect confidence that I could win. I had confidence in my trainers, and I was confident that the fight would be a square one. The outsiders gave us a fair show, and that was all I wanted. So far as Ryan is concerned, I want to say this: I've had several good men who couldn't fight me four rounds with the gloves. Ryan fought me nine rounds with bare knuckles."

Of all the theories to account for the defeat of Ryan, that advanced by a Chicago paper is the most ingenious. It claims that as I hail from Boston, I was most likely imbued with the culture of that locality, and had the plan laid, in case of finding myself in close quarters, to interest Paddy with an exposition of Professor Tyndall's atomic theory, and then slug him under the ear when he was not looking.

The news of the result of the fight was received in my native city about half-past twelve o'clock, and I am told the scenes around the bulletin boards of the newspaper offices on Washington Street were almost indescribable.

At first a report was bulletined at one of the offices to the effect that Ryan had won the fight. This, of course, created no enthusiasm; but when, a few minutes later, that bulletin was torn down and one in its stead put up giving myself the victory, men screamed and cheered and indulged in all kinds of antics of delight.

The following verses, written by a humorous admirer are appropriate here:

> Just fancy what mingled emotions
> Would fill the Puritan heart
> To learn what renown was won for his town
> By means of the manly art!
> Imagine a Winthrop or Adams
> In front of a bulletin board,
> Each flinging his hat at the statement that
> The first blood was by Sullivan scored.
>
> Thy bards, henceforth, O Boston!
> Of this triumph of triumphs will sing,
> For a muscular stroke has added a spoke
> To the Hub, which will strengthen the ring!
> Now Lowell will speak of the "ruby,"
> And Aldrich of "closing a match,"
> And Longfellow rhyme of "coming to time,"
> Of "bunches of fives," and "the scratch."

Ryan had five friends to my one, and a good many of the outsiders - a class of low-lived fellows who are the bane of the prize ring - tried their best to do me, even offering Madden $4,000 and putting the cash in his hand, if he would give me something to put me out of condition. They then went to a person in New Orleans and offered him $2,500 if he would get me out of the way, - kill me, if necessary.

These persons did not belong to Ryan's party. They were outsiders who had lots of money on the fight, and were bound to win at all hazards. After the victory, I was treated like a lord in New Orleans.

On the evening of February 9th, I started for Chicago with Billy Madden, Joe Goss, Pete McCoy, and Bob Farrell, where I was billed to give an exhibition, under the management of "Parson" Davies, at McCormick's Hall February 11th. Just before leaving New Orleans, I suddenly thought of a promise I had made to sit for an instantaneous picture at a photograph gallery. Almost at the last moment I tore myself away from my friends at the St. James Hotel. They tried to prevent my going,

Scituate, Massachusetts training headquarters of John L. Sullivan, 1883.

fearing that I would miss the train; but I said that, having given my word, I would keep it. As the train with the sleeper attached, which had been specially engaged for the party, moved off from the city, loud cheers for "Sullivan" rent the air.

The journey from New Orleans was an ovation. The people along the line of the road had information of the train that would carry our party. At every station where a stop was made immense crowds surrounded the cars, and clamored for a sight at "the great pugilist." I did not appear, however. In our party was the well-known sporting man familiarly called "Big Steve." He is of great stature, and when the crowds became unduly clamorous, to appease their curiosity, he was led out on the platform and introduced as "Sullivan." This joke was several times repeated, and on each occasion Steve made a speech. The result of this was, that I got the reputation of an orator as well as a fighter between the Crescent City and Chicago. A comical thing happened to Pete McCoy: he was left behind at Cairo, where he was accidentally caught in the crowd that gathered at the station to see our party go through.

At Chicago our party was received by a large crowd. We were lionized everywhere, and most of the leading saloons and billiard rooms had signs out notifying the public that "Sullivan" would visit them during certain hours of the evening. "No one would ever guess from his appearance," said a Chicago paper, "that he had been through a mill within a week. He appears to be in the flower of health and spirits."

From Chicago I went to Detroit and gave an exhibition there, and from Detroit to Cleveland, from Cleveland to Pittsburgh, from Pittsburgh to Philadelphia, and from Philadelphia to New York. At Philadelphia I gave several sparring exhibitions in Old Liberty Hall and in the Art Industrial Hall, and then left for New York to receive the stakes.

Having arrived in Boston after my battle with Ryan, my friends living at the Highlands and vicinity gave me a rousing reception in the Dudley Street Opera House. The pleasures of the evening opened with a variety entertainment under the management of John B. Duffy. At the close of the entertainment several persons, noted among the sporting fraternity, appeared on the stage, and presented me with an elegant gold watch and chain inscribed, "Presented to John L. Sullivan by his friends of Boston Highlands, March 9, 1882", and also with a splendid horseshoe of wax flowers, 18 inches in height, and set in a gilt frame.

Shortly afterwards I issued the following challenge which ought to satisfy all challengers:

BOSTON, March 23, 1883

There has been so much newspaper talk from parties who state that they are desirous of meeting me in the ring that I am disgusted. Nevertheless, I am willing to fight any man in this country, in four weeks from signing articles, for $5,000 a side; or, any man in the old country for the same amount at two months from signing articles, - I to use gloves, and he, if he pleases, to fight with the bare knuckles. I will not fight again with the bare knuckles, as I do not wish to put myself in a position amenable to the law. My money is always ready, so I want these fellows to put up or shut up.

JOHN L. SULLIVAN

A large crowd, estimated to from 6,000 to 8,000, attended the benefit tendered to me in the American Institute, New York, March 27th. Billy Madden came on the stage and made an offer of $100 to any man who would stand up before me for four rounds. William Borst said: "George Rooke is willing to spar Sullivan in a 24 foot ring pitched on the floor."

I then came forward and said: "I am willing to spar Rooke on the stage; it is as fair for me as for the other."

Madden increased his offer to $200, but Rooke did not respond. An unknown man was found who offered to stand up for four rounds. I said: "I do not want to hurt the man, but I will give him $25 and spar him."

This was acceded to. The unknown proved to be Jack Douglass, a blacksmith. In the first round, which was short, I did all the hitting in a light manner. In the second round I landed a right-hander on Douglass' left ear, which caused him to stagger against the ropes. Douglass wanted to quit, but was induced to spar another round. After a few light blows given by me, I sent in three left-hand blows on Douglass' face, and the latter threw down his hands.

April 20th, I gave an exhibition at Rochester, New York. It was stated that one or two good local hitters were willing to stand before me for $100, but when called upon, none of them came to the scratch. The crowd of hissing, jeering roughs, numbering some 1,500, hooted "Fraud!" till finally, John McDermott, a light-waisted, small-chested fireman of No. 4 Engine Company, agreed to accept the terms. Everybody was astounded to see him give a good, lively, first round without himself getting a single blow, though three times I struck hard enough to have knocked his head off, but for his cat-like dodges. The crowd yelled with delight. Before the end of the second round the wind was knocked out of the plucky amateur whom I floored in two minutes, punishing him till he was limp as a rag as soon as he was up and at it again. The second minute of the third round settled McDermott as a completely-beaten man, though he dodged my blows wonderfully well under the circumstances. Of course I did not take all the advantage I might have taken of the fireman.

From the day that I defeated Paddy Ryan up to the time when Jimmy Elliott was knocked out by me, I had what the *New York Sun* termed "a series of picnics." On the Fourth of July, 1882, I gave a "picnic" at Washington Park, offering half the receipts to anybody I could not stop in four rounds, Marquis of Queensbury rules. The challenge was accepted by Jimmy Elliott, a boxer of high pretensions and good ring record. Both hard and soft gloves were offered to him, and he chose the former. He was seconded by Johnny Roche and I by Madden. Cleary, the noted Philadelphia pugilist, was accepted for referee. Elliott was taller and fully as heavy as I was. As soon as time was called, I let go my left and landed on Elliott's body; the latter countered, and hard fighting followed. I then knocked him an over the ring, and sent him flying off his feet amid the yells of the crowd. The second round was far more desperate. I punished him terribly, landing with left and right on Elliott's nose and neck until Madden begged me not to hit him again. In the third round Madden told me to finish him, but to be careful and not knock him out forever. He was knocked out in this round by just such another blow as I gave Paddy Ryan at Mississippi City the previous February. I then made Elliott a present of $50. Over 5,000 persons were present, and they appeared to have been well satisfied with the manner in which things were conducted; and so ended my "series of picnics."

CHAPTER FIVE
TWO "ARTFUL DODGERS" FROM ENGLAND

In my encounter with Joe Collins, better known as Tug Wilson, who had been imported from Leicester, England, for the purpose of "pulverizing" me, the match took place on the evening of July 17, 1882, at Madison Square Garden, New York City, when Wilson, by his floor-crawling and hugging, managed, with the assistance of Chambers and the bad decision of the referee, to stay the four rounds. It was evident to the 12,000 people who witnessed the contest, which could hardly be called a fight, that Wilson did not have the ghost of a show.

My encounter with Tug Wilson offers a striking exception to the concentration of local interest in local mills, while at the same time it has flooded the market with valuable information to sparrers, which might, under other circumstances, have been forever sealed in the bosoms of the possessors. "The splendid hitting powers of one of the contestants and the patience and Christian fortitude of the other" formed a fruitful source of conversation among the exponents and lovers of the noble art. One of the first to be approached on the subject was the rotund Billy Rice, the hero of a thousand attacks on the pages of old almanacs. When asked for his opinion of the fight, Billy's face for the nonce assumed a serious expression, and he gave unmistakable evidence of being wrapped in moody contemplation. When he had sufficiently grasped the importance of the subject, Billy prefaced his remarks with a spasmodic cough, and, striking an attitude, commenced:

"Big fight, sir, big fight! Want some points, eh? Couldn't have come to a better man. Do a little slugging myself. See that for style!" continued the now thoroughly aroused artist, as he aimed a vigorous blow, straight from the shoulder, at a visionary antagonist. "Good, eh! Well, Sullivan's better. Now, right here, without entering into a philosophical disquisition on the combination of forces, the logic of one of his blows would knock the big hammer at Wolwich silly. The only wonder in the world is that Wilson wasn't transformed into a regular pigeon house. You see, Sullivan knows what he's about, and when that arm runs away, then the conventional hostility of a government mule sinks into insignificance. Oh, he's a daisy, and in full bloom, too! As for Wilson," continued the artist, contemptuously snapping his fingers, "he wouldn't do for a sand-bag. He was badly pummeled, but just think what a heap of court-plaster can be bought for $4,000!"

"Shades of St. Patrick!" said Mike Price the minstrel. "What a hitter, Plunkctt, my boy," said he to an attorney who sat by his side, "Sullivan comes from Ballysimon, and bejabers he's the boss. What tinder hiven ever possessed Wilson to face him! Why, it is as bad as if you stood agin me. He's a straight hitter; it comes from the shoulder."

Suiting the action to the word, the over-appreciative Michael unconsciously dealt the interested attorney a blow in the side that doubled him up like a jack-knife. At the critical moment the assailant resumed the reading of the paper, when a prominent clergyman entered, and after the usual salutation, inquired the news.

"What a glorious fight!" exclaimed the enthusiastic athlete.

"Fight! Where?" inquired the astounded clergyman.

"What! Not heard of the fight?" said Mike with a profound look of astonishment and supreme disgust.

Ex-Senator Tim McCarthy was found engaged in earnest conversation with a number of friends, expatiating at length upon the features of the fight. "It's no use, boys; science backed by brute force tells every time. Jimmy Elliott stood up to Sullivan only to be knocked down as if he had been struck by the piston rod of a locomotive. Wilson went in merely for the money, and he got it by sticking to Sullivan as long as he could, and when he went to grass he took the full benefit of his knockdown."

Another match having been made between us, to take place in the same garden, I began at once to get myself in condition, having learned a lesson from my over-confidence and carelessness in my first match, for which I never took a day's training.

The second match was prevented from coming off by the authorities. The whole affair, however, taught me a lesson I have never forgotten.

Subsequently, there was a match made between Tug Wilson and Elliott, and a forfeit of $500 a side put up to fight according to London prize-ring rules. Tug Wilson sailed for his native shores, and his backer, who was Richard K. Fox of the *Police Gazette*, forfeited the stake money. That was the end of Tug Wilson's career in America, and very little has been heard of him since. The feelings of his financial victims are expressed in the following:

> "Tug Wilson has got his level. He is keeping a public house
> and performing solos on his own trumpet. He is better at blow-
> ing than at blows. He didn't thrash any one over here, and did-
> n't wait long enough to get thrashed by Elliott or Sullivan or
> Rooke. He made a masterly but inglorious retreat, ungratefully
> leaving in the lurch those who had been his best friends.
> Sullivan, they say, is going to make a trip over there, and Tug
> may be put to the test in a way that may make him shake in his
> boots. Over here we have fighters who fight and don't talk. The

best that England has sent us yet is Tug - the kind that talks for
$7,000, and doesn't fight for a cent."

I am quoted as saying that my principal incentive to a European tour
was a desire to again meet Tug Wilson. "The power of Victoria's court,"
adds an admirer, "will not protect the expert dodger when John meets him
the second time."

Having seen the last of this "artful dodger," I started out with a variety
show and athletic combination, under the management of Harry Sargent
who first brought Modjeska before the public. The variety portion of the
show consisted of the American Four - Pettengill, Gale, Daly and Hoey -
Georgie Parker who is now Pettengill's wife, Annie Hart, who is married
to Billy Leslie, Harry Sargent, sleight of hand performer, Edwin Bibby who
was at one time champion catch as catch can, Graeco-Roman wrestler
William Hoefler, champion club swinger, who took part in the wrestling
with Bibby, Bob Farrell and Pete McCoy in their boxing bouts, Billy
Madden and myself. Billy Madden, who did the talking for the company,
was asked:

"What are the terms of the agreement?"

"That Sullivan and I shall spar six nights a week for 20 weeks at $500
a night. We went down to ex-Judge Dittenhoefer's office today and signed
the articles. Sargent, they tell me, is a good manager. He is going to run
a 'bang up' variety company with John and I as stars. He paid us a week's
salary in advance. He pays John and John pays me. I got tired of being
manager, so I turned star. We go out on September 4th, and show for 20
weeks."

"Five hundred dollars is a large sum to receive for 15 or 20 minutes
work at night."

"That's nothing," said Madden. "At the rate Sargent is paying us, it'll
take over three weeks to make what we made in one night at Madison
Square Garden."

The combination appeared September 4th at Newark, on September
9th at the Academy of Music, Philadelphia, on the 12th at Scranton, 13th
at Pittston, 13th at Wilkesbarre.

At Fort Wayne a great deal of excitement was caused. It had been
rumored that Shang Donohue, "the tripper of Cornellsville," would face
me and attempt to win the $500 which was the sum offered at this time
as a prize for standing out the four rounds. The crowd was greatly disappointed when he did not appear, but they soon got satisfaction by witnessing the scene which is described by the following account of a spectator:

"Madden and Sullivan came on the stage, when there was a

great commotion in the audience near the entrance. A tall, muscular fellow had forced his way by the doorkeeper, insisting that he would meet Sullivan, and he wanted that $500. "He weighed over 200 pounds, and looked equal to the task of tackling anybody.

"'I'll box this world beater!' shouted the unknown, as he pushed his way through the crowd. His appearance created a great sensation.

"'Here is a customer for your champion!' shouted one of the spectators.

"'Mr. Sullivan will box anybody,' said Billy Madden. And then to the stranger: 'Sullivan will box you, sir, if you will come and get ready, and if you can stand up before him for four three-minute rounds, here is $500,' brandishing five $100 crisp notes.

"'I'll take it, anyhow,' said the unknown. 'I threw over Farmer Babcock's steer when they wanted to shoot him. I lifted over 800 pounds, and there is no fighter can whip me in four rounds, especially with boxing gloves.'

"'Did you ever fight anybody?' inquired Madden.

"'Well,' replied the new would-be champion, 'I never fit 'cording to rules. I was going to fight Joe Coburn once, but I left the town afore he arrived. Tom Allen and I was going to have it up in Cleveland, Ohio, once, but I did not stop over night, and we never met. I intended to fight Paddy Ryan when he was in Cleveland, but it was not Ryan's fault the fight did not take place. I tell yer what I did do, though. I lifted tho whole double corner of a stake and rydered fence one day. Josh Myer's colt's leg got fast, and when Dave Gould was going to kill his bull and they could not corner him, that fist (showing Madden a bunch of fives that would not have disgraced Tom Spring) knocked him stone dead.'

"Madden, Bob Farrell, and Pete McCoy smiled in wonder.

"'Well,' said Madden, 'Mr. Sullivan has been looking for a pugilist like you for some time, but he's never yet found one.'

"'I am the man, then,' said the unknown, bracing up; 'bring on your man. I have read how this yer Sullivan raised a hen coop on Paddy Ryan's neck, and how he knocked in the head of a steam biler at Boston, and I often thought how I would like to have been Tug Wilson, and to have received that hay cart full of silver dollars for letting him pound me.'

"'Well, you are satisfied to meet the champion, are you?' said Madden.

"'Well, you see I've been slinging a sledge hammer all day, bouncing it against an anvil, and I should like to box him without any gloves, for I am not used to wearing them mufflers; but I will go it anyway.'

"'Don't you think you had better have a doctor or a surgeon brought in?' said Bob Farrell.

"'I think if the gentleman is going to meet Sullivan, he had better send his measure for a coffin,' suggested Pete McCoy.

"Madden then escorted the rustic giant to the dressing room, and he stripped. Madden looked in amazement when he saw the muscles and the great physical development of the Indiana giant, and rushing up to Bob Farrell and Pete McCoy, said with a wink: 'Why, this fellow will murder Sullivan.' Then turning to McCoy, he said in a stage whisper: 'I guess we had better postpone this meeting.'

"In an instant the burly blacksmith was alert, 'No, No, sir,' said he, 'I am going to whip this champion, want that $500 to buy wrought iron when I go to Pittsburgh, and I'm bound to have it.'

"'Alright,' said Madden, 'our man is ready.'

"In a few minutes the ambitious pugilist was prepared. He stripped well, displaying well-formed limbs and well developed chest, and weighed about 180 pounds. As soon as the manager announced that Sullivan's challenge had been accepted and that the great Unknown was to meet him, the announcement was greeted with loud cheers. Sullivan stepped on the stage and was followed a few seconds later by his opponent.

"'He is quite a big fellow, Billy,' said Sullivan, 'but I'll double him up with a couple of punches.'

"The Unknown eyed the champion eagerly, but did not appear at all nervous. When all was ready Sullivan stepped up to the center of the ring, and the Unknown's friends told him to do the same. The men shook hands and the next instant there was a great slugging match. The Unknown was devoid of science, but he let go his right and left at random, sometimes landing on Sullivan's body or face, but more frequently missing or falling short. Intense excitement prevailed as Sullivan bored in and delivered several crushing blows on the Unknown's jaw, but he did not flinch. He swallowed the medicine good-humoredly. All of a sudden he made a desperate effort to plant his left on Sullivan's nose, but the champion stopped it, and quickly crossing him, knocked the Unknown all of a heap into his corner. He gamely came again and received another dose, and was fought down. Time was called, and both pugilists were loudly cheered. Sullivan had only been making sport for the crowd, but on time being called for the second round, he got at work in earnest. He banged the Unknown a terrific one with his right on the neck. His antagonist rushed in to clinch, but in an instant the champion jumped back, and then, feinting with his left, gave the giant yahoo a swinging blow with his right, which landed on his left ear with tremendous force. The Unknown reeled and fell senseless on the stage. Time was called, but the countryman was still asleep. When it was announced that the Unknown could not fight any longer, Sullivan was greeted with loud cheers.

"Stockwell, which is the Unknown's name, did not know whether he was asleep or awake when he came to and wanted to know if he fell off a barn! He says he was never cut out for a prize fighter, and says he is now very glad that when he went to Cleveland some time since, to meet Paddy Ryan and fight him, he chanced to leave before the ex-champion arrived."

The entertainment given by our combination was varied a little in Buffalo, where we appeared October 20th, by a match between myself and a Buffalo boy named Henry Higgins, who thought he could down me within the prescribed 12 minutes. He stood up like a little man, but it was evident to the audience that he was no match for "the hard hitter from Boston." One or two good passes and "wipes" by Higgins were applauded loudly, but after that it was "simply a question of mercifulness on Sullivan's part." The third round winded him badly, and time was called.

The Theatre Comique, Washington, where we showed November 17th, was packed. "Mr. Alfred McDowell came forward and announced that Mr. Mike Collins, who had positively agreed to test the slugging powers of Mr. Sullivan, had failed to put in an appearance. Colonel Shelbaker, however, not to disappoint his audience, had scoured the district and found a man who was willing to stand in front of Mr. Sullivan." He then presented Mr. P. J. Reintzel, who lives in Georgetown. He was formerly driver of a herdic, but is now a blacksmith. He was nearly my size, and when he appeared it was believed that there would be a good exhibition of the "manly art." The blacksmith, however, stated that he was not an adept at the gloves. I didn't strike him more than one good blow, and that was the first. The novice, however, played the drop game and went to grass six times in a minute and a half, and when he was getting up the last time I plugged him in the nose and drew blood. The show was brought to a sudden termination by the appearance of Lieutenant Arnold and a squad of police, who forbade any further proceedings. I at once dropped my hands, and the blacksmith was taken away by the guardians of the peace, evidently glad that the interruption had occurred. December 10th our combination appeared at Charley Davies', Argyle, Chicago.

Jimmy Elliott and I were to have sparred at Chicago, December 22nd, my undertaking being to knock him out in four rounds, but the authorities prevented the meeting.

Says a dispatch dated New York, December 28, 1882:

"The stamping of 10,000 feet in Madison Square Garden sounded like the roaring of the ocean surf in a storm as John Lawrence Sullivan skipped up the steps leading to the elevated ring occupying the center of the building this evening. The champion wore a pea jacket and light yellow trunks. He climbed the ropes, walked to his corner, and threw aside his jacket. His white skin outlined the muscles, thews, and sinews, that gave him his strength. A few seconds later the shining pate of Mr. Joseph Coburn appeared above the edge of the platform. The old champion never looked better, even when training for a fight.

"Pop Whitaker, master of ceremonies, in a stentorian tone of voice, roared: 'Now we will have a gentlemanly wind-up. Mr. Joe Coburn,' waving his hand toward Mr. Coburn, who bowed, - 'Mr. John L. Sullivan,' waving toward Sullivan, who also bowed.

"The giants then arose and approached each other as light of foot as panthers. Their white boxing gloves sawed the air. They circled each other like falcons at play. Then Sullivan's left flew out like a stone from a catapult. It was neatly stopped by Joe, who stood on the defensive. The falcon-like play was resumed. Again and again Sullivan launched out his left, and was neatly foiled. The interest of the spectators was breathless. The pugilists were smiling. Coburn stopped Sullivan's passes so elegantly that one of his friends shouted, 'Go in, Joe, go in.'

"The hot blood mounted Sullivan's cheek. He stopped spurring and turned toward the front of the house. His dark eyes flashed fire. 'Gentlemen,' said he, 'this is a friendly set-to between Mr. Coburn and myself. There is to be no knocking out. Some day, possibly, I may oblige you by killing a man for you. It may be Mr. Mace's unknown, and it may be some one else.'

"The champion turned and again confronted his antagonist. The fencing was resumed. Coburn rallied and twice tapped Sullivan on the ear with his right. The cheering was terrific. The old duelist had made the first hit. An exquisite display of science followed. Coburn stopping a score or more of direct passes, and old Pop Whitaker called time. The men returned to their corners and readjusted their gloves. They were not in the least blown. Alluding to Sullivan, a friend said:

"'He can't spar like he would spar if he was wicked. No big man can.' At the second bout the giants sprang for each other like old gamecocks. For a minute they revolved like figures in a kaleidoscope, then Sullivan bent forward and touched Coburn on the ribs, ducking his head as he did so. Coburn countered on the muscles of his back. Sullivan straightened and tapped Coburn twice on the nose. Joe crossed on Sullivan's ears. Sharp rallies, diversified with ingenious fibbing, followed. Out of the wilderness of this scientific display, Coburn laid his glove on the side of Sullivan's nose, and kept it there for a full second. The champion gave ground, and was followed by Joe, who tapped him in his turn twice on the proboscis. Amid lively countering Pop called time, and the men again retired to their corners. They were panting from their exertions. Sullivan ground his feet in the chalk under the rounds of his chair, and old Pop Whitaker shuffled himself around and used his one hand and a crash towel in wiping their faces.

"'Now, gentlemen,' said the old man, after the lapse of a minute or more, 'shake hands and wind up.'

"The masses of muscle, bone, and sinew, skipped for each other like Colorado cicadas. They got down to real work. The soft spots of the gloves on the hard flesh could be heard in every part of the great hall. Old Pop Whitaker began to dance like a man strung on electric wires. It was give and take. The men came together like two gamecocks on the wing, and skipped away on the rebound as elastic as rubber. The white gloves flew in the air like corn popping in a griddle. Exquisite feints and the sharpest rallying were followed by close countering.

"There was no 'slugging,' and no effort at chancery. The spectators were delighted. At times you could have heard a pin drop, and again the uproar was so great that you could hardly hear yourself talk. The rallying grew sharper, the countering became heavier, and the men were fast becoming winded, when Coburn, of his own accord, seized Sullivan by the hand, and the friendly set-to was ended."

We gave an exhibition at Troy, New York, January 29, 1883. The entertainment wound up with a bout between Joe Coburn and myself. In response to calls for a speech, I advanced to the footlights and said: "I don't know what to say that will be of interest to you except that I am going to New York City next week to make a match with the half-breed, Slade, and if it is made, I hope to win."

During the evening the question "Where is the Troy Terror?" was frequently asked, but Eagan failed to put in an appearance.

In Boston, at the Mechanics Institute, I had on the 19th of March, 1883, a benefit which netted over $15,000. During the exhibition, I sparred with Steve Taylor, Joe Coburn, and Mike Cleary. Fifteen thousand persons were present. William J. Mahoney acted as master of ceremonies. It was said to be "the largest and most noteworthy sparring exhibition ever given in New England."

When I sparred with Joe Coburn, I used my left hand only. At the finish of the three short rounds, Coburn returned to his dressing room and remarked to those present, among whom were Mike Cleary, Arthur Chambers, Billy O'Brien, and several other well-known sporting men, that Sullivan was a bullock and didn't know his own strength. Said Coburn, "He could lick a ton of Maces and Slades."

Under the management of Jimmy Wakely, of New York, I made arrangements to meet Mitchell who was imported from England especially to "knock out the Boston Giant," at Madison Square Garden, May 14, 1883. I sparred him three rounds. In the first round I was knocked down. This has never been explained thoroughly to the public until now, and is best done in the language of Mr. Hugh Coyle:

"What about Mitchell knocking Sullivan down in their fight?" was asked of this gentleman.

"Sullivan says his legs got crossed, and Mitchell hitting him knocked him down as you would knock over a chair. A noted sporting man in Chicago was twitting Sullivan about it one night in the

Joe Coburn

Palmer House, Chicago. Sullivan explained, but the gentleman laughed. That aroused Sullivan, and he offered to bet $1,000 that he would stand in his usual position with his hands tied behind him, and let Mitchell hit him twelve times without once knocking him out of position. The bet was not taken."

I got up immediately and went at him like a bull at a red rag. In the third round I had him helplessly on the ropes at my mercy. Inspector Thorne and Captain Williams, who is now inspector, interfered and stopped the proceedings. I said:

"Captain, let me have one more crack at him."

"John, do you want to kill him?" he asked.

When Mitchell recovered, he made all sorts of bluffs, and Captain Williams said:

"You go to your dressing-room. You are a lucky individual that I stepped in and saved Sullivan from killing you."

The event was the biggest of its kind. The doorkeepers had a night of it. People jammed, and elbowed, and bolstered one another along as

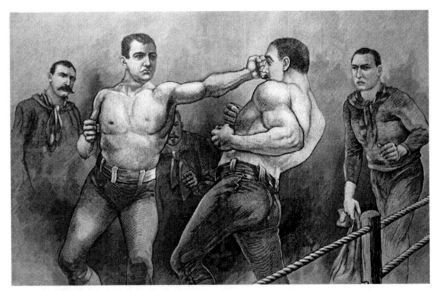

Charlie Mitchell versus John L. Sullivan, 1883.

though their hopes of happiness depended on an early glimpse of the "fist slingers."

To use the words of a spectator, "Men who doze in obligatory pews on Sunday to the soothing accompaniment of a clerical homily, struggled eagerly to see these Christians pound each other. Men eminent in the higher walks of life lent the warrant of their presence to an exhibition of fistic skill which for once was stripped of the attributes which make such shows reprehensible. Staid, half-frightened mortals - evidently strangers to such gatherings - pressed their way through the rout of sporting-men and turf-loungers, with their eyes on the platform and their hands on their watch-pockets. A single he-looking female appeared at the gate, scrutinized the shifting throng, heard some unscriptural quotations, and then buried her emotion in the rain and darkness without."

At 20 minutes past eight the exhibition began. Madison Square Garden was then a sight. "There was no semblance of a seat, of a bench, of a box," said the same spectator, "but every foot of board, every oval of leather, every stretch of flooring, presented one continuous and uninterrupted expanse of human heads."

Just beside the platform sat ex-United States Senator Roscoe Conkling. At the end of the reporters' table was Mr. Charles A. Dana. Mr. Lawrence Jerome and a cluster of club men were beyond the platform, while "Fisticdom " was represented by its subjects in swarms.

"The fight was a good one," said Billy Edwards after the battle was over. " Only one thing can be said about it. Mitchell is a very good man, but he met another who is his superior all the way around."

"The contest," said Jim Cusick," only proves the old saying that a good little man cannot whip a good big man."

"I always like to hallo with the underdog," said Roscoe Conkling. "Mitchell was unquestionably overmatched."

Said a listener to the ex-senator's remarks to a group of friends, when the great Conkling had passed beyond hearing, "Did you ever hear the boxing story about Conkling and the late Secretary Chandler?"

"No; give it to us," said one of the group.

"When both were members of the Senate, they were accustomed to meet at each other's house after tea and put on the gloves with each other. It happened that at one meeting the New Yorker sent the Michigander to grass in so very bad a way that the latter ruminated long and deeply over his humiliation and studied how he should have his revenge. He hit it.

"In due course of time Conkling was invited to Chandler's to a private tea, nobody being present save one of the latter's constituents, a Mr. Elmer, of Ypsilanti. After the tea and muffins were disposed of and the cigars were lighted, Conkling began bantering his host about his discomfiture, and finally proffered him satisfaction with the gloves. Chandler had a lame wrist and declined, but seeing that his guest had been anticipating some fun and was disappointed, suggested that his friend Elmer would put on the boxers. Elmer was a little shy about it, but Conkling promised not to hurt him, and the two men were soon facing each other on the dining room floor. In a flash Conkling was bowled over, and it was done so 'slick' that Chandler insisted that his colleague must have slipped; but the senator had scarcely faced his adversary the second time before he was sent spinning into a corner.

"'Never mind about hurting, go in Conk,' yelled Chandler; and the New Yorker, a little flushed, went at it again. Then he got a pounder that laid him in a confused mass among a pile of chairs, and the fun was over.

"'You should have put me on my guard, but it's all right, and how much did you give him?' was Conkling's parting salutation to his host, who was shaking the whole block with his laughter.

"The secret was that Chandler had sent to New York for one of the boys, and the Michigan 'constituent' was one of the most noted sluggers in the country."

In regard to Mr. Conkling, I am proud to say that he was a warm and constant adherent of mine, attending every exhibition that he could where I appeared, and always dropping in to have a chat when he came near my headquarters in New York.

CHAPTER SIX
VICTORIES WITH THE GLOVES

"Do you think that you and Slade will fight?" asked a friend.

"Why, yes," said I, "he was brought 15,000 miles by Mace to try and lower my colors, and it won't be my fault if he is disappointed. I'm prepared to gratify him at any time, from one week to three months from the date of signing articles, for $5,000, or $20,000, a side. I had rather fight for the latter sum than the former. I don't want any six months about it, as his backer proposes."

It was the general opinion of the crowd assembled at the Mace-Slade exhibition, just before my battle with the latter, that Slade was no match for me. "He'll make a good marker for Sullivan, that's all," said Joe Elliott.

"Slade does well enough with his friend Mace," added Billy Edwards, "but let him go before such a terrific hitter as Sullivan, and the tricks Jem has taught him won't count for much, Sullivan would soon knock them out of him."

Charlie Johnston said: "As far as I have seen, I should judge this big fellow was a pudding for Sullivan."

A crowd greater in point of numbers, and of the same mixed character like that which assembled at the same place to witness the memorable four-round glove contests which I had with Tug Wilson and Charles Mitchell, congregated within the walls of Madison Square Garden, New York, on the evening of Monday, August 6, 1883, when an event took place which the sporting public had long wished to see, - a fight in the old style did not seem among the possibilities, - "a combat in the latter-day pugilistic fashion between John L. Sullivan and the importation from far-distant New Zealand, Herbert A. Slade, a Maori half-breed." The latter, it will be remembered, was brought to the States by ex-champion Jem Mace, at the instance of an individual who has scoured a great part of both hemispheres in search of a pugilist, who possessed the qualifications necessary to compel me to step down and out from the position to which my fighting qualities had elevated me.

He had arrived at San Francisco late in December, 1882, and for some time afterwards the papers throughout the country had been full of flattering descriptions of his physique, and glowing accounts of his deeds of prowess at the antipodes. There was no denying that he was a strapping young fellow; and, as he possessed a fair reputation as a wrestler who was quick, skilful, and strong, it was reasonable to suppose that if he had any ambition to gain fame as a fistic artist, and showed ordinary intelligence and aptitude, he must, under the training of Jem Mace, develop into a clever boxer. It was blazoned forth by his importer, that he had come here expressly "to fight Sullivan for the championship," and a large sum of money and a challenge was issued to me; but the conditions embodied therein were of a nature that, as was well known to the Slade party, would not meet with my approval. As they would not consent to treat on a fair basis, no match resulted. On the strength of the challenge, however, the Mace-Slade Combination managed to make money, for all save the person who started the troupe on the road, during their not very lengthy traveling tour.

The Maori is described as a larger man than I. His frame is angular and powerful, and his motion somewhat slower than mine. His face is dark. His carriage is erect and graceful. He is a veritable Hercules, with a chest and arm that recall statues of the Roman gladiators of an earlier day. His weight was, at this time, 236 pounds, and his height six feet one and three-eighths inches.

The following is a condensed account of our contest at Madison Square Garden, as given by a close observer:

"Time was called. The men approached and shook hands. Both had removed their undershirts. Sullivan's flesh looked hard and firm, and he appeared in good condition. Slade looked larger than Sullivan and heavier, but his flesh had a soft appearance. Slade's face wore an anxious look, while Sullivan's had a contented appearance. After cautious sparring of a few seconds, Sullivan delivered his first blow squarely on Slade's countenance, following it by another on the neck, driving him into his corner. A storm of cheers greeted this performance. The men were soon at close quarters, and rapid exchanges took place. 'Break,' was called by the referee. They then sparred for the opening, which Sullivan obtained, and he drove the Maori, finally knocking him down. Springing up, the two again clinched, but the Maori soon had enough, running to the ropes, Sullivan assisting in the movement by a heavy blow on the back of the head and neck. A well-directed blow sent the Maori between the ropes and off the platform headfirst. The Maori soon regained the platform, and the three minutes expired. While sparring, Slade appeared 'winded,' while Sullivan seemed all right.

"In the second round Sullivan beat Slade all around the ring, knocking him down twice. Slade had his 'bellows to mend.' Sullivan in fine form.

"In the third round Sullivan led off with a terrific right-hander square in the face, which staggered Slade. The two clinched, but Sullivan, breaking away again, rattled away upon his antagonist, whose replies were weak. The Maori was finally sent sprawling upon the platform. He appeared dazed and unconscious of his surroundings. Sullivan stood over him. Inspector Thorne and Captain Williams then rushed on the platform to stop the fight. Slade made their interference unnecessary. He had 'enough.' He was helped to his corner and the gloves removed. Sullivan discarded his gloves and shook hands with Slade. The champion was loudly cheered."

After the victory over Slade, I started on an eight months' "knocking-out tour," leaving Boston on September 26th for New York, and leaving New York on the 27th, with Al Smith as a manager, and Frank Moran to look after my interests with the different boxing shows. We took in most of the principal cities in the United States clear to British Columbia. The company consisted of Herbert Slade, the Maori, Steve Taylor, Pete McCoy, and Mike Gillespie. To quote a remark made by a fellow fond of dipping into ancient history:

"This modern Hercules had two of the famous pugilists whom he had vanquished in the ring, if not chained to the wheels of his chariot, at least present to pay homage to his prowess, while two of the lesser athletes, the ablest of their rank in the American Olympics, also attended upon the champion, Mr. Hugh Coyle, who was advance-agent, and had formerly been with Forepaugh's show."

"Between you and me," said a warm admirer of Slade to an interviewer, "the Maori is playing a big game in starting out as a member of the Sullivan combination. Jem Mace is as cute out of the ring as in it. He found out that his pupil had but one chance of ever downing the Boston wonder, and that was to learn how to guard off that tremendous rush with which he knocks men out. This whole Sullivan tour is but the carrying out of one Mace had mapped out for Slade had he beaten Sullivan. As it was, Mace dropped out and Sullivan stepped in. Mace put as much distance as possible between himself and the party, and kept quiet.

Now, there is more in Slade than you suppose; Sullivan knocked him clear over the ropes when they met, but Slade turned round to let him do it. He wants to fight and he is the coolest man in the country. Sullivan is excitable, and if a man would stay with him in the ring for 20 minutes he would lose his head. That is the idea that Mace and Slade have, and when this tour is over Sullivan will have to fight or back down. That is the objective point in the whole matter, and I am surprised that Sullivan don't get on to it. Al Smith knows it, but he is not a big fool and don't want to lose one of his big cards. If Sullivan finds it out he will lick the Maori while he can. When Slade gets all the knowledge Sullivan will give him, and all the tricks that Mace knows, he will whip any man in the world. Don't publish what I've told you, but mark me, Sullivan will be challenged at the close of the tour."

This is a sample of the gossip that was put into the newspapers about this time, but the tour proved it groundless. Its mention now gives occasion to explain something of the relations between Mace and myself.

Speaking of Mace's challenge to myself, Al Smith, as reported in the *Cincinnati Enquirer*, said:

> "The truth of the matter is this: when Mace was here before I was his firm, fast friend, and was his umpire when he faced Coburn in Canada, and until I saw Sullivan I thought he was the best man in the world. When he first talked of meeting Sullivan, which was before the Maori went against him, he came to me and said:
>
> "'I want to meet this young fellow, Sullivan, but I don't want to be knocked out. It would break my heart if I was. Now, I want you to fix it so I won't.'
>
> "I told him it was no use to talk to Sullivan on this subject, but he urged me, saying:
>
> "'Won't you see him and tell him that after the four rounds are over, I will get up and say he is the best man I ever met, and the coming champion.'
>
> "I replied: 'Jem, why not go against him on the dead square? We can pack Madison Square Garden at $2 a ticket for common seats. It will hold $20,000, and suppose you do get knocked out, we will split the receipts in two with you and you will have $10,000 for your trouble.'
>
> "He asked me to give him until next day to think it over, and he did so. The next night he met me and urged me to see Sullivan about his proposition, as it would break his heart to be knocked out. To oblige him I went to Boston, where Sullivan was training for his fight with the Maori, and delivered Mace's message, saying, as I did so:
>
> "'Now, do as you please about it.'
>
> "'There is only one thing I will do about it,' answered Sullivan, 'and that is I will do my best, and let him do the same. All I have ever made has been by doing this, and I won't quit to oblige Mr. Mace.'
>
> "When asked if he would meet Sullivan then, he said: 'Not for the Bloody Bank of England.'
>
> "After Sullivan beat the Maori, Mace resumed his challenges. One day I met him and said: 'Jem, you had better accept our proposition. You are getting to be an old man and in a year or two no one will believe that you will have any chance to fight Sullivan. You had better make this $10,000 while you

can.' He refused again to meet Sullivan on the square, saying that he was the wonder of the world, and it would break his heart to be knocked out by him. When he issued his challenge to meet Sullivan in three matches, he said to me:

"'Don't mind what I say or do, I have to make some money, and this is the best way to do it.'

"John would be only too happy to meet him with the gloves, but it would have to be on the square."

During the trip I offered $1,000 to anybody who could stay four rounds, Marquis of Queensbury rules. There were 59 men who tried to stay the specified number of rounds, all of whom met defeat in a most decided manner. I cannot remember the names of all these would-be victors, but the principal aspirants I shall give in the order in which I knocked them out, as I narrate the chief events along the way.

Time and time again, while traveling through the country and offering $1,000 to any man who would stand before me four rounds, I have had men approach me who wanted to attempt to do that. Where I thought, in my judgment, that a man could make any show whatever, I have always obliged him with a trial, of course, knocking him out eventually. In some cases it took 20 seconds, in some cases longer. A great many times while traveling under the management of Mr. Al Smith, some poor fellow would be put forward by his so-called friends who, thinking they would have some fun out of him, would want him to spar with me. Rather than do so, I have put him before Pete McCoy, or Slade, or some other member of my combination, and let them settle it to his and his friends' satisfaction. I never yet wanted to meet a man whom I considered physically inferior to me, and I never would consent to knocking a man out simply for the amusement of his so-called friends, unless I thought him physically somewhere near my equal, but on the other hand I would not spar him; and time and time again, where I have seen that a man wanted simply the money, or a little money for sparring me, I have made him a present of $25 or $50 rather than to spar him. I never could see any fun in beating down weaker men than myself, especially if it was to afford amusement to a lot of blackguards.

I never had any objection to meeting with gloves any strong, healthy young men who wanted to contest for boxing honors, for I appreciate their position as one in which I found myself on starting out. I know full well that reputation does not make the man. I want to give every young man a chance to prove what he is. I remember in 1880, two years before I fought Ryan, I challenged him personally to fight me at Music Hall, Boston, and he ignored me and belittled me as much as he could. His reply to my challenge was, "Go get a reputation." I had none at that time, but in the two years from 1880 to 1882 I proved to the public and everybody in general

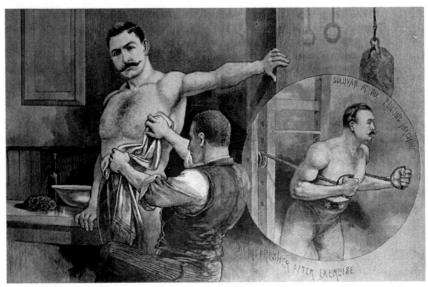

Sullivan in training, circa 1883.

that I was at least deserving a chance.

As this brings me to a point in my career which forms a kind of connection between my fighting and my sparring accomplishments with the gloves, the following from John Boyle O'Reilly, who was an authority on both of these, may be timely:

> "The superiority of Sullivan lies in his extraordinary nervous force and his altogether incomparable skill as a boxer.
> "In what does his extraordinary skill consist? In hitting as straight and almost as rapidly as light; in the variety and readiness of his blows; in standing firmly on his feet and driving his whole weight and nervous force at the end of his fist - a very rare and a very high quality in a boxer; in movements as quick and purposeful as the leap of a lion. He can 'duck' lower than any feather-weight boxer in America; he can strike more heavy blows in 10 seconds than any other man in a minute, and he watches his opponent with a self-possession and calculation that do not flurry with excitement, but only flame into a ravening intensity to beat him down, to spring on him from a new direction, and strike him a new blow every tenth of a second, to rush, hammer, contemn, overmaster, overwhelm, and appall him.
> "Sullivan enters on a fight unlike all other men. From the first movement his action is ultimate. Other boxers begin by sparring; he begins by fighting - and he never ceases to fight. But

from the first instant of the fight, Sullivan is as fierce, relentless, tireless as a cataract. The fight is wholly to go in his way - not at all in the other man's. His opponent wants to spar; he leaps on him with a straight blow. He wants to breathe; he dashes him into the corner with a drive in the stomach. He does not waste 10 seconds of the three minutes of each round.

"And look at the odds he offers, and offers to all the world! They are not 10 to 1, nor 20 to 1, but nearer to 100 to 1. Observe, he will not only defeat all comers, but he will defeat them in four rounds - in 12 minutes! And this is not all - he will defeat them with his hands muffled in large gloves.

"The chief reason why boxing has fallen into disrepute is the English practice of prize-fighting with bare hands, and under improper rules.

"The American champion, Sullivan, has done more than attempt to defeat all pugilists who came before him; he has made a manly and most creditable effort to establish the practice not only of sparring, but of fighting with large gloves. The adoption of gloves for all contests will do more to preserve the practice of boxing than any other conceivable means. It will give pugilism new life, not only as a professional boxer's art, but as a general exercise."

CHAPTER SEVEN
GREATEST "KNOCKING-OUT TOUR" ON RECORD

"What are the sensations of a man on being knocked out?"

"I have never been knocked out myself, as the public well know, but as I have put so many other men to sleep after this fashion, I have had a good chance to find out what their feelings were. The most effectual point, to reach a man to knock him out, is right on the point of the chin. In explanation of this, the doctors tell me that point is connected with the spinal column, and the effect for the time is to paralyze the brain though not effectually to weaken him. The sensation, as it has been described to me, is about the same as that felt by a man who has been under the influence of ether and is coming out of it. A man's mind, they tell me, seems confused, sick, giddy. He has no feeling of pain, but simply a sense of numbness or deadness which renders a man *non compos mentis* for the time. To verify what I have said about there being no pain, I can mention several instances where men have come to after having been knocked out, and instead of complaining of pain asked various questions, showing that they were simply insensible to all feelings or acquaintance with the surroundings. I have heard men ask very different questions. For instance, one fellow at Nashville, Tennessee, that I had knocked out, came to in about 20 minutes, and the first thing he said was, 'Did I win?' Another man that I had knocked out said, 'When do I go on?' not remembering anything about fighting. I think, in fact I am sure, that the effect of a man's being knocked out is not as serious as people think, and leaves no mark or lasting damage."

This reply of mine to a question often asked of me will be found to have an interest in connection with episodes in my long knocking-out tour which I am about to describe.

My first experience at Baltimore, where we opened, September 28, 1883, was being interviewed by the writer of the following, in which, for the humor of contrast, he took liberties with my style of expression:

> "Sullivan is stopping at the Carrollton, and all day yesterday, whenever he appeared, he was the cynosure of all eyes. He has the appearance, in citizen's clothes, of being a well-built, heavy, thick-set man. He was approached by a representative of The American, who tremblingly asked the privilege of grasping his hand, after Al Smith, his manager, had done the honors. The slugger granted that privilege and extended his capacious

paw, which closed like a vise upon the tender fingers of the reporter.

"'Mr. Sullivan,' asked the news-gatherer, 'how do you manage to do such terrible execution with your strength and skill?'

"'What der yer say?' growled the giant. "'I am desirous of ascertaining how you manipulate your digits and the other component parts of your general make-up with such force and accuracy as to succeed in annihilating every opponent you have yet encountered!' ejaculated the scribe.

"The slugger closed his eyes, drew a long breath, but deigned to say nothing.

"After waiting patiently for some minutes, the reporter again plucked up courage and went for the slugger once more.

"'You have, from all accounts, become such a terror that no one can be induced to stand up before you for the requisite minimum of time prescribed by the articles of your standing challenge. Will you be kind enough to divulge the information as to whether you will cross the briny, and there, in England, defy the roast beef and plum pudding champions to meet you on their native heath?'

"Sullivan, at this tirade, appeared staggered, and gazing askance at the puny stripling, clenched his fists, and seemed to be on the verge of having a fit. The state of affairs was becoming alarming for the reporter. The slugger looked as though he were becoming aroused, and the scribe was at his wit's ends, but plucking up courage he said:

"'Do you think Miller will be powerful enough to cope with you, and have you ever dreamed of the day arriving when you will admit yourself a defeated man?'

"It was fortunate that Al Smith was at hand, as Sullivan fell over in a faint. When he recovered he was asked the cause of his sudden illness and exclaimed:

"'I'll be blowed if that newspaper man didn't knock me out.'

"This was all he could say, and his manager does not think he will recover for several days. What hurts him so badly is the fact that all the big fighters in the country have succumbed to him, and yet he, the hero of a hundred battles, was forced to yield to a poor, weak, every-day newspaper reporter."

The same scribe, in writing of our exhibition, said:

"A number of rounds were fought, in all of which, except the last, 'the slugger' did not let himself out, but allowed Slade to give a fine exhibition of the manly art. Slade countered and cross-countered in splendid style, and his work was well done, but there was an inward feeling to the spectators that Sullivan was not trying. In the last turn Sullivan showed something of his ability to drive a man before him with his patronymic blows. He drove Slade across the stage to the edge, and then only refrained for fear Slade would land upon the heads of the orchestra."

Another writer in the same city wrote:

"The engagement of Messrs. Sullivan and Slade closed at Kernan's Monumental Theatre last night. The sparring matches which they have given to the three immense audiences have been greatly appreciated. Probably over 10,000 persons visited Kernan's Theater during the engagement of the Sullivan Combination, besides the crowds which nightly gathered around the carriage which conveyed the wonderful pugilist from one part of the city to the other. When the sparring exhibition was over, an immense crowd gathered at the rear entrance of the theater on Front Street. All cheered lustily for the champion as he made his way to his carriage."

After our combination appeared at Altoona, October 16th, the *Tribune* of that place said: "None of Sullivan's admirers will die happy until he is elected to Congress."

Without admitting any aspirations of that sort, I think it worth noting on the part of the profession that John Morrissey, the foeman of Poole, Yankee Sullivan, and Heenan, was elected to Congress, and that John Gully, who conquered the "Game Chicken" in the presence of King William IV, was chosen a member of the first Reformed Parliament.

This latter result came about in a rather curious way. He had just declined the suggestion of standing for a constituency, when, offering to lay long odds to a large sum against two events on the turf, a sporting nobleman agreed to take him on condition that he would add a third contingency; namely, that he would be elected for the new Parliament, the proposer being unaware that he had already refused the distinction.

"Done," cried Gully; and he at once took measures by which he was elected from Pontefract.

The Irish poet, Tom Moore, wrote this witty epigram on the result, the joke of which is in the fact that the word Pontefract means *broken bridge:*

"You ask me why Pontefract's borough should sully
Its fame, by returning to Parliament Gully;
The etymological cause, I suppose, is
His breaking the bridges of so many noses."

On October 17th, our combination gave an entertainment at McKeesport, Pennsylvania. The Opera House where we appeared was well filled. One number of the program consisted of sparring between Steve Taylor and Mike Gillespie. Taylor weighed about 200 pounds, while Gillespie, who is styled "a scientific sparrer from Boston," tipped the beam at 165 pounds. Taylor had a big advantage over the little one, and contented himself with stopping Gillespic's blows.

Occasionally Mike would counter on Taylor, and every time this was done, the audience would howl with delight. So great was the contrast between the men that one of the spectators yelled for Gillespie to stand on a chair or else put his glove on a broomstick. After sparring for the three rounds and a wind-up, the men retired. The regular program was interrupted at this stage by Mr. Moran stating to the audience that he had a surprise for them.

"It is customary for us," he said, " to offer $250 for any man who can stand up in front of the champion for four rounds, Marquis of Queenshury rules. This has induced one of your local boxers to come forward and ask to be given a trial."

At this the audience fairly went mad. They yelled and hammered each other on the backs in their glee at the prospect of seeing a real set-to with "the ideal thumper" as one of the parties.

As a spectator put it:

> "Sullivan has waved his red flag, exultingly in the face of the brawn and muscle of every Eastern city where he has appeared, and to be met by a man in McKeesport who wanted to meet him must surprise the champion himself. "Mr. Moran then waved his hand for the gladiators to toe the mark. From the left entrance came the champion; from the right emerged James McCoy. The latter is a puddler from Sharpsburg, and a local slugger of some repute. He said, previous to going on, that he had been anxious to meet Sullivan for years, and that he did not believe any man could knock him out in four rounds. When Sullivan stepped out the audience forgot to applaud, and a murmur of admiration was all that could be heard. His physique is that of an Apollo. He shows a depth of chest that cannot be duplicated, perhaps, in the world.
>
> "He gave one sweeping glance at the audience, and then turned to see the man 'who wanted to meet him.' The contrast between them was painful. Mr. Moran said:
>
> "'I pity that man, but he was well warned.'
>
> "McCoy, like all the others, was bared to the waist. He weighs 160 pounds, and his broad chest is covered with tattoo work representing flowers, anchors, white and blue snakes, and wide-mouthed dragons. His eyes increased visibly in size as he surveyed the lion-like bearing of the invincible Sullivan. The reptiles seemed to be in motion on his quivering chest, but, despite this, he stepped forward with firmness and shook

hands with the champion. McCoy opened the picnic by reaching for Sullivan's mouth. The blow was a very weak one, and made no impression on the Bostonian further than to start him laughing. McCoy evidently felt highly elated at this achievement of hitting the great slugger in the mouth, but his term of exultation was of very short duration, for the next instant Sully tapped him an easy one with his right hand, and then delivered a similar compliment with his left. Neither of the blows looked like a very vicious one, yet the latter was sufficient to send the receiver sprawling on the stage. He stirred uneasily, raised his head, and requested his friends to pull him into the flies. Sullivan stood undecided for a few seconds while the crowd cheered, when he suddenly strolled off the stage. His first remark was:

"'I was afraid to hit him where I intended to. I would have broken his jaw.'

"The official time of the round was 20 seconds. Afterwards, when he had time to think of his exploit, McCoy unburdened himself with, 'Well, I always wanted to meet Sullivan. I never thought any man could knock me out with gloves; but holy murder! I never thought any man could hit as hard as he does. A little of such thumping goes a good way. You can bet that hereafter it will take very little champion to do me, but I can say what few men can, that I fought with the champion of the world.'"

I had tried hard to persuade the man to keep away, but he was determined. I was afraid to hit him hard for fear I would kill him. We showed at East St. Louis, November 3rd. When I stepped on the stage, Mr. Moran, the time-keeper and master of ceremonies, announced:

"An unknown desires to win the $500 offered by the management to any one who will stand before Sullivan twelve minutes. The unknown has been advised to put on the gloves with some other member of the company, but he insisted on trying conclusions with Mr. Sullivan, and he should be accommodated."

The name of this candidate for fame was announced to be Jim Miles, alias "Gipsy Brady." Mr. Miles came forth, and the crowd, when they had sized the little fellow up, thought it was a good joke. He came to East St. Louis with the express purpose of having a "go at Sullivan." He said to his friends:

"I can hold my own against any man in St. Louis, including Mike Collins and Tom Allen, and no one on earth could stop me in twelve minutes."

Miles only weighed about 135 pounds, and was not over five feet, seven or eight inches in height.

"He's a fool to tackle Sullivan," shouted several among the spectators.

The "Gipsy" went at me pluckily, but my first blow sent him sprawling on the floor. He got up and staggered around in a dazed condition, but struck out wildly at me. I followed him around the stage and inside of four seconds he was on the floor again.

"Don't hit him any more, Sully!"

"He's crazy!"

"Take him!" was heard among the crowd, who stood on tiptoe, breathless with excitement. The chief of police jumped on the stage and separated us. Miles turned to his timekeeper and asked, "Isn't it two minutes?"

When informed that it was only 20 seconds, he made another lunge at me, when I caught him a blow under the chin and knocked him clear off the stage into the left wing, where his head struck between the rounds of a ladder. The fellow was, however, still game, and, although about half dead from pummeling received, would have toed the scratch once more if not held back.

In St. Louis, November 4th, I pitched five innings for a picked team against the St. Louis club. Five thousand persons were present.

At the finish, I was surrounded by a great crowd, and found it hard work to reach the dressing room. The Maori and I escaped from the ballpark by way of a rear entrance, and it was not until we had gone some distance that we discovered that a cigar-box containing a part of the day's receipts had been left behind. We returned to the park on the run and recovered it. I received, as my share, 60% of the gate receipts, which amounted to about $1,425.

There is a State law in Missouri which prohibits public sparring and boxing exhibitions, but our company paid no attention to it, and gave an exhibition in the People's Theatre, November 5th and 6th. The next morning, as the members of the combination were making ready to leave town, Steve Taylor and I were arrested, charged with violating the law above referred to. We gave bonds to appear in the court of criminal correction on December 16th. Our only alternative was to abandon the California trip, or forfeit the bonds. Of course we preferred the latter.

We gave exhibitions at Chicago, November 15, 16, 17, and 18, drawing enormous gatherings.

"I don't suppose," said an authority on such things, "that there ever was a troupe that traveled drawing such large audiences."

There were between $1,800 and $1,900 cleared in two nights. In one exhibition given at the hall of Battery D, there were over 9,000 spectators, and the interest on the occasion may be judged by the fact that 4,800 of them were willing to be standers.

"Truth told," said a spectator, "it was an audience of no mean aspect: Long John's periods, Oglesby's eloquence, Harrison's thrusts, and Finnerty's phrases, have erstwhile crept around the rafters and echoed from the dome of Battery D Armory; but the enthusiasm of a dozen political campaigns was last night concentrated around the ring which held two hundred and twenty-five pounds of the most remunerative brand of Boston culture."

The following lines tell the story of a Hoosier from South Bend, Indiana, who stood before me for a few passes, the fatal ending being, of course, only a humorous conceit of the rhymes under what might be claimed as poet's license:

"A long and lean Hoosier ascended the stage,
And stepped to the front with a grin;
Removing an ulster, which showed signs of age,
He said he would like to begin;
While Sullivan, properly sizing his man,
'Advanced with his left,' as they say,
Remarking: 'I'll touch him as light as I can,
By giving him Battery A.'

"But John's lightest touch, it is safe to suppose,
Weighed not a pound less than a ton,
And so thought the Hoosier, whose prominent nose
The slugger had landed upon.
The Hoosier arose and again made a pass,
But ere you could say, 'One, two, three,'
A blow from the Boston boy sent him to grass,
And John remarked: 'Battery B.'

"Adjusting three teeth and removing an eye,
The Hoosier, in terrible plight,
Laid over the ropes half determined to die,
Or, perhaps, to seek safety in flight.
But, cheered by the crowd, he came up with a smile
When ' time ' was announced for round three,
Receiving in very weak action and style
The contents of Battery C.

"Now wail for that Hoosier whose unhappy end
Remains in a word to be told,
And wail for the mourners today at South Bend,
Who gaze on those features so cold.
The coroner's 'quest has removed every doubt,
And soon on a tombstone you'll see:
'Here lies a poor Hoosier completely knocked out -
A victim of Battery D.'"

A Chicago paper relates the following grotesque episode:

"Sam Corcoran is a big, bluff brakeman on the Northwestern. He is so good-natured that everybody likes him, drunk or sober. Sam's great hobby is harmless jokes. He is always playing some little pranks on the boys. His future jokes will be few and far between. Saturday was Sam's beer day. He and two friends had been imbibing quite freely when they struck the Tremont barroom. Two men stood at the bar chatting. One was facing the entrance, but the other, who wore a silk hat, was looking directly in the opposite direction, toying with his glass as he talked. Now, one of Sam's favorite tricks was to slip up behind a man and tip his hat down over his eyes, making him look like a prizefighter and feeling anything but comfortable. The nicely brushed hat caught Sam's eye the minute he opened the door. He wasn't in the habit of tackling strangers, but this was too tempting an opportunity to be lost. Moreover, Sam wasn't quite sober. So motioning his friends and the gentleman's companion to keep quiet, he tiptoed softly up behind; then quickly rapping up the rim of the glossy hat with his left hand, he gave it a solid thump with his right. The stranger pushed up his hat with both hands and turned quickly around. Sam took just one glimpse, then he made two monstrous jumps, one of which was over the table to the door, through which he fired himself as if shot from a gun. The spectators were so astounded at this unheard-of action that it took them a full minute to catch their breath. Then they turned around. The man in the glossy silk hat was John L. Sullivan."

At the close of one of the performances, Charles E. Davies, the "parson," stepped into the "ring." He had been sitting with Paddy Ryan near the center of the hall. He was greeted with cheers. Advancing to the ropes, he said:

"You are all doubtless aware that John L. Sullivan has issued some challenges to Paddy Ryan. He has offered Ryan one half the receipts for a set-to with soft gloves, the match to take place in San Francisco in one, two, or three months; or, in the event of Ryan's failure to accept that proposition, Sullivan has declared that he would give Ryan the gross receipts of the house if he (Sullivan) failed to knock him out in four rounds, Marquis of Queensbury rules.

"Well, I am here tonight to say on behalf of Paddy Ryan that he accepts Sullivan's challenge. [*Cheers.*] Tomorrow I will be happy to meet Al Smith who represents Sullivan, and draw up articles of agreement and such stipulations as are necessary. The meeting will occur in San Francisco. I am assured that there will be no objection to the match on the part of the authorities. There will be a fair field and no favor, and may the best man win!" [*Applause.*]

On the next night it was announced that Ryan and I had signed articles of agreement for a glove contest in San Francisco. We gave an exhibition at St. Paul, November 25th, when Morris Hasey, of that city, undertook to face me. Hasey was a railroad engineer, six feet in height, and weighed 195 pounds. He had a local reputation as a vigorous and plucky man with his fists, but he was less than a reed in the wind.

"It is indeed surprising," said a spectator, "that Sullivan could knock out any man of like build so easily."

Said Hefey, afterward, "If you want to know what it is to be struck by lightning, just face Sullivan one second."

While showing at Davenport, Iowa, December 4th, Mike Sheehan, a blacksmith, was brought to the front and presented to me as "the strongest man in Iowa." He was 35 years of age, and stepped on the stage to win the $250 offered by me to any man who would stand before me four rounds. He wore pants strapped to the waist, with bare body above. He was accompanied by two grown sons who acted as seconds. The local striker and myself shook hands (gloves). Sheehan put up his fists. I pushed down those fists with my right, and with my left tunked Sheehan on the right side of his nose, and he threw his two hands to his face and looked at me in perfect amazement. It was pitiable, but very laughable. After a little loss of time, Sheehan approached me again. Down went his guard again, and a light blow fell upon his left cheek and turned him partly around, and, quick as lightning, a cuff under the left jaw fairly sent him spinning towards the rear of the stage. The $250 was no object now, and Sheehan began pulling off his gloves and walking toward the north wings, behind which he disappeared, feeling of his nose the while. Mr. Sheehan was a very powerful man, a very skillful worker at his trade, but he lacked training as a boxer. I gave him $100 for his gameness, and he retired to his family a wiser and better man.

Just before the exhibition, his wife, on learning of his intention to meet me, came to the hotel and begged of me not to meet her husband, as she was the mother of five children and did not want a murderer for her husband, as she expected her husband to kill me. During my career as a boxer and a pugilist, and during my travels throughout the different countries in which I have appeared, I have been reported a number of times as having been shot; this fortunately has never occurred. And to be candid, newspapers to the contrary, I have never yet had anybody threaten me or attempt to shoot me. The reports that have been circulated throughout the country to that effect have come principally from over-zealous reporters who wish to work up some sensational news.

My method of self-defense is such that I do not need any weapons except those that Nature gave me, and they answer my purpose. There was a little incident that happened in Denver, Colorado, where we appeared on Christmas Day that makes me refrain from ever handling a gun or a revolver, or ever tolerating their handling in my presence. I have done some shooting at birds and other objects, the same as any sportsman, and I am a fair shot, for an amateur. The incident to which I refer happened in the hall in which we were showing at Denver. I saw a two-barreled gun lying upon the table, and when I picked it up one of the attaches of the hall told me it was not loaded. I pointed it at Mike Gillespie, one of the party, and playfully pulled the trigger. The barrel was not loaded, very fortunately for Gillespie. In trying the other barrel I aimed at the table which stood in the room, pulled the trigger, and if ever a table was thoroughly blown to pieces that one was. Had I pulled the trigger on that barrel, when I pointed it at Gillespie, at first, the chances are I would have killed him. In fact, after the table had been blown to pieces with buck shot it was fully an hour before we could make Gillespie believe I had not shot him, and he ran around crying, "I'm shot, I'm shot." Any of my readers who may have the experience of making Gillespie's acquaintance, can imagine for themselves, how comically he would act. To attempt to describe his actions is impossible, but as long as I live I will remember his dancing around the room. It was some days and weeks before he got over the fright. I realized at once the danger, and never since then have I fooled with a gun.

A great many accidents have occurred just in this way. Thank God, I was not obliged to use the old excuse, "I didn't know it was loaded!"

In Leadville, Colorado, two days after Christmas, we had a grand reception. Large banners were hung across the streets and in the saloons bearing the words, "Sullivan, the Champion, is Leadville's Guest." "The event of his arrival here," says a local newspaper, "was even more important, as indicated by the number of people in waiting and the enthusiasm they displayed, than would be the appearance of either General Grant or General Sheridan. At the Union depot an immense crowd of people had gathered, and, as Sullivan edged his way through to the carriage, he was greeted with such pleasant expressions as 'Well, if he ain't like his picture!' 'Isn't he a darling!' 'Look at the neck on him!'"

At Butte City, Montana, where our company exhibited, January 14, 1884, I defeated Fred Robinson in two rounds.

February 1st, I knocked out a big Frenchman at Astoria, Oregon; he was a fisherman on the Columbia River, and Mr. Frank Moran, my master of ceremonies on that trip, tells the story in a rather amusing manner. Mr. Moran says: "When Sullivan met the Frenchman, I was sent in with the gloves for him to select; his trainers had rubbed him all over with oil of some description, and had wrapped four yards of blue flannel around his stomach (he was a big fellow and weighed about 340 pounds). After seeing the Frenchman and offering him the gloves (he could not understand English), they called the mayor of the town, who was an Irishman, and they then selected the gloves. On my return to Sullivan's dressing room, Sullivan asked me if I had seen him and what he looked like; I told him I had, and that he was bigger than the building; Sullivan said, the bigger he is, the bigger the fall. So I ordered both men to get ready, introduced both to the audience; time being called, both shook hands. Sullivan led with his left, catching the Frenchman on the forehead and knocking him down; he had 10 seconds to recover in, in which time he recovered his feet again; Sullivan crossed him with his right hand and knocked him down and out; he remained on the floor 15 minutes, in which time he came to, and broke away from his seconds and ran towards the back of the building, and striking the brick wall at the back of the building, head first, knocked himself out again for 20 minutes. After the show was all over, he insisted on seeing Sullivan and shaking hands with him. He was brought to Sullivan's dressing room, and in broken English said that he had broken boards with his fist, but Sullivan could break stone walls. The mayor asked him what he thought when Sullivan first hit him; he said, the first punch he got, he thought he saw a French soldier on horseback; the second, he thought the whole French army was after him."

I beat George Robinson in four rounds at San Francisco, March 6th, Robinson repeatedly falling without a blow.

"When I see a plain, ordinary senator or representative go on the rampage trying to do up the press gallery," says Colonel Sterett, "I am reminded of the manner in which a friend of mine in Texas whipped John L. Sullivan. His name was Marks, Al Marks, a cotton screwer in Galveston, one of the strongest men and gamest fighters in Texas. Sullivan came down there on a tour and offered $500 to any man who would stand in front of the gloves three rounds. Marks accepted the challenge. After the contest, two weeks or more, I interviewed Marks, and this is the way he told his story: 'As I walked up to the stage, people cheered me, and I felt pretty proud. I was going to put my hands up against the great Sullivan. I felt sure I could whip him, but when I got into the ring and John L. stood in front of me he appeared to be a heap bigger than he looked from my seat. But the people cheered me, and I determined to astonish him right from the jump. So after we had shaken hands I let him have a good one right in the jaw. Sullivan looked at me in a surprised sort of way, and I saw that I had his heart broken. Said I to myself, "This man has his match at last, and he knows it. He is afraid of me." So I gave him some more hard knocks. John L. looked at me almost appealingly. He tried to stop my blows but he was slow and clumsy. Said I to myself, " Marks, you are a made man. You'll whip this fellow easy. He is so slow with his paws that you can batter him all to pieces." But I made up my mind I wouldn't knock him out till near the end of the third round. I didn't want to rob the people of their sport. At the end of the round I asked Sullivan how he was getting along, and he looked kind of scared and said only tolerable. In the second round I gave him several more hard ones and he continued to look scared. I said to myself it was ridiculous for this man to be posing as the champion of the world, and determined that in the next round I'd put an end to his absurd pretensions. About the middle of the third round, just as I was getting ready to do Sullivan up, I saw another sort of look come into his eyes. He looked like some wild animal. In the next second he caught me under the left jaw with his light and lifted me up from the floor till my toes barely touched. At this his terrible left caught me on the other side of my face, and' - I'll have to finish the story," continued Sterett, "for Marks didn't know much about the subsequent proceedings. When he had raised his man clear of the floor, just as a football player lifts the ball preparatory to a kick, he hit poor Marks a crack which knocked him over the ropes and down into the orchestra, where two chairs and three violins were broken and where Marks was picked up unconscious. Sullivan thought he had killed the man and went and hid himself in the wings of the theatre."

This "knockout" occurred at Galveston, Texas, April 10th.

The arrival of our party at New Orleans, April 12th, for the first time since I won the championship of America in that section, drew the following from the *New Orleans Times-Democrat:*

"The wild desire to see Sullivan, and the enthusiasm displayed at the mention of his presence in the city, contrasted strangely with his reception here some two years ago, when he came without notice, and was simply regarded as a strong young fellow, who had the pluck to stand before a terror like Paddy Ryan. Sullivan kept his own counsel, did not try to make any friends, and was hardly thought of, except as a victim to Ryan. At that time, it can be truly said, he had very few friends indeed; in fact, his real friends could be counted on the fingers of a man's hand. Now, however, the scene has changed, and his 'few friends' have increased to such large proportions, hundreds of men now speak of the champion with the remark, 'You know I was his friend here, when everybody was down on him.'

"In an interview with a reporter, the champion was asked how much he would have to reduce to meet Thompson.

"Sullivan's face assumed a disgusted expression, as he said, 'He doesn't mean business. He 's working for reputation, and is backed by Duncan C. Ross. They want to dictate the terms to me, the champion, and have their own stakeholder and referee. I'll give Mervine Thompson a chance, though, when I get up his way.'

"'He relies on his wrestling a great deal.'

"'Well, what does wrestling amount to,' said John L., contemptuously,' after a man gets a few thumps on the jaw? But I will fight him, Marquis of Queensbury rules, and, by mutual agreement, allow him to wrestle. I am not afraid to wrestle. That's the kind of talk they used to give me about Ryan's wrestling. I don't like the London prize-ring rules, as they admit of too much monkey business. The Marquis of Queensbury rules give a man every chance he wants.'

"Sullivan gave his exhibition at the St. Charles Theater. The St. Charles is one of the largest in the country, but it was literally packed with people. The exhibition opened with a passage between Mike Gillespie and Steve Taylor. They closed in four rounds and gave the stage to Charles Bixamos, the wrestler, and Pat Kendrick, a local lightweight boxer. They drummed away for three rounds.

"Then Sullivan had a couple of rounds with Pete McCoy. Pete was very quick, and got in some handsome licks. Once Sullivan showed his great power by putting aside a pass from McCoy with so much force and vigor that Pete spun around like a top and nearly fell over the footlights. His quickness of movement is shown in his rounds with lightweight men. He seems to be as active and as light as the best of them."

At Chattanooga, Tennessee, where we appeared April 24, 1884, there was a widely circulated report that the John L. Sullivan advertised to spar was an impostor. When I appeared on the stage the chief of police and one of his officers demanded that I should establish my identity. It was said that I "raved like a mad bull" at what I called an "outrage." I said to the officers, "If you don't believe I'm Sullivan, you just send any man in the house on the stage, and if he faces me five minutes I'll give him $1,000. There's but one Sullivan, by Sancho! And I'm that man." I was identified and the show went on.

At the exhibition at Memphis, April 28th, a young physician of the town, who was up in athletic sports, called on me, and wanted to know if I offered $1,000 to any man that would stay before me four rounds. I informed him that I did offer that amount, and he said he had a man, Fleming, that would meet me. He brought his man around, and after the money ($1,000) was put up in a responsible man's hand in the audience, Fleming was brought to the stage, a big, strong fellow, who required but one punch of mine to knock him out. He was knocked out in 20 minutes, and was taken to his dressing room, and had not entirely recovered when the show had closed. The first word that he spoke after coming to was to ask his friend, the doctor:

"When am I to meet Sullivan? "

When he was informed that he had met me, he asked, eagerly, "Did I win?"

This was the shortest glove fight on record, lasting but two seconds.

Dan Henry was beaten by me in one round, at Hot Springs, Arkansas, April 29th. I made my usual offer of $1,000 to any person who would stand before me four rounds, Marquis of Queensbury rules. Henry was a stalwart Irishman, six feet in height, and weighing 190 pounds. His ambition to vanquish me asserted itself in the inaugural exercises, and he sparred vigorously. Being deficient as a tactician, Henry was knocked out the first round, but he evinced no disposition to retire until he saw he would be badly used up.

At Nashville, Tennessee, May 2nd, I met Enos Phillips, a youth of about 20, and 150 pounds in weight, at the Grand Opera House. Phillips endured my blows for two minutes, and, although thrice driven into the wings of the stage, manfully toed the mark for the fourth round. He had been punished so severely that he was taken off the stage by force.

William E. Stern, the local boxer, had been advertised to meet me, but he backed out.

The tour of the combination closed at Toledo, Ohio, in May. It was during this tour that Paddy Ryan forfeited an engagement for a combat to which he had challenged me when in Chicago. I made several ineffectual efforts to induce Mervine Thompson, the Cleveland Thunderbolt, to meet me, and, failing in this, returned to Boston, thus ending the longest, most eventful, and most profitable tour of its kind on record, the total receipts being a little over $187,000, with expenses of about $42,000.

CHAPTER EIGHT
BIG GLOVE ENGAGEMENTS

After I came back to Boston, I appeared at a benefit tendered to my old friend, Tom Denney, at which I sparred three men, winding up with Denney in a friendly set-to. On May 30, 1884, I was to meet Mitchell under the management of Al Smith, but did not prepare for the contest, as I had been led to believe that Captain Williams refused to let it come off. However, I was obliged to make my appearance at the exhibition, and excuse myself to the public, as I was in no condition to fight. I then went back to the hotel. Smith sent over what was supposed to be my share of the gate money, which was about $1,000. I refused to take it, and told him to give it to some public charitable institution, or to return it to the persons who had paid for admission. At that exhibition there were a great many counterfeit tickets in circulation, and while the hall was nearly filled, there was, in reality, very little money in the house. The show had been very badly managed, and it was fully an hour and a half after the doors had been opened, before the managers found out, or even suspected anything wrong about the tickets. Some parties had counterfeited the tickets, and were disposing of them on the outside at the regular prices, and in some cases were charging more.

When it was discovered that counterfeit tickets were in circulation, it was too late to do anything about returning the money. Mr. Smith said it was impracticable, for, as he stated, we did not have money enough to go round, that is to refund to each man in the house; and if we attempted to refund the money we had received only, the chances were that those who had actually paid for admittance would not get their money back, and the people who had come in on bad tickets would be the ones to whom we should probably have refunded. This was an unfortunate affair, particularly for me, and much as I regretted it, as I have explained, we could not see our way clear to make matters right.

I did not meet Mitchell for the reasons above stated, and also because I was incapacitated through sickness, caused by my own fault. I received a dispatch stating that even if the fight were allowed to come off, Mitchell would not be in fix to meet me. I got this dispatch in Boston, and thinking the match was off, I grew careless in eating and drinking, and was thrown off my guard.

My next contest was with Professor John Laflin whom I met at Madison Square Garden, November 10, 1884, and whom I defeated in the middle of the third round, for the receipts of the house. My manager was Pat Sheedy. The referee was Mike McDonald, of Chicago, the well-known politician. Laflin was seconded by Billy Edwards and Arthur Chambers, two well-known, ex-lightweight champions. I was seconded by Patsey Sheppard, the well-known lightweight, and Colonel Tom Delay, a personal friend of mine.

Wrote a New York correspondent at the time:

> "If John L. Sullivan had received the necessary majority of electoral votes to proclaim him president, the homage paid, by the successful party, would have been scarcely less than that accorded him by the multitude of people of all classes who gathered in and about Monico Villa, at 146th Street, November 9, 1884, the day previous to his fight with Laflin.
>
> "Such a crowd had never before been seen in the locality. They came in buggies, coupés, dogcarts, barouches, and sulkies; Sullivan's constituents from Boston were present en masse, and all were willing to back their pugilistic townsman in any amount - from a dollar to the Bunker Hill Monument. Two Boston brokers expressed a solid admiration for the champion, by offering to bet any part of $20,000 that he would defeat Laflin the next evening.
>
> "Nearly a hundred ladies sent their cards to Sullivan's room during the day, some begging him to appear in the parlor, while others wished 'just to see the fine fellow.' All cards were returned to the fair admirers of the Boston boy with a polite, but firm, refusal to see any ladies."

"There was nothing in the fight between the pugilists, Sullivan and Laflin," said a spectator, "which seemed more intensely interesting than the smile on Laflin's face right after Sullivan had hit the countenance squarely in the middle. Laflin is a coarse and burly, yet good-looking, man, and from the beginning of the encounter there had been an air of lofty condescension on his part, as if to say: "'I am letting myself down to this fellow's level for this occasion only.'

"You probably have seen accounts of the match. This particular blow was struck straight from the shoulder with all of Sullivan's might, and it was easy to imagine that the gloved fist sunk so far into the face that the nose was flattened. However, the visage rebounded into place, like a hollow rubber ball when you stop squeezing it; but it was left for an appreciable moment in a terribly distorted condition, then shaping itself into the sickliest smile that human features ever conformed to. The grin of the ballet girl, whose toes are excruciating, gives a very faint idea of it."

In spite of hugging and crawling, Laflin was knocked out.

Said a special dispatch, dated New York, November 15, 1884, just before my contest with Greenfield:

"John L. Sullivan is the biggest man in town. The pilgrimage to the wayside inn, just outside of the city limits, where he makes his headquarters, is made by hundreds every day. Sporting men of high and low degree, in wagons and afoot, make their way to the house and wait patiently, sometimes for hours, until the champion returns from a walk. The lamentable feature of these gatherings of worshippers at the shrine of the slug-god is the presence of boys in throngs. Imagine the burning desire of the little rascals to grow up into prizefighters! They have gone into training every one of them, as shown by the striding, rapid gait, with which they walk to the tavern from the nearest streetcar line. Yesterday about noon a stout, rosy-faced young fellow with evident sporting proclivities was seen rushing in the direction of the inn at a 2.12 gait.

"'Johnny, are yez going to dinner?' asked a passer.

"'Dinner be damned; I'm going to see Sullivan,' was the characteristic reply.

"An audacious urchin asked Sullivan what he ate and drank.

"'Blood, nothin' but blood,' was the reply. 'I drain a boy about your size three times a day.'

"The anxious inquirer escaped with no delay, but the words of the illustrious man spread among the lads with pugilistic aspirations and they got the further belief somehow that beef blood from a neighboring slaughterhouse really composed most of his diet. A consequence is that they go in numbers to the abattoir in question, where the butchers provide all the blood called for. The boys take it from a tin cup while it is yet warm from the slaughtered beasts, and some of them are able to gulp down half a pint without stopping for breath.

"Not all of the callers are rude. The story is told in the tavern (although I don't endorse the language) of a girl's morning visit. She sent in her card.

"'Show the duffer up,' the champion said, without looking at the card.

"''T ain't no duffer, sir. Anyhow, I guess not, cause it 's a girl.'

"'What's her sort?'

"'Daisy.'

"'Rise her up.'

"'But she said she'd wait in the parlor, if you'd be kind enough to see her there.'

"Sullivan loafed down to the public parlor, not more than half awakened from his heavy sleep, and loomed upon the startled vision of as dainty a little lady as ever surrendered her slender figure to the entrapments of fashion. She rose and advanced timidly to the giant whose face relaxed none of its characteristic scowl, and showed crimson spots left by several blows in the previous night's contest.

"'Our church is to hold a fair,' the girl said, 'and I am on a committee to solicit articles to place on sale. I thought you might be willing to contribute a few autographs.'

"'A few what?'

"'Autographs, you know, - your signatures, your name written on slips of paper by yourself, if you please. We could sell them for one dollar apiece.'

"She did not know that the ideal manner of the successful slugger is most threatening when he is amiable. When Sullivan glowered savagely down on her she wouldn't have been surprised if annihilation had instantly happened to her.

"'Of course, Mr. Sullivan, if it would be distasteful to you, don't do it,' and she shyly retreated backward keeping her mild eyes fixed on his because she had read of that method as the only one for getting safely out of a wild beast's cage.

"'Oh, what yer givin' me?' he exclaimed; ' I ain't no good at writin', but I'll have Dave Maloney make as many autographs as ye want.'

"The missionary explained why that plan would not do. Pen, ink, and paper were brought, and with great toil Sullivan signed his name twenty times over.

"'I always like to do all I kin for religion,' said he as he took one of her hands and most of the forearm into his capacious grip, 'an' I hope you'll find chumps to buy these things.' The soft smallness of her hand seemed to complete the conquest, and he very savagely added, 'An' if ye can arrange a set-to betwixt me and one of your fellers, I'll put on the gloves for the cause, an' you shall take the gate money.'

"The sweet missionary melted out of the room, satisfied that she had risked martyrdom for the Church."

On the same day that my popularity was thus recorded, Pat Sheedy, Richard K. Fox, Alf Greenfield, and myself, with our backers, waited in the neighborhood of Jefferson Market Court for Captain Williams to come and arrest us. Inside, Inspector Thorne had been making an affidavit that he had reason to believe, and, moreover, did believe, that one Sullivan and one Greenfield proposed to "engage in a fight or contention without weapons, commonly called a ring or prizefight," in Madison Square Garden on Monday evening, and that "one Sheedy and one Fox are instigating and abetting that felonious purpose." Justice Jake Patterson signed four warrants, and Captain Williams came out and got us. A crowd followed us. Greenfield wore a four-button cut-a-way coat and dark trousers, and carried a silver-headed cane and a brown derby hat; a diamond horseshoe sparkled in his salmon-colored tie, and his cheeks were rosy. The majestic Colonel Spencer, who was once a candidate for dis-

trict attorney, appeared for the defense. He made Inspector Thorne iden-
tify the papers in the case of Mace and Slade, who had been arrested on
similar charges and discharged on *habeas corpus* by Judge Donahue.
Colonel Spencer followed the line of the preliminary examination in that
case. First, he elicited that Inspector Thorne's affidavit was made on
hearsay, and then called me. I was sworn, and sat down in the witness
chair. I was requested to give my name, which I did, and the examination
went on:

Question - "Are you the person mentioned in this affidavit as having
    some sort of an engagement at Madison Square, Monday
    evening?"
Answer - "Simply a scientific exhibition of the manly art of self-defense."
Question - "Have you any animosity against Mr. Greenfield?"
Answer - "None at all."
Question - "Do you intend, during that exhibition, to inflict upon Mr.
    Greenfield any damage?"
Answer {Laughingly.) - "Pshaw, - no ! We were merely going to spar sci-
    entifically, - not hurt each other."
Question - "Is there any prize put up beyond what people are willing to
    pay to come?"
Answer - "No, sir."
Question - "Is there such a thing as a science of self-defense treated of
    in books?"
Answer - "Yes, sir."

"Sign your statement," said Clerk Sellman, as I concluded; and, as I
hesitated, the clerk said, with a smile:
"You can write, can't you?"
"I can," said I, laboriously putting my signature to the paper.
Then Alf Greenfield came up smiling.
"Hi was born in England," he said, "hand know Mr. Sullivan slightly.
Hi 'ave made harrangements with 'im to give, you know, what you call a
scientific hexibition."
"Have you any enmity toward Mr. Sullivan?" asked the lawyer.
"Lord bless you, no!" said Greenfield, closing his eyes and shaking
his head, "hi don't hintend 'im hany 'arm."
At this everybody grinned, and Greenfield continued:
"We would use the hordinary boxing-gloves, which, you know, his
very soft."
"Sign your name, please," said Clerk Sellman.
"Beg your pardon," said Greenfield, "but, you know, hin hour country
we don't 'ave a chance to learn, but hi can make my mark," and he put a

big X at the bottom of the sheet.

Pat Sheedy said he was my manager and not my backer and that he had been to an expense of $1,700 or $1,800. Colonel Spencer said that if the justice decided to hold us, he would take the matter before the Supreme Court on a *habeas corpus*, and have the question settled once for all. Justice Patterson paroled us until the following Monday at 3 P. M., by which time we were told the decision might be looked for.

At Madison Garden, some seven days afterwards, November 17, 1884, I met Alf Greenfield, when the police stepped in and interfered in the second round. I had Greenfield at my mercy. The referee was Charles Johnson of Brooklyn, now my backer, who award-

Alf Greenfield

ed the decision to me. We were both placed under arrest and held under bonds to appear in court the following morning. A jury was empanelled to try the case. Superintendent of Police Walling endeavored to make it a case of prizefighting, but he was unsuccessful. The jury brought in a verdict of acquittal.

On the 12th of January, 1885, at the New England Institute, Boston, I again met and defeated Greenfield in four rounds, for receipts, 65% and 35% ; I received 65%, having the best of it, according to the decision of the referee, whose name was Keys, of San Francisco. Greenfield repeatedly asked me to let up on him, which I did. Afterwards, during a conversation between Jack Burke and myself, at which he was present, he stated to Burke that "Sullivan could beat himself, Burke, and Mitchell, in the same ring, before a number of spectators, at an exhibition held in Boston."

On January 19, 1885, I met Paddy Ryan at Madison Square Garden, New York. I allowed him one half the profits of the house as a favor, to assist him to get some money. The contest was stopped at the end of about 30 seconds, by Inspector Thorne and Captain Williams, before we got thoroughly to work, it being the idea of these two officials that the contest would be too brutal. It was the opinion of Ryan's friends that he would have made a better showing than in his first contest with me, at Mississippi City. Previous to putting up our hands, I was warned by Inspector Thorne that if any hard blows were struck he would stop the contest. In reply, I said, "You can tell that to Ryan, yourself. As for me, I will hit him as hard as I can, and try to knock him out the first punch I give him, and you can stop it whenever you like."

The fact in regard to this contest was that Ryan came to see me at Monica Villa, my training quarters, and asked me to give him a show to make a few dollars. Through a liking for him I consented to give him 50% of the gate receipts, but I would have endeavored to do the same thing I did before had it not been for police interference.

After the contest with Ryan I returned to Boston, and stayed at home for a few weeks, when I agreed to meet Dominick McCaffrey, at the Art Industrial Hall, Philadelphia, March 30, 1885. I went to Rentz's Park and commenced to condition myself for this contest, but both McCaffrey and myself were arrested, and placed under $10,000 bonds each. This prevented either of us contesting in that city, as it was punishable by law. The receipts for this affair, which was under the management of William Corney and John Clark, of Philadelphia, were returned to those who had purchased tickets for admission.

On June 13, 1885, at the Chicago Driving Park, I defeated Jack Burke in a five-round contest, Marquis of Queensbury rules for 65% and 35%. I received 65%, although I never trained a day for this event and had two carbuncles the size of large cherries on the back of my neck. Notwithstanding my condition, I demonstrated to the audience that witnessed the contest that Burke was but a mere boy in my hands.

After this contest I returned to Boston and had no sooner settled down than I was challenged by Dominick McCaffrey for a contest to take place at Chester Park, Cincinnati, on August 29, 1885. A well-known gentleman by the name of George Campbell came to Boston to make the arrangements for the match. He said that he had to guarantee McCaffrey $1,000 before he would meet me in the ring. I said, "I will meet McCaffrey under one condition only; that is, that the winner of the contest is to receive all the money." That was agreed to by Campbell and myself, and it was also agreed that Campbell should receive 40% of the gate receipts for getting up and managing the show, as it did not concern me what arrangements he would or did make with McCaffrey.

In this contest I was successful as I had been in all of my others, receiving something like $5,200 and being declared winner by Billy Tate of Toledo, Ohio, who was referee.

Some friends of McCaffrey, who had been connected with certain sporting newspapers, went to the home of Billy Tate in Toledo, Ohio, offering him a sum of money to withdraw his decision, which he would not do, nor could he be induced to accept a bribe from these scamps. McCaffrey then tried to live on this reputation, by trying to gull the public, stating that he had stayed six rounds with me and that I was unable to knock him out.

During the contest his brother came on the stage and pulled a revolver and used a lot of epithets saying: "If you hit my brother again I will kill you." He was then landed over the ropes by some of the spectators who had witnessed the affair and quietly made to understand that the contest would go on without any interference from him. This occurred in the third round. He might have been seriously dealt with but for the better judgment of calmer and cooler heads, who had come to see the contest and see fair play.

One little incident in my career, which has never been told, might have finished me. It happened while I was returning from the place where I was supposed to train to fight McCaffrey at Cincinnati. Right here I might say my training for that event did not amount to anything, and that instead of taking off flesh I actually gained it. We were located at a little town called Searsmont which is 12 miles from Belfast, Maine. I went there by train, that is, left Boston I think about eight o'clock in the morning and got to Searsmont about eight o'clock that night, which made quite a journey by rail. When I came back I had determined to come by boat or steamer, for there is a very fine line of steamers running between Maine east-shore towns and Boston.

We left Belfast in the evening, or late in the afternoon, and stopped at several places to pick up passengers going east. At one place we stopped, I have forgotten the name of the place now, an elderly gentleman and lady, evidently his daughter, came aboard. They had been attending a camp meeting which had taken place at the town from which they got on the boat. They both seemed more or less fanatical on religion, particularly the woman.

After they came on board I was introduced to them both and noticed their actions. The woman was evidently somewhat crazy, for she several times attempted to jump overboard, and was kept from so doing by some of the passengers; finally she went overboard, and the cry went up from the ship, "A man overboard."

I ran to the stern of the ship, and saw her floating at some distance. As we sailed on, I climbed over the rail and was within one second of being overboard, clothes and all. It came to me so quick that I did not think; but my first impulse was to save the woman. All the passengers grabbed me, and with the assistance of my trainers tore my coat tails off, and stopped me from jumping overboard. I finally got back over the rail and jumped into the life-saving boat to row to her assistance, and again I got myself in trouble, for I was ordered out of the boat, and one of the regular crew for life-saving purposes took my place. The steamer was stopped, and the boat crew rowed back fully a mile and got her. Had it been a man, he would undoubtedly have been drowned, but the woman's clothes bore her up, and lying flat upon her back, in which position she was found by the crew, saved her life. She was unconscious when the boat brought her to the ship, but the ship's physician brought her around all right. I do not know what my experiences would have been if I had got overboard, as I intended to, for, being a woman and somewhat crazy, she might have made trouble for me in the water; but I am a good swimmer, and I think I could have saved her.

I then returned to Boston, and started traveling with Lester and Allen's Minstrels, opening up on September 20, 1885, at a salary of $500 per week, posing as statues of ancient and modern gladiators. In this business I continued until May, 1886. I was with them 21weeks at the salary of $500 per week; afterwards I became a part owner, from January, 1886, up to May, 1886, when I closed in Chicago. I endeavored to make a match with Mitchell in Chicago, under the management of Pat Sheedy, which, however, fell through on account of the citizens appealing to the mayor to prevent the contest from taking place. Before this I went to Mt. Clements to get myself in condition for the contest, and received a dispatch from Pat Sheedy that negotiations were off for the contest, as I have mentioned, for reasons stated above.

I then returned to New York and formed a partnership with William Bennett in the saloon business, where I was hounded and pestered to death by one Frank Herald, of Philadelphia, who was aspiring to the championship honors. Through the loud-mouthed talking of one Edward Mallahan, in endeavoring to bring the contest at Ridgewood Park, the authorities interfered, preventing the meeting from taking place. The party then started for Pittsburgh on the six o'clock train, to gain an unearned reputation by trying to inform the public that I was afraid to meet Herald. A friend of mine heard of their intended departure, informed me of their underhand work, and put me on my guard. I immediately left on the seven o'clock train, an hour later than they, arriving in Pittsburgh the following morning, then through the management of Tom Hughes, who arranged all preliminaries, we met that evening in Allegheny City, across the river from Pittsburgh, in the rink. I gave Mr. Frank Herald enough in the first round. This was on September 18, 1886.

Before this time I challenged any man to fight for from $5,000 to $10,000 a side, depositing $1,000 with the New York *Clipper*.

I now placed myself under the management of Mr. Pat Sheedy who organized a combination, for which Joe Lannon and Steve Taylor, George La Blanche the marine, Jimmy Carroll and Patsy Kerrigan, were engaged. The combination opened in Racine, Wisconsin, from whence we went to Minneapolis and St. Paul, and several other cities, on our way to San Francisco. When I reached San Francisco, I arranged a glove contest with my former antagonist, Paddy Ryan, from whom I won the championship in 1882. We met in a public contest on November 13th, in a San

Francisco pavilion, and I knocked Ryan out in the middle of the third round. The gate receipts of said contest reached between $9,000 and $10,000, Ryan receiving $2,600 as a solace for his second defeat.

On my return from 'Frisco, having stopped at numerous cities to give exhibitions, I arrived at Minneapolis, January 18, 1887, where I met Patsy Cardiff in a contest of six rounds, for 75% and 25% of the gate receipts, the winner to receive 75%. I let drive my left in the first and opening round. I had gauged my man wrongly, and hit him on the fore part of the head as he was ducking (a term used in boxing), and broke a bone of my left arm, which the doctors called the radius. I continued the other five rounds, at the expiration of which I was declared winner and received the seventy-five per cent. In endeavoring to explain to the audience the reason for my not being able to bring the contest to a finish before the six rounds had expired, as they supposed I would, it was utterly impossible to get a hearing; therefore I left the stage and went to my dressing room. I put on my clothes as best I could, went to the Hotel Nicolette in Minneapolis, and sent for two surgeons to look at my arm. It was then about 11 o'clock in the evening. The principal doctor in the place consulted with another physician. During this time I had suffered the most excruciating pain and my arm had swollen to twice its natural size. It was then three o'clock in the morning, and, after sending for two splints, they concluded that my arm was broken and agreed to set it.

I left the city next day and went through Dakota up into Winnipeg, Manitoba, with my combination of boxers. They gave exhibitions and I appeared at the shows. The audience were not satisfied at seeing me in citizen's clothes, but demanded to look at me in tights. Returning from Winnipeg to Minneapolis, I had the same doctors look at my arm. This was two weeks from the time they first saw it. They then put it in felt splints. At the time of this accident, I wish to inform my readers that the thermometer was in the neighborhood of twenty or thirty degrees below zero, and to the fact that I was not acclimated I attribute the breaking of this bone. I had just come from a warm state - California - into a cold one.

From Minneapolis I returned to Chicago, where I stopped one day as Mr. Sheedy wished me to see a surgeon there. I thought it would not be necessary, and told him I would wait until I got to New York, and I would see Dr. Louis Sayers, who is one of the greatest surgeons living. On my arrival in New York I called at his residence at the corner of Fifth Avenue and 30th Street. I showed him my arm, and, to my surprise, he made the remark that I could not button my collar or tie my necktie, as the arm was in bad shape. The part of the hand which should turn down in its natural position, was facing upwards, towards me. In consequence of this, he had to call both of his sons, Louis, Jr., and Ridgeway, who are also in the profession, to hold my arm around the muscle, and then, taking hold of

Special Champion Belt, presented to John L. Sullivan on August 8, 1887.

my hand and shaking hands with me, he broke my arm and reset and locked it in a plaster of Paris cast. In this position I carried it for five weeks.

Starting out on the 28th of March, 1887, again under the management of Pat Sheedy, I gave exhibitions, opening at Hoboken, New Jersey, and sparring with my partners, who were Joe Lannon and Steve Taylor. I sparred, giving exhibitions in several of the large cities, up to the Fourth of July, my last exhibition being given in Hartford, where I umpired a game of ball between the Hartfords and the New Havens. At the finish of the ninth inning, Joe Lannon and myself gave an exhibition of the manly art of self-defense, thus closing the afternoon's performance. On my return to Boston, a grand testimonial was given me August 8th, at the Boston Theatre, where I was presented with a magnificent gold belt, containing 397 diamonds, and valued at $8,000, by the citizens of Boston and many warm and admiring friends as a token of esteem, and for the honor in which they hold my undefeated name. This magnificent belt was gotten up and manufactured by a New York firm. The diamonds in it were furnished by Lyons, of Maiden Lane, and all who have seen it pronounce it to be the greatest and nicest piece of workmanship in that form that has ever been gotten up for a champion. This belt is my own personal property, and to be held and handed down to the generations of my future relations.

The description of the belt is as follows: It is 48 inches in length and 12 inches in width, and is the largest piece of flat gold ever seen in this country. It was about 12 inches square when started, and weighed about 2,800 pennyweights. It took about three months to complete it. It contains a center plate, two boxing panels, an eagle panel, and a harp panel. These panels are studded with diamonds. My name on the belt is composed of 250 stones.

CHAPTER NINE
FROM NEW ENGLAND TO OLD ENGLAND

The morning of October 27, 1887, it eight o'clock, I sailed from my native city for England on the Cunard steamer "Cephalonia." My object in making the trip was "money, glory, and revenge." My manager was Mr. Harry S. Phillips, a well-known sporting man of Montreal, with whom I signed a contract for a year. Accompanying me were Jack Ashton the Providence pugilist, Mr. John Barnett, a personal friend who acted somewhat in the capacity of companion and secretary, and my manager, Mr. Harry Phillips. I was given a rousing send-off by the sporting men of Boston, who engaged two tugs and followed the steamer some distance on her way. My cabin was literally filled with floral pieces, and I was made the recipient of numerous other presents. My father and brother saw me off, and the former waved me a last "good-bye" with the colors I wore when I won the championship of America from Paddy Ryan. My sporting friends cheered themselves hoarse as the tug left the wake of the big steamer, and fired a salute with two brass cannons they had taken on board.

I arrived in Liverpool, England, on the 6th of November, Sunday afternoon, at two o'clock, on which occasion I was met by many prominent members of the sporting fraternity (among whom were Arthur Magnus, Alf Greenfield, and Johnny Curran), outside the harbor by a special tug chartered by friends. We disembarked at the Liverpool landing, and when we stepped from the tender we were cheered by thousands with the utmost enthusiasm. The crush was so great that it was deemed advisable to form a bodyguard so that I might make my way to the four-in-hand that was in waiting to take me to the Grand Hotel. My admirers were ambitious and tried to take the horses from the carriage that was to take me to the hotel, but they were dissuaded from doing so and the hotel was reached in safety. A large number of friends were in attendance there to welcome me.

I had the distinction of having interrupted the ordinary traffic both in London and Liverpool. The crowd that followed me through the streets was described as a "multitude."

I had brought the belt that had been presented to me to display at all the exhibitions I intended giving in England, Ireland, Scotland, and Wales, but the Custom House officers wanted to claim 120 pounds - $600 - for admitting it into their country. This I refused to pay as I intended to take the belt back with me to my native shores. Consequently, the British did not have the opportunity of seeing the magnificent emblem which I had to leave in the Queen's bonded warehouse until I set sail for America on the 12th day of April, 1888. On the day after my arrival, Monday, Mr. Harry Phillips and his wife, and Jack Ashton and I left the Grand Hotel at Liverpool for London and proceeded to the Lime Street station for the London & North Western railway. Although but a short distance had to be traversed, the throng was so dense that it was with difficulty our party reached the terminus. The train left the station immediately amidst the cheers of the spectators.

At a station called Crewe the crowd assembled to see the great "knocker-out," and in their anxiety to catch a glimpse of me a number of people climbed to the roof of the carriage. This was repeated at Rugby and at Willesden, but the admiration and gazing that I encountered from the time of my landing was eclipsed at Euston, where fully 5,000 persons had assembled at the station. The appearance of the "American" was a signal for loud cheering and hurrahs from the people, amongst whom were Jimmy Mace, Jack Baldock, Young Bill Goode, Bat Mullins, and Tom Lees.

The crush was so great here that it was impossible to reach the carriage that was provided for me, so I jumped into the first carriage that I saw close at hand. Then it seemed as if the whole crowd must get into that one carriage, so many entered it that the bottom fell out, and I discovered to my astonishment that it was a "funeral coach." It did not take me long to seek the brougham that was in waiting for me. I jumped in, and there met a friend by the name of Harry Bull, better known as "Chippy Norton." We then drove to the *Sportsman* office on Fleet Street, outside of which the crowd was so great and eager to get a glimpse of me, it was with difficulty that the police were able to clear the way. Having finished my business with Mr. Ashley, who was proprietor of the *Sportsman*, the celebrated sporting paper of London, and in fact of all England, I was obliged, in order to get away, to address the audience from the windows of the *Sportsman*; I thanked them for their kindness and for their hearty reception in this my first visit to their country, and told them I would be glad to meet them all at the exhibition that I proposed giving on Wednesday evening, November 9th, at St. James Hall, which was to be my first appearance on any stage, or in any hall, in that country.

On the evening of November 9th, about 1,800 people were present in St. James Hall, London, to witness the first appearance in England of your humble servant. My appearance on the platform, accompanied by Jem Smith, was the signal for a prolonged outburst of cheering. Each of us was, in turn, introduced as the man, who, in his own country, was considered the champion of the world. In acknowledging the cheers, I said:

"I thank you, one and all, for your kind welcome, and I hope I shall always deserve it, so long as I remain in your country. I may furthermore state that it is my wish to defeat Mr. Smith, just as it is his wish to defeat me. I hope you may have the pleasure of seeing us box, and so demonstrate which is the better man. [*Cheers.*]

In response to loud calls, Smith briefly said:

"I shall do my best to beat Kilrain, and then to beat John L. Sullivan."

This is the notice we received next day:

> "As the two champions stood together their differences of build and height were very apparent, Smith being much the shorter. Sullivan stands five feet ten and one-half inches, while Smith is only five feet eight and one-half inches. In chest measurement the two men are forty-four inches and forty-two and one-half inches respectively. After some interesting boxing matches, Sullivan again appeared, and had three rounds with Jack Ashton, of Providence, U. S. A. Ashton is a lighter weight than Sullivan, but of about the same stature. It was universally admitted that the four rounds were a fine exhibition of sparring. While both men were remarkably quick and agile, the rapidity and springiness of Sullivan's movements created the deepest impression, and evoked universal admiration. It can readily be understood, even by those who saw no more than last night's exhibition, why few of the American champion's antagonists have been able to keep the field after the third or fourth round. Once an opportunity occurs he delivers a perfect bombardment of blows with a speed which the eye can scarcely follow. In attack he seems literally to throw himself upon an opponent with puzzling and disconcerting suddenness and impetuosity. Sullivan was a good deal 'winded' with the effort, which was only natural to a man so much above his proper weight when in condition. Jem Smith watched the encounter from a seat on the platform with close attention."

I then started on a tour giving exhibitions in Birmingham, Liverpool, Manchester, Newcastle-on-Tyne, Leicester, Nottingham, Derby, Sheffield, Preston, Oldham, and various other cities in England. The places in Ireland where I appeared were Dublin, Waterford, Cork, Limerick, and Belfast; and in Scotland the towns were Glasgow, Dundee, Aberdeen, and Edinburgh. The only place I visited in Wales was Cardiff, where I gave an exhibition and met an ambitious boxer named Samuels who, after the second round, cried "quits," and said he had had enough.

My descent upon Birmingham was at once made known to a few hundred of my most ardent admirers, who received me at the railway station with such rough cordiality as would have dismayed a man of softer mold, and who roused the peaceful inhabitants of the town from a wonted apathy by dashing up Corporation Street after the open vehicle in which I rode, with ecstatic shouts of "Sullivan!" "Hooray!"

I at once held a reception at the Stork Hotel. It was quite in the American fashion, recalling Martin Chuzzlewit's encounter with the interviewers: "Up they came with a rush! Up they came, until the room was full, and, through the open door, a dismal perspective of more to come was shown upon the stairs."

Said a local writer: "Sullivan took the rush of 'idolaters' very quietly. He observed, in fact, that the same thing happened to him every day at home."

The two nights' show at Birmingham brought together over 19,000 people. A writer in the *Birmingham Gazette*, commenting on my appearance in that town, says: "Kilrain and Mitchell have, however, been completely snuffed out by the arrival in Birmingham of John L. Sullivan. The name of Sullivan has been a household word in the mouths of pugilists on both sides of the Atlantic for years. It is small wonder, then, that his admirers - and they are many - should give him a welcome scarcely accorded to a royal prince."

I arrived in Cardiff from Nottingham by the 2:50 train. Considerable amusement was created by the expectation raised among the crowd, who awaited me at the station, by the arrival of several trains before that from Nottingham. Passengers leaving the station had to pass between several ranks of expectant sightseers, and the comments on the physical peculiarities of each individual, as he ran the gauntlet, were neither pleasant nor edifying, but very amusing. One tall gentleman caused a flutter when he emerged from the station exit, but a second glance revealed some serious defects. "That's not Sullivan!" shouted a rough voice, "he's groggy on his pins!" A very little man, with a meek face and a huge shawl, was immediately backed to the extent of several hundreds of pounds to "knock smoke out of Sullivan in the first round," and an unsuspecting policeman, who followed, came in for quite a demonstration.

At last, however, our party arrived, and we made our way to the carriage in waiting. We were loudly cheered, and it was with some difficulty that our conveyance reached the Royal Hotel, where we stopped while at Cardiff. It was said at the time that even Mr. Gladstone, when he came to Cardiff the previous summer, failed to draw a larger or more decent crowd than that which thronged to meet me. "It is a somewhat noteworthy circumstance," continued the same authority, " that here, in the very metropolis of 'good little Wales,' a prizefighter should prove as great an attraction as a truculent radical ex-Prime Minister."

"You don't attach much value to the diamond belt in the possession of Kilrain?" was asked of me in Cardiff.

"No," I replied, "it is only a dog collar. As I said before, its real value is only about 30 pounds, and if I win it I intend to offer it for competition among the New York boot-blacks."

On December 8th a dinner was given at the Pelican Club by Founder Wells to Phillips, Ashton, and your humble servant. After the banquet Ashton and I had a bout, and when it was over we were getting ready to go home when a gentleman, faultlessly arrayed in a capecoat, glittering patent leathers, and a crush hat appeared upon the scene.

"I would like to speak to Mr. Sullivan a moment," he said picking me out from the men present.

"I am at your service," I said.

"I have the honor to be the bearer of this message," said the stranger, handing a note to me. I tore open the letter and read:

ST. JAMES BARRACKS

My Dear Mr. Sullivan,

I have great pleasure on behalf of the officers of the Scots Guards in inviting you to breakfast in our mess room tomorrow at 12 o'clock, and subsequently to meet His Royal Highness the Prince of Wales, who has repeatedly expressed the desire to make your personal acquaintance.

Very Truly Yours,

CLIFFORD DRUMMOND,
Captain Scots Guards

This is what the papers published in regard to the affair:

"After reading the note Sullivan lit a fresh cigar, put on his coat and, turning to the bearer of the note, said:

"'Well, tell the Prince and Drummond I won't disappoint them.'

"Then turning to his friends, who expected to see Sullivan duck under his honors, he remarked:

"'If the Prince was not such a sociable, nice fellow I would not go there tomorrow, for I'm dead tired, and this means getting up early.'

"At midday of the day assigned, all the private hansoms in London were driving like mad down Piccadilly and rattling up to the St. James barracks, where the meet was to be.

"The son of a well-known peer placed his hansom at the American champion's disposal, and said out of the fullness of his heart:

"'Ah, you are too kind,' when Sullivan remarked that he would not mind him crawling in alongside, as it were.

"In the mess room, Captain Drummond, the ideal of Ouida's guardsman, with whom all are acquainted, received the transatlantic slugger. Captain Drummond presided, with Sullivan on his right, Phillips on his left, next to whom were Lord Randolph Churchill and Sir Gordon Cummings.

"In addition to the full roster of officers of the Scots Guards, there were present many officers of the Grenadier and Coldstream Guards. Cold salmon, hot cuts and cold joints were served, washed down with bitter ale, porter, half-and-half, the light French wines on the top not being in great demand. Evidently most of the soldier gentlemen were in training for some event. The history of the prize ring was twice told, from the Homeric days of Epeus down to Tom Sayers and Heenan, whose healths were drunk in silence.

"Shortly before three o'clock word came that the Prince had arrived at the Fencing Club across the way. Breakfast was immediately adjourned and prize-ring history saved a third recital. The Guards' gymnasium is a gem in its way.

"The fighting ring is a model and the fencing spaces admirable. The walls are adorned with pictures of good guardsmen who have gone before. Standing in front of an open wood fire toasting himself was the Prince, dressed in a cut-a-way black coat, gray trousers, drab gaiters, and thick-soled walking boots. He was smoking a cigarette, not an American, by the way, for as he subsequently remarked, 'The only thing American I don't like is the American cigarette.'

"Sullivan entered the room, dressed quietly in black, demure, and as innocent to all appearances as a Sunday school superintendent, and as self-contained as a young lady who has seen several seasons.

"'There comes Gentleman John,' ran the whisper among the officers, who agreed that the only thing they would like to have changed about Sullivan was his birthplace.

"Sir Francis Knollys skipped forward and said:

"'His Royal Highness desires very much to meet you, Sullivan. May I have the honor of presenting you?'

"'You may; I reciprocate heartily the sentiments of the Prince.'

"Neither the pugilist nor the Prince were in the least bit stiff or formal in their manner, as they met and shook hands right heartily. The Prince immediately took away the frigid nap of newness from the acquaintance by saying that he felt as if he had known Sullivan many years, whereupon John L. reciprocated by remarking that, next to Jem Smith, the Prince of Wales was the man he had most wanted to see in coming to England. Then the Prince looked Sullivan over carefully, Then Sullivan did ditto, and they again shook a shake of mutual satisfaction.

"The Prince was in very good trim for a man who had opened five fairs, three bazaars, gone to seven funerals by proxy, and laid two cornerstones, in a week. He immediately referred to his trip to America before the war, and how in Detroit he had had his first real scrapping match.

"'It was a stand-off,' he remarked. 'My eye was darkened, and the other man's nose was red.'

"'I see,' remarked Sullivan, with professional nonchalance, 'you got what we call a baptismal black eye, while the other fellow received his claret christening.'

"The Prince then referred to some of Sullivan's big fights, particularly that with Paddy Ryan. The fighter blushed as he heard the soft words of praise from the Prince's lips, and turned the conversation glibly by asking the Prince if he put up his 'dukes' much now-a-days.

"'Oh, no. I am too old,' said the Prince.

"'I don't know, of course, how you feel,' said Sullivan, 'but you look as young as Jack Ashton.'

"'No, I do not spar at all now,' continued the Prince. 'But my eldest boy, who is down in York with his Lancer regiment, punches the bag half an hour every morning before breakfast, and my second son, George, the middy, is a regular slugger, at least so the officers of the ship, the "Dreadnought," tell me. I never sparred very much myself, but I believe in the manly art, and, like most fathers, am endeavoring to bring my boys up in the way I should have gone.'

"Then the sport began, and the Prince, pugilists, and peers craned their necks into the arena where Bat Mullen and Jack King, two promising bantams, were pecking away at each other. Sullivan turned to go towards the dressing room and came face to face with Jem Smith, the English champion.

"'How are you, Mr. Smith?'

"'Splendid weather we are having, Mr. Sullivan.'

"'For blind men, maybe, but it does not suit me,' said Sullivan, who is not partial to fogs.

"Then the two men shook hands for a minute or two, and came to the conclusion, if professionally they were not fated to smash each other out of recognizable shape, the friendship of Pylades and Orestes would be nowhere compared to theirs.

"Smith and Greenfield then pummelled each other in" good style. Smith is in admirable form, the very picture of what fighting trim should be. The only fault which the greatest stickler for form could find on Smith is that he is a little too stiff.

"Just as the audience, which did not, however, number over 40, were becoming impatient for the upper crust of the pugilistic pie, the electric light was turned on, and out into the garish glare Sullivan and Ashton strode from their dressing rooms into the ring.

"'Gentlemen,' said Phillips, 'I have the honor of introducing to you John L. Sullivan, the champion of the world, and Jack Ashton, a fine fighter, who will soon be heard from.'

"Jem Smith winced when he heard the words champion of the world.' But as his Royal Highness paddled his hands together, all present applauded.

"Both boxers wore emerald-green tights - green as that of the grass fields of Galway - and dotted all over with harps and medallions of famous Irishmen, from the days of great Brian-Boru down. Then the set-to began, and I have never seen Sullivan in a better one.

"Manager Phillips and the World correspondent drew near to the Prince, whose eyes were dancing with delight at the fine spar.

"'He is the quickest big man I ever saw,' was the first drop of wisdom which fell from the Prince's lips.

"Then John L. landed one of his terrible left-handers full in Ashton's face. The sound was like that of a falling forest monarch in the north woods.

"'Ah,' said Phillips, with a Mephistophelian smile, 'what will happen when he meets Smith?'

"'Sullivan has the weight, the height, the reach, and undoubted pluck,' continued the Prince.

"'That put together generally wins the fight, does not it?' insinuated Phillips.

"'Well, of course I am an Englishman and want Smith to win. That is, of course, officially I disapprove of prizefighting entirely, and would be grieved if it came off in the United Kingdom.'

"After the set-to was over, the Prince again led the applause, and was heartily seconded. He went up and shook hands again with Sullivan, hoped that he would meet him again, and, with an amused smile said, 'I wish you much luck while here, Mr. Sullivan.'

"Some hours after the peers of the realm and hard hitters had vanished, like the baseless fabric of a dream, the writer called on Sullivan at his private lodgings and asked him what he thought of the Prince.

"'He is a nice, sociable fellow,' said the slugger, 'with splendid manners; he is a splendid good, all-round man. He is the sort of man you like to meet anywhere, at any time.'"

At the Pelican Club, 19 English peers, of whom 13 were earls, were present. I was made a member of the club, an honor which I esteem very highly, and which other Americans have been unable to procure. The meeting between myself and the Prince inspired such humorous lines as the following:

Ho! Britons, raise a joyous shout,
Give voice in thrilling tones,
Accompanying your song throughout
With banjo, harp, and bones.
The olive branch floats on the breeze,
Peace marches in the van;
The Prince's hand has had a squeeze
From John L. Sullivan.

Perchance some day the Prince will king
Become, when value much
Enhanced to that same hand shall cling
Which Sullivan did touch.
The loyal throngs, as on they pass,
Shall step with more élan
To kiss the hand which got the squeeze
From John L. Sullivan.

"All ordinary boxers arc paid for pleasing the prince, but Sullivan meets him on a basis of equality, and, in fact, better than that, comes to him as a benefactor, and will treat him to a grand sight, and teach him all he can about boxing, to quote his own words, 'free gratis.'

"Sir William Gordon Cummings called on Mr. Phillips, on behalf of the Prince, to know how much money 'so great a man as Sullivan' would expect. He was told by Mr. Phillips that both himself and Sullivan would be glad to treat the Prince as a friend, but that they would not accept any money from him. When asked if Sullivan would not accept some little token from the Prince as a souvenir of the occasion, Mr. Sullivan said probably he would, and Sullivan tells me now that he will do so rather than hurt the Prince's feelings. Sullivan is just in condition to show the Prince what a man should be physically. He is looking in almost perfect condition. His face is clear-cut, and, on being weighed last night, he barely turned 210 pounds stripped, which is less than he has weighed for years. Sullivan is arrayed in style to do credit to the country which he represents fistically.

"The big fellow astonished the king that may be with such a display of fistic power as he had never before seen; but, great as this display was, it was insignificant in comparison to the lesson he taught the snobs and snoblings of this country, who are ever ready to bow the knee to, and approve of, anything if it is only 'English, yeh know.'

"Sully wasn't a bit abashed in the presence of majesty. Titles and offices count very little with him, and seeing in the future king of England an unpretentious-looking gentleman, he was respectful, but perfectly self-possessed. Albert Edward, who

Edward VII

must often wish that men would be natural with him, not merely polite, or, still worse, adulatory, cringing, or sycophantic, was
taken with the American champion's poise, as was shown by
the admiration he expressed for it after they had parted."

The Pelican Club presented me with a valuable pin and waistcoat
buttons to match. My reception in Dublin, December 11th, was mar-
velously enthusiastic, and brought forcibly to my mind the fact that I was
in the midst of the warm-hearted people from whom I am proud to claim
descent. Not fewer than 15,000 people had gathered at the steamboat
landing, and their cheering when our party made its appearance was
something to remember. Two full brass bands were there, also, and vied
with each other in the energy and enthusiasm with which they played
"See, the Conquering Hero Comes!" "The Wearing of the Green," and
other complimentary and patriotic tunes. Our party proceeded to the carriages awaiting us and started for Grosvenor Hotel, headed by the two
brass bands. Progress was slow, for the crowd pressed against the carriages and caused confusion, but the hotel was reached at last, and we
went quickly inside.

This was not the end of my reception, however. The crowd had no
intention of clearing off until they had heard my voice, so they shouted
and cheered for "Sullivan," and the bands kept up the enthusiasm, until I
stepped forward on the veranda in full view of the multitude. One mighty
shout went up, and then there was momentary silence, for it was seen
that I was about to speak.

The address was not long, but it was appropriate to the occasion. "I
thank you," I said, "for your kindness to me this evening. As a descendant
of Erin's Isle, I will endeavor always to prove myself worthy of your attention and to uphold the honor of my father's native land." Tumultuous
cheering followed, and then the band struck up again and marched off,
followed by the bulk of the crowd. I was much moved by the warmth of
this reception in the land of my forefathers. I also met enthusiastic receptions in Waterford, Limerick, Belfast, and Cork.

One of the most interesting things connected with my tour in Ireland
was a visit to the spot called "Donnelly's Hollow," in the Curragh of
Kildare, where the famous Irish champion, Donnelly, vanquished Cooper.
Travelers visiting the Curragh are taken by proud natives to the scene of
the famous battle. The footsteps of the champions are still plainly visible.
"They are preserved in this way: Every visitor, especially those who love
the 'noble art,' puts his feet in the ancient marks, which are thus preserved and deepened in the soft green sod." The position of the men, as
they began the fight, are pointed out. "And over there," say the guides,
"just outside the ring, stood Miss Kelly, who wagered thousands of

pounds on Dan Donnelly."

"Donnelly's Hollow" is probably one of the most perfect natural amphitheatres in the world. Here, on the sloping hillsides, could stand or sit a hundred thousand men to behold a dramatic scene; and here, on that day, was assembled a greater crowd than had ever witnessed a boxing contest since the close of the Olympic games.

This is from an English paper:

> "At last America has sent us a great entertainer of the male variety. We have had Booth, and Adonis Dixey, and all the men of the American drama, but none have shone. Sullivan, however, comes to us as a sunbeam to shed his lustrous light upon sportsmen and others. Marquises have entertained him at dinner, and barons have drowned him with refreshment. When enumerating the qualities and accomplishments of Sullivan of America, please do not forget to mention that he fights."

It will be remembered that I arrived in London November 7, 1887, and gave my first show at St. James Hall two days afterward. During my tour, I gave 51 exhibitions, including that before his Royal Highness the Prince of Wales and the one before the Pelican Club. The tour was a grand success financially, as well as in every other respect. During it I cleared 5,000 pounds, which is an extraordinary sum, considering the condition of the kingdom and the small wages paid workingmen. In no instance did I go to any town without receiving a hearty welcome from the local sporting fraternity, and the receptions accorded me in London, Liverpool, Manchester, Dublin, and several other places, surpassed anything heretofore heard of. In the first show given, over 500 pounds were taken in, while at many places people had to be turned away.

In Scotland I met with particular success in Edinburgh, Glasgow, Dundee, and Aberdeen.

As to the substantial appreciation which I met in Ireland, I can say that I made more money in one week there than in six weeks in England. Among other things I received there were a tweed suit, 17 blackthorn sticks, four jugs of whiskey, a beautiful design in shamrocks, and 45 letters asking me to give benefits for charitable institutions.

It is not necessary for me to plead guilty to running after royalty in order to mention the interest manifested by ladies of the royal family in England. I have frequently seen Princess Christine and her daughter in their carriage, and they used to look after me when the coachman pointed me out. I have seen the Queen near Windsor, and on more than one occasion, together with a companion, she looked out to see me as I passed along, and made comments which I did not hear. A pardonable appreciation of their sex, rather than of their rank, must be set down as my warrant for telling these things. My tour in Great Britain was closed with an exhibition at Portsmouth in January, 1888.

CHAPTER TEN
BATTLES ON BOTH SIDES OF THE ATLANTIC

"While Sullivan was winning golden opinions in England, starring the provinces, Mitchell," says a newspaper correspondent, "was snarling out challenges to him by the dozen. The big 'un pays just as much attention to them as the great mastiff in Landscer's picture of 'Dignity and Impudence' does to the little cur tha' is barking around him."

Perhaps it would be better if I had continued this course, but I was led into a match to fight the bombastic sprinter boxer, foolishly giving away everything in the match in his favor.

On November 29th I met Mitchell at a well-known sporting resort, and signed articles for a fight for 500 pounds, under London prize-ring rules, and in a 24-foot ring. Neither the time nor the place of meeting were mentioned in the articles signed. They were to be arranged between the seconds, namely, Phillips for me and Pony Moore for Mitchell. Among those present at the time were Mr. Allison, the editor of the *Sportsman*, and Messrs. Harding, Bennet, and Morton, American sporting men. After H. Bull, the well-known bookmaker of Newmarket, had been chosen as stakeholder, the drawing-up of the articles began, which, even under the skillful treatment of Allison, was no easy matter. Mitchell disputed every article, and the transaction took three hours. When he came into the room where I was sitting, he turned around to his train of friends and followers, and said:

"Now, boys, I have got him."

I only laughed. One by one the articles were agreed to, I giving away every point without demur until it came to the size of the ring.

"It must be a 24-foot ring," insisted Mitchell, who saw in this a loophole to get out of the match.

"You are not signing for a foot-race, Mitchell," said Phillips.

"And I am not a sprinter," remarked Sullivan.

Mitchell insisted, however, and just as he thought the contest spent on the rock of contention, I said:

"Alright, my boy, let it be a 24-foot ring. You'll find even that too small to skulk in when the day comes."

Mitchell's countenance darkened. Then I insisted that the liberty of choice of time and place given the seconds should be limited by two conditions: that the contest must come off within 1,000 miles of London, and not clash with any of my previous engagements.

"I had to do this," I said, "because when the time came Mitchell would insist on fighting in China."

During the whole two hours, Mitchell had been taunting me in the most outrageous manner. Finally he called me a dirty rogue. I sprang to my feet, and this time my blood was up.

"Come on, you young whelp. I have two carriages downstairs. You get in one and I will take the other and we'll drive to the nearest vacant space, and there I'll knock your head off."

Mitchell smiled sickly and followed me a little way towards the door. Then Allison interposed and I was hurried away. I left, saying, "All right, I will wait until I meet him; but when I do, I'll give it to him all the worse for waiting."

The fight took place on Baron Rothschild's grounds at Chantilly, March 10, 1888. I wanted to fight this sprinter in a 16-foot ring, knowing well that his tactics in a 24-foot ring would be to run around or to lie down, which he did at every opportunity afforded him in the fight. I wished to prevent this cowardly and unfair business. It is a well-known and established fact that in all my career as a boxer or fighter, I have always fought my opponent manfully and fairly. In this fight with Mitchell I was fouled a number of times by being spiked repeatedly by Mitchell. Of this the referees seemed to take no notice.

One of the witnesses of the fight was Pony Moore, Mitchell's father-in-law, who stood with a face puckered with anxiety and nervousness. When I got my right across and Charley dropped, Pony cried, "There goes my boy."

Knockdown blow the second brought forth, "There goes my house."

And when for the third time Charley was floored, "Pony," in an agony, exclaimed, "and there goes the estate and everything."

For the first four rounds it looked odds - as Baldock has since said, long odds - on the "big fellow."

In the fifth round, when I was swinging the right, I caught Mitchell at the back of the head and severely bruised the muscles of the right arm. Still Mitchell seemed afraid to stand up to the fight. In the 10th round, when he was continuing his tactics, I said in disgust, "Oh, don't run around the ring."

"First blood" to Mitchell was claimed in round eight, to which I replied, "You can have it." He said, "Well, there is nothing in it but to decide a bet."

Running and dropping was his game, and to such an extent did he practice the former that, when the fight was over, a track like a sheep run was to be noticed all around the ring. Once he dropped without a blow and received a caution, and after this he went down a number of times for a mere tap.

Had I desired to practice the tricks of the London prize-ring rules I had good opportunities to do so by giving my weight to Mitchell, but I tried my best to avoid falling on him. Mitchell adopted a saving game throughout.

Before starting he had admitted having a great task before him, and when he went into the ring he did not go to win my 500 pounds, but to save his own, which, thanks to the big ring, the weather and my accident, he succeeded in doing.

In this fight I was unfortunately in the worst corner where the rain beat incessantly in my face and body, causing me to become chilled, and I refused numerous times to partake of any brandy which my seconds insisted upon my taking.

The termination of the fight was brought about by Mitchell's second, Jack Baldock, who stepped into the ring and said, "Shake hands and call it a draw." I said, "Let us fight a couple more rounds," but everybody said "No." Mitchell and I then retired from the ring.

On the road, while retiring from the scene of the fight, we were arrested by gendarmes who pointed revolvers at our heads. We were taken to a place called Senlis where we were brought before a tribunal, and the gendarmes gave in their charges against us. The outcome of this episode was that we were locked up from seven o'clock Saturday evening until one o'clock Sunday before the French authorities would accept bonds for our release. Being satisfied that we would appear in court the next day, they admitted Mitchell and myself to bonds. After our release we both met our friends, who fortunately had not been locked up, going to a hotel across the road, and the party, consisting of a dozen Americans, Englishmen, and Frenchmen, sat down to a sumptuous breakfast. The party included Harry Phillips, Jake Barnett, Edward Holske, William O'Brien, "Pony" Moore, Jake Baldock, Kilrain, Mitchell, and myself.

Only a few in the party knew that I did not intend to stand trial, having already made up my mind to leave Senlis by the first train for Paris, and then to go by way of Calais to England. When the officials came to suspect my intentions they increased our bonds from $800 to $1,600 each.

My reason for not appearing in court or wishing to stand trial was that, some two months before this event, Kilrain and Smith (Jem Smith, then champion of England) fought in France, and during the battle a gentleman named McNeil, who had gone over to see their fight, and to do the reporting for the Sportsman of London, lost his life by either falling overboard or being foully dealt with. The facts have never been found out. The English press dealt very severely with the French authorities for not investigating the case of this well-known sporting writer. This being so, I did not wish to stand trial, as I was afraid that I would be dealt severely with for coming over into their country, or, to use a technical phrase in pugilism, trying to "pull off this fight" there Therefore, I took the boat at

Calais to Dover, and arrived in London, England, the following morning.

From London I went to Liverpool, and stopped with a friend of mine, Arthur Magnus, who had accompanied me home and had been a witness of the fight - if fight it could be termed. The following morning the papers contained an account of my trial. My sentence was three days in a French prison and two thousand francs fine.

"Tell me," said a reporter interviewing Mr. Magnus after our return to England, "whether the arrangements for the combat were satisfactory."

"Yes, they were good, with the exception of the backwardness of the Mitchell party in selecting the ground, as agreed upon."

"Was Mitchell careless about his movements in France?"

"I should think he was - the most careless man I ever saw. In Amiens, he walked from day to day all over the town without any attempt at concealment, as if he didn't care whether the police got 'wind of it' or not."

Yes, the fight, as you say, was a walking tournament the greater part of the time. Mitchell did not face Sullivan as he ought to have done. He danced continually around the ring. This, of course, must have been his plan; there can be no doubt about it.

"In the fifth round Sullivan disabled his hand with a blow at Mitchell's head. Only the round before this, Mitchell was knocked down and completely dazed by one of the champion's right-handers. So I leave you to judge what a mishap it was to Sullivan to be compelled to fight practically with one arm."

"Could Mitchell have tired out his opponent with his tactics?"

"I honestly believe he couldn't. His blows were not strong enough to tire any one out, and even in his disabled state Sullivan could have kept it up as long as Mitchell."

My fight with Mitchell was the last event of any note in my first trip to foreign countries. I embarked on the 12th day of April on the steamship "Catalonia," for Boston, arriving after 14 days' sail, and meeting with a grand ovation from my friends, who came down the harbor to welcome me home.

Two weeks after arriving home, I acted as master of ceremonies for Billy Mahoney, the well-known sporting man and politician of Boston, at a benefit given to Joe Lannan in Music Hall. Ten days later I was tendered a testimonial at the same hall, on which occasion I sparred with Joe Lannan and Jack Ashton.

After that I formed a partnership with John B. Doris, the circus man, and Milton Dray. Our combination included a traveling circus of well-known acrobats and tumblers, and lady and gentleman riders of the sawdust ring. Jack Ashton and I appeared in a sparring bout at each performance.

After the conclusion of the circuit, I sojourned for about two months at Nantasket Beach. Then I went from the southerly side to the northerly side of Boston Harbor, spending some time at Crescent Beach. Here I was taken very sick, as may be judged from the fact that I had typhoid fever, gastric fever, inflammation of the bowels, heart trouble, and liver complaint all combined.

During this sickness I was obliged to keep my bed for a period of nine weeks, leaving it on Monday, the 15th day of October, 1888, the day I was 30 years of age. On the day before, Sunday, I told my doctor, Dr. Bush, that on the following day I would get up, as I had made up my mind to do so, and that if I had to meet the inevitable, I would die at my father's house in Boston. His residence at that time was

Jake Kilrain

No. 8 Parnell Street. My doctor advised me not to do this, as "it would be suicide," he said. However, I did not heed his advice, and that evening took a carriage and was propped up and driven to my father's house, which was 10 miles from where I had been taken sick. During this illness I had been given up on two occasions by doctors. I had five before having Dr. Bush, but, under his treatment, I came out of my sickness a new man.

From this sickness I contracted what the doctor termed incipient paralysis, having no use of my legs except with the assistance of crutches, which I had to use for six weeks. During this period I was rubbed continuously twice a day with oil and some other preparation ordered by my doctor. I also took electric treatment.

Being challenged by Kilrain, after this dreadful sickness, to fight for the championship of America, I agreed to do so, and made the match on the seventh day of January, the fight to take place on the 8th of July, 1889. In company with my representatives, I met the representatives of Kilrain at Toronto. Kilrain was not present.

Everything being satisfactorily arranged by his representatives and mine, we took our departure for New York. I then came to Boston, where I stayed for a couple of months, and again went to New York, where William Muldoon was accepted as my trainer, owing to the willingness of Charley Johnston, my backer, and James Wakley, who was also interested in my half of the match. I went to his place in Belfast, New York, to train

Building the ring for the Kilrain fight - Richburg, Mississippi, Monday, July 8, 1889

for the memorable event. Mike Cleary, the well-known boxer and pugilist, and as game a man as ever stepped into a 24-foot ring, assisted Muldoon in training me for the contest, and helped put me in good condition.

During my training with Muldoon we had a little misunderstanding, but after a day we were led to bury the hatchet. My training under these men consisted of long walks, fighting the football, throwing a 10-pound ball, using dumbbells of four pounds each, skipping rope, and going in swimming.

At the time I trained for my Kilrain fight at Belfast, New York, the whole of western New York and Pennsylvania was flooded through that memorable Johnstown flood. The river running through Belfast was filled with debris from all the upper country, and was quite a sight to see. Frequently during our training we went in bathing and swimming. This, of course, was very dangerous, especially as the river was flooded. At the time we were there, a young man named Lauk called on us and went bathing, very unfortunately for himself, for in attempting to make his way through the falls or over the dam, he lost his life. His body was found some miles below.

We never knew exactly how he came to his death, but supposed that he struck some rock beneath the surface, which stunned him. We were

very careful after that about venturing into the water. After the flood had subsided somewhat, we sent one of Muldoon's dogs through the rapids several times, and I went myself, and came very near getting seriously injured. I scraped my shin very severely by striking against a rock. It was several weeks afterward before I fully recovered. I thought at the time that it would be more serious than it was, and might interfere with my fighting with Kilrain, but fortunately it did not. My shins at the time had not fully healed from the effects of the foul spiking which Mitchell had given me in my fight with him in France. Spiking me as he did was against all rules, and had I claimed foul on that account, I undoubtedly would have been entitled to the fight on these grounds. He spiked me so severely that my shoes were full of blood, and I still bear the marks of those wounds. There are five large scars on my shins yet.

I arrived in New Orleans on the morning of the 4th day of July, and located at Mrs. Green's private boarding house. Being given the use of the Young Men's Gymnastic Club, I took there what exercise was necessary to the muscles to keep them in active condition until the day of the fight, which was the 8th day of July.

The fight took place at Richburg, in the State of Mississippi. The Kilrain party, as well as my own, took a special train on the Queen & Crescent Railroad on Sunday, the 7th of July. They were guests of Charles Rich, while I was quartered at the house of Mr. Smith, who was foreman for Mr. Rice.

The battle was fought on the estate of Charles Rich. Kilrain was seconded by Charles Mitchell, the bombastic sprinter, and Mike Donovan, of the New York Athletic Club, and John Murphy of Boston was bottle hold-

er. I was seconded by Mike Cleary and William Muldoon, and had for bottle holder Dan Murphy. After all the preliminaries had been arranged, Kilrain won the toss for corners and selected the southeast. I had the opposite corner. The referee was John Fitzpatrick, a well-known politician of New Orleans, and at the writing of this book mayor of that city. The timekeeper for the Kilrain party was Bat Masterson, of Denver; and for me Thomas Costello, of Cleveland, officiated. Finally we were assigned our corners, and the order to get ready was given. Kilrain advanced to the center of the ring and I met him, and each man placed $1,000 in the referee's hand on himself to win. The bet being made we were ordered back to our corners, and we received the call and orders of the referee to step to the middle of the ring, shake hands and return to corners.

The referee said, "Get ready," and "Time." The hostilities commenced then, and without a blow being struck, Kilrain won first fall by throwing me with a cross buttock, ending the round. On going to my corner I remarked, "If that is his game I will fool him," and on time being called for the second round Kilrain attempted the same thing, but I was ready for him and threw him heavily to the ground, fooling him and giving Mitchell the laugh. This spoiled Kilrain's chances of wrestling and he gave it up in despair.

Time being called for the third round, we both advanced to the center of the ring, and on Kilrain running around his corner, I caught him, hitting him a right-hand punch under the heart, following it up with a left-hand punch on the top of the head, injuring my left hand slightly, and virtually, if I do say it myself, winning the fight right there and then, and ending the round by knocking Kilrain down. In the succeeding rounds, there being 75 of them, Kilrain either went down to avoid punishment, or was knocked

down with my blows, right and left handed. His tactics were pursued in endeavoring to tire me out, and were according to the advice of his seconds. Mitchell, in particular, gave him lessons in his method of dodging me when I fought him in France.

Now, from the best of my remembrance, I think it was in the middle of the fight that I took a drink of cold tea in which a little whiskey had been put. Joe Coburn, thinking there was not enough whiskey put in, left his seat, and coming to the corner, put in more whiskey than I could hold. There being too much liquor in the tea, and my stomach being in such a good condition, I threw it right off. My opponent's friends, seeing this, said:

"Go at him, Jake; you have got him."

I said, "Come on."

Kilrain said, "Give it up, John; I have got you."

I said, "Come on and fight."

With the encouragement of his seconds, he came close enough to me to be knocked down, thus ending the round. From that time, Donovan, who was one of Kilrain's seconds, played between the two corners of the ring, keeping Kilrain between himself and Mitchell, and I had to fight him out of his corner repeatedly; Donovan acting like the umpire of a baseball game, rather than like a second in a fight.

During this fight it was Kilrain's intentions, through the advice of his seconds, to keep in the ring by repeatedly falling or being knocked down, it being the only resort or hope he had of winning this fight. He was carried to his corner by his seconds during all the rounds. I walked to my corner, and being asked by my seconds to sit down on a chair provided for

me, refused, saying:

"What is the use of sitting down? I have to get up again," and I remained standing in my corner, talking with my seconds and friends.

When asked to go on and finish Kilrain, I laughed, and said, "Let me stay! They say a man who can hold me half an hour can lick me. I will show these fellows that I can stay and make as long a fight as anybody else, if that is what they call fighting."

I did this more to satisfy the newspaper men who had styled me a hurricane fighter and not a stayer. I proved conclusively in this fight that I could stay as long as I liked, and could have finished this man at any time, as the fight was all my own. I was fighting an hour and 20 minutes when I was asked by Muldoon how I felt.

I said, "I never felt better in my life. How long have we been fighting?"

Muldoon said, "About an hour. How long can you stay, John?"

"Until tomorrow morning, if it is necessary," I replied.

This was all in the sun at 120 degrees. Kilrain resorted to all the tricks imaginable. He had spiked me and tore my right shoe wide open, so that the blood oozed through the shoe on to the grass. I found no fault about this, and never made it known to his seconds or to anybody else at the time.

Every one could see what Kilrain's game was. In throwing him later, in one of the rounds, Kilrain, in falling, threw his foot up and caught me with his spike, tearing my tights open. Upon which I turned to the referee, and said:

"Make that man fight fairly."

The referee warned him not to let that occur again.

He was finished five rounds before they threw the sponge up, and I was more scared than anybody for fear that I had killed him, as in each fall that he had made during the last five rounds it looked as if his neck had been broken.

In the third round, after the right-hand punch, on being taken to his corner, he said:

"My God, I am licked. He is too strong, too powerful, and can hit too hard."

Before he had entered the ring that morning, he had told a prominent physician, Dr. J. A. Dougherty, of Philadelphia, who had been engaged by the Kilrain party to look after and attend to him in case of his being injured in the fight, that he felt so strong that he thought he could punch a hole through the wall. The doctor examined him before allowing him to enter the ring, found his pulse to be normal, and his condition in every other respect to be of the first order. These are facts that are well known, and can be substantiated by Dr. John A. Dougherty, who is a well-known member of the Athletic Club, located near the Schuylkill, in Philadelphia.

The same doctor, who had attended him after the fight, found that he was severely punished and hurt internally, and has since told me that it looked as if Kilrain would never get over the beating that I had given him. He stated to me that he had given him a number of grains of morphine and drams of brandy, injected hyperdermically, to alleviate his suffering after this defeat. It is a well-known fact that he stated to several of his friends that it was the mistake of his life to ever have allowed himself to be so foolishly led into making a match with me.

On the breaking up of the crowd after the fight was over, we went for the trains that were in waiting on the sidetracks to take us back to New Orleans. Kilrain went back on the press reporter's train with Mitchell and some others, theirs being the first train to pull out.

I got into one of the other trains, which did not start for fully an hour later. During our stay on the train, a passenger who was standing on the platform said he heard in the distance the coming of a train, and gave the alarm, saying that the militia were on this train. This caused quite a stampede among the passengers. I with my fighting togs on and a big coat around me, jumped through the window of the car, regardless of the pain which my hands were giving me. They were swollen to three times their natural size. I never knew how I got through that window, it being a surprise to myself as well as to everybody else. I ran over into a thicket. When some friends who had brought over my street-wearing apparel appeared, I put on my pants and coat, found it was a false alarm, re-entered the cars, and after 15 minutes' stay, we were on our way to the city of New Orleans. We arrived there about 10 o'clock in the evening. I went to my private boarding house, took a hot mustard bath and soaked my hands, but I bore no marks, with the exception of a little scratch under my right eye, and a small sore on one side of my lip. After my bath I had supper consisting of chicken, cold meats, and Bass's ale. I sat up until about one o'clock with my friends.

The next morning I took a ride, and went around visiting my friends throughout the city. To my surprise, on returning that evening, I was informed that the sheriff of Mississippi had arrived in New Orleans with a warrant for my arrest, as well as Kilrain's, for breaking the laws by fighting in the State of Mississippi. Through the aid of some friends I succeeded in eluding this official by engaging an engine and one coach; and with my backer, Charles Johnson, I bade adieu to New Orleans, running through on this special car to Grad Bay, Alabama.

Accompanying us were William Muldoon, Pat Duffy, Mike Cleary, Budd Reno, John Kilkenny, and two of the railroad officials, whose names I do not remember. We laid over at the above-named place, and, going into a little store where provisions, notions, and groceries of all kinds were sold, we asked the proprietor and proprietress to get us something to eat. They were alarmed, not knowing who we were, and, judging from our appearance, I suppose they were afraid we would walk off with their store. However, after smooth talk, when they had found out who and what we were, they prepared a meal for us, setting down before us that well-known Southern dish - ham and chicken - in their own peculiar style of cooking. It tasted as well as any meal I had ever eaten, and I have indulged in my lifetime in the finest table luxuries that life has ever afforded.

Having finished our meal, we waited for the fast express from New Orleans, which we boarded, and on it met some of our friends who had come along. We all sat down and talked about our escapade, and, as we smoked our cigars, we thought how lucky we were to escape from the authorities of Mississippi.

When we pulled into Nashville, Tennessee, I was lying asleep in a stateroom, and was awakened by a war of words between the police and my friends. One of the former said to me as I awoke:

"What is your name?"

I told him my name was Thompson.

"Well," he said, "I think your name is Sullivan."

I stoutly denied this, and still said my name was Thompson.

They said, "We have a warrant for your arrest."

I asked them to show it, but they could not. They claimed, however, that they had a telegram from Governor Lowry, of the State of Mississippi, to arrest Sullivan and his party. I refused to be taken out of the car, upon which the officers drew their revolvers - there were eight of them - and, pointing them at me, two of them put handcuffs on my wrists, after which they tried to drag me from the car.

There were so many officers that they were in one another's way, and could not move me. I took it for granted that some of them would forget themselves and make a target of me, and not feeling disposed to die at this early stage of the game, I consented and went with them. They then took me to an old jail in which was situated the office of the chief of police. He was one of the party who had made the arrest.

This office was more like a rat pen than anything else; and the jail, filthy as it was, was filled with negroes and whites. This arrest took place at 10 o'clock in the morning. Charles Johnson, my backer, was the only one who stayed behind to keep me company, thus showing that he was a true friend in need. A friend of mine, who happened to be in the town, got the best lawyers in the place and brought them to me. I stated the facts of the case, and got their opinion to see what might be done in this matter. They got out a writ of *habeas corpus*, and took me before Judge Allison, who was a very liberal-minded man, and who, after hearing both sides of the case from the lawyers, ordered my discharge, and said I was not to be interfered with, and that I should go unmolested out of the State of Tennessee.

My legal and other expenses of various kinds in this matter were $4,500. Judge Allison was in no way connected with this matter, and did not receive one dollar for his action in the case, although he was accused in the newspapers, at the time, by some malicious person, of having been bought off to turn this "burly pugilist," as they termed me, loose.

They did not consider a pugilist anything more than a brute, and thought a man of muscle and science could not be gifted with brains as well, and on this account I wish to show to my readers and to the public in general, that there is one, who, while in the line of a professional pugilist and boxer, is quite capable of informing them through the medium of this book, that he is gifted with ordinary ability, and is conscious of being something more than a pugilist. I want them also to understand that, while not of an egotistical nature, I have a fair amount of common sense, and, with a Boston public school education, can give an intelligent opinion on almost any subject, and conduct myself as a gentleman in any company.

Leaving Nashville, Tennessee, we will go on with the rest of our story which brings me to the city of Chicago, where I made a stay of one week in the company of friends, informing them how I was being chased by the efforts of Governor Lowry who was offering one $1,000 reward for the apprehension of myself as well as Kilrain. After my sojourn in Chicago, I with a friend of mine, James Curly by name, a well-known sporting man of that city, took the train for the city of New York.

On arriving in New York I went to Brooklyn, to the place of my backer,

Mr. Charles Johnson, who had left me a week previous in Chicago to see how matters stood in the field, and to see what progress he could make in having the matter of my arrest fixed up in a manner that would be agreeable to Governor Lowry and the other authorities of Mississippi, and to show that, as a matter of business, I was compelled to fight in that state as the Kilrain party had won the toss for the choice of ground, and had named Richburg, Mississippi. I had to accept and go there to fight, or else be called by the world at large a coward; therefore, I went there to fight, and not to break the laws of the State of Mississippi, or in any way to defy the proclamation issued by Governor Lowry.

Leaving Johnson's in Brooklyn I went to New York, where I made my home and headquarters for some time, meeting all the prominent newspaper men of the city.

After a stay of two weeks in New York, I was informed that a requisition had been granted by Governor Hill, who is now United States Senator, for my return to Mississippi. I was arrested by Inspector Byrnes and treated in a very kindly manner, as he has always been a great admirer of mine, and has witnessed all my exhibitions of a knockout character in Madison Square Garden. I was in durance vile that night, and the next morning engaged as my attorney DeLancy Nicoll who tried to have the case postponed, and to have me admitted to bail, as I wanted to go home to see my mother, in Boston, who was very sick at that time and not expected to live. Being refused bail by Judge Morgan, who was the acting judge upon this occasion, I consented to go back to Mississippi, through the advice of my counsel, so that I could demand bail. I started back the next morning with Sheriff Childs of Mississippi, in whose charge I was, and Thomas Adams, one of Inspector Byrnes's men, and a friend of mine by the name of Matt Clune. We left New York on Thursday, and arrived in Jackson, Mississippi, Sunday afternoon at two o'clock, where I received a great ovation from the citizens, who were all in sympathy with me, and all my friends there, among them Colonel Jones Hammonton, who did everything in their power to intercede with the Governor in my behalf. I put up at the Edwards House.

The sheriff who had charge of me was a nice fellow, and had fulfilled his contract and kept his word with
me, stating that I should not be locked up. He manfully carried out his promise until some jealous-minded individual went to the Governor's mansion and told him that I was to hold a reception at the Edwards House.

The reception consisted of my being introduced by Colonel Jones Hammonton to the ladies of the city, and they one and all shook hands with me in a most cordial manner until I thought they would take my arm from its socket. The Governor, on hearing of this, sent for the sheriff, and had ordered him to take me to jail, but being a good fellow he gave me free access to the jail yard, where I could walk around and smoke.

Colonel Jones Hammonton, hearing what the Governor had done, went up and had a long talk with his Excellency, desiring that I should be given the freedom of the city.

In a very short time I was taken back to the Edwards House where I stopped until morning, when my lawyers, Judge Tyler and Mr. Green, got out a writ of *habeas corpus*, demanding that I should be taken to the county where my "crime " had been committed. The name of the judge, before whom this writ was tried, was Campbell. He had ordered me brought back to Purvis, Mississippi, which was the county seat, at which place my offence, as it was termed, was committed.

I was brought back to Purvis, taking the train that evening at five o'clock from Jackson, and arriving in Meriden the following evening. The Governor also boarded the same train, and, meeting Judge Terrel, who was holding court in Meriden, ordered him to dispense with court and go to Purvis and try this special case.

We left Meriden early the next morning, arriving in Purvis about eight o'clock the same evening. Sheriff Childs handed me over to Sheriff Cottel, who was sheriff of that county, he (Childs) being relieved of any further charge of me. I was obliged to remain three weeks in Purvis, as it took them that length of time to empanel a jury to try and convict me. This they accomplished, and, my sentence being twelve months in the county jail, I made an appeal to the Supreme Court, giving bonds for $1,000 to appear there the following June.

My lawyers made objections to the unfair trial I had received at the hands of this jury. They convicted me of prizefighting, and some two months later, when Kilrain was brought back for the same charge, they convicted him of assault and battery, showing their ignorance and partiality in this affair. This jury, which consisted of all shapes and styles of the human type, would have made a good picture for some of our comic illustrated papers.

My lawyers, now taking care of this part of the affair, after the appeal from the lower court to the Supreme Court, kept me informed how my case was progressing, and, not knowing what time it might be called, I remained idle almost a year, with the exception of five or six weeks that I traveled with a show called the "Paymaster," in which Duncan B. Harrison was starring, and gave sparring exhibitions with Joe Lannan. I received the sum of $1,000 per week for my services, and Joe Lannan $300 per week as his salary. Being informed by my lawyers that on June 19th my case would be tried, as it had been referred back from the Supreme Court to the Circuit Court, I returned to Purvis. The case was referred back on the grounds that I did not have a fair trial.

I met the same judge and district attorney, whose name was Nevil. They informed me that if I would plead guilty to prizefighting, they would fine me, and that the fine could not exceed $1,000, as that was a statute law. I stated that if they would say that in the presence of Colonel Tom Ford, who was one of my lawyers in the first trial, and any other friend, I would go in the morning and plead guilty to prizefighting. It actually cost me $18,670 to get out of this fight. What it cost Kilrain, I do not know, but on account of my being the victor, and having a reputation for "throwing money away," they made me settle in good shape.

After having settled my case in the South, I remained about New York during the summer of 1890. In July or August I formed a co-partnership with Duncan B. Harrison to appear with him in a play called "Honest Hearts and Willing Hands." We opened in August, 1890, at Niblo's Garden, New York, and made a tour of the country, appearing in all the principal cities throughout the United States, clear through to San Francisco, California. I appeared in all cities as an actor, which was my first attempt in the histrionic line, and made money everywhere.

As it would be impossible to give here the diverse comments of the papers on my performances, perhaps the following from a member of the profession will be fitting as a substitute.

When I played in Cincinnati, April 21st, of the present year, Madam Modjeska, seated in a box at Henck's Theater, witnessed the performance of "Honest Hearts and Willing Hands," and seemed to enjoy it very much.

When asked how she liked my acting she replied: "Oh, I like him very well, indeed. He speaks his lines naturally, and one likes that bluff, hearty manner. It is in keeping with the part. Of course, he hasn't the gracefulness of gesture and business, but he is very good."

Asked about the sparring exhibition, the good woman didn't just know about it, and she wrinkled her brow in puzzling to answer: "It looks so rough, and they might get hurt, but I suppose they would have to take their exercise anyway."

My career has brought me frequently into a position to make the acquaintance and form estimates of many interesting members of this profession. In regard to this a Chicago paper gives the following facetious account of an encounter with one of them. Of course allowance must be made for the writer's lively imagination:

> "Two stars of the first magnitude clashed together last St. Patrick's Day somewhere in the aristocratic region of Michigan Avenue. It was a dazzling display to the watchers of the skies, making the weak-eyed sun hide his diminished head, and totally eclipsing the splendor of the far-famed aurora borealis.
> "At that time Venus and Mars were observed to be in con-

junction by the loungers on the lake front. As Danny Shay soulfully whispered, 'Bedad, the sight of the pair uv them wud warrim the cockels of yer heart; to persave the Graycian Goddess uv Love an' the divastaten man uv war together wuz a komplayte cure for sore eyes.'

"As John L. Sullivan, the champion of the world and the only human pile-driver in that arduous and noble profession, was leaving the auditorium, he encountered the beauteous Lillian Russell entering the rotunda.

"After her morning constitutional down Michigan boulevard Miss Lillian looked as fresh as a May morning, her eyes sparkling and a big bunch of green ribbon fluttering on her breast. It was, indeed, as Danny Shay so truthfully observed, a meeting of the gods on high Olympus. Like the transit of Venus or the birth of such another sprinter as Curly Charley Mitchell, it occurs only once in a hundred years.

"For a moment the champion beauty and the champion boxer faced each other in silence, as if sizing up each other's strong points. The champion was a trifle groggy as he beheld the dazzling array of loveliness. Then the beauty blushed, averting her face and turning her dewy eyes to the floor, and the champion feinted with his deadly left, removed his stovepipe with his right, and, bowing, murmured, abashed, in a classic Back Bay whisper:

"'I throw up the sponge. I couldn't knock her out in four rounds. She's prettier than Rosy O'Neill's picture that Maggie Cline is turning toward the wall every night down at Tony Pastor's, for fifty a turn.'

"'Ah! Good morning, Mr. John L.,' began the beauty in silvery tones, frankly extending her gloved hand and bathing the champion in one of her glorious violet glances that cures the grippe, and which nearly knocked him into a trance.

"'Let me grasp the hand of the great John L.,' murmured the radiant Lillian, with charming candor. 'Won't you? Please do; that's a good boy.'

"'Why, certainly,' quoth John, taking the proffered palm and squeezing it so tight that Lillian winced till the tears came to her eyes. 'Don't spring such chestnuts as that on me,' said John. 'Every one I meet wants to grasp my hand; it 's getting monotonous. How are they coming, Miss Lillian? I hope I haven't hurt you,' John ventured to remark, as if sparring for wind.

"'They are arriving in gondolas,' murmured Lillian, sweetly; 'and with a rapidity that is extremely gratifying; but I won't shake hands with you in a hurry again, Mr. John L.; you've a grip like a bear. We're turning them away over at the Columbia. There's breathing room only, and precious little of that, Alf Hayman tells me,' continued the queen of comic opera getting down to business.

"'Same case here; Joe Baylies claims you can't keep them away from the People's this week with cannons; the house is so full they bulge out of the window and hang on the fire escapes by their eyebrows. Chicago's a great town. There's only one New York and that's Chicago. Let me think. Last week the aldermen wanted to give me the freedom of Chicago, but I refused. I was holding out for the compressed air franchise, but that was gobbled up by Mr. Bacon, so Mayor Washburne couldn't let me have it. But you bet I'm due for the next franchise or there'll be trouble; and the mayor has promised, so has Tim Scanlan, to let me in on the ground floor.'

"'By the way, Mr. John L., where 's your green ribbon this morning? Shame on you, sir! Don't you know this is St. Patrick's Day? You'll never be elected president if you go on this way.'

"'Why, that 's a fact,' groaned John, ruefully; 'shiver my timbers, but I forgot all about it. They'd murder me over in the unterrified 19th ward if I loomed up without a sprig of green in my buttonhole - What'll I do to square myself with the populace?'

"'Oh, I'll save you from being slaughtered,' returned Airy Fairy Lillian. 'I want you to whip James Corbett, and win that $50,000. Sabe, Mr. John L.? Let me pin this piece of green to your lapel. Stand straight; I won't hurt you, so don't get frightened. You're too big to cry; there we are. Now, Mr. John L., you wear my colors, go in and win, and knock out all the telephone fighters down at New Orleans next September.'"

As a diversion, at intervals between boxing and theatre engagements, I kept alive my youthful interest in baseball, by acting as umpire, pitcher, or in some other capacity on special occasions. There is a droll account of one of these occasions which appeared in the *New York Morning Journal:*

"Mr. John L. Sullivan astonished everybody in Philadelphia by appearing this morning in a full Quaker habit. He came out in front of the Continental Hotel wearing a long drab coat, cut of 1702, and a wide brimmed hat, and sat down in a comfortable armchair. School children who passed by said, ' See the good old Quaker! What a pious man he is!' Mr. Sullivan's face had a serious expression softened by a look of benevolence.

"'Get on to him!' said Arthur Chambers's Pet to Ovvney Geoghegan's Chicken, as the two gentlemen approached the hotel.

"'Blast my heyes!' said the Chicken, 'hif that h'aint hold George Fox 'imself; 'owsomehever, it may be Villiam Penn.'

"The two men stood still and looked at Sullivan a moment with wondering eyes.

"'Ullo, Villiam Penn, watchyer doin' hin them togs; watchyer racket?' said the Chicken.

"'Good morning to thee, friend Chicken; hast thou had any 'scrap' this week? Was the referee kind to thee in that last scrimmage in Brother Hezekiah Doolan's dog-pit with Bill Chandler's Ghost?'

"'Hennybody 'ud know you was ha Quaker. Wat makes you so fly? Wy 'ave you got hon them church regimentals?' continued the Chicken.

"'Well, you see,' said Sullivan, 'that if I was in Rome I would do as the Romans do, so when I'm in Philadelphia I do as the Quakers do. The landlord told me that a good many representatives of the old Quaker families would probably call on me today, and so out of respect for their feelings and in courtesy to them I have put on this costume.'

"'Well,' said Arthur Chambers's Pet, 'if you were in Mexico would you do as the Aztecs do? If you were among the Choctaws would you do as the Choctaws do? If you were among the cannibals would you call for a piece of parboiled missionary on toast? The Quakers are the Aztecs of Philadelphia.'

"A good many old Quakers called on Sullivan during the forenoon, and were received by him with plain old-fashioned courtesy. They spoke of him pleasantly as the 'fighting Quaker.'

"About one o'clock Sullivan called a cab, driven by a Quaker, and drove down to the City Hall, where the mayor and Colonel McClure were waiting to receive him, Colonel McClure was in full-dress suit, and had been waiting patiently for three hours, as he had expected the distinguished guest since 10 o'clock. Mr. Sullivan entered the room containing the portraits of the mayors and of Revolutionary heroes. As he came in, Washington, Franklin, and the other pictured worthies seemed to shrink in size. Owney Geoghegan's Chicken accompanied Mr. Sullivan.

"Colonel McClure advanced to meet the great pugilist and shook hands with him warmly.

"'Who is that?' said Sullivan pointing his umbrella at a faded picture on the wall.

"'That,' said Colonel McClure, 'is Washington.'

"' Wash - ? Who was Wash -' asked the Chicken of Sullivan in an undertone.

"'Sh' - said Sullivan. 'He was a terror. He had a big scrap with Cornwallis at Yorktown and knocked him out in two rounds. No police interference. Referee said 'twas fair, and George took the stakes and the colors.'

"'And who is that crank?' asked Sullivan, indicating another portrait with his umbrella.

"'That is mad Anthony Wayne,' said Colonel McClure, 'one of

our Pennsylvanians.'

"Mr. Sullivan, Colonel McClure, the mayor and Ovvney Geoghegan's Chicken, after a few moments of conversation about the Revolutionary War and the part Pennsylvania had taken in it, walked into the mayor's office and partook of an elegant lunch.

"Sullivan and the Chicken left the City Hall at three o'clock surrounded by thousands of people. As Sullivan was walking in Chestnut Street a little policeman about five feet high blocked his way and insisted on arresting him for gathering a crowd on the street. Sullivan was bullied by a bandy-legged policeman at the baseball grounds yesterday, and thought that it was about time to curb the Philadelphia police. He picked up the belligerent policeman, put him under his arm and marched down the street with him for a block, and set him down on a water plug, an immense crowd following."

CHAPTER ELEVEN
PACIFIC OCEAN VOYAGE

Early in 1891 I arranged a trip to Australia, and sailed June 26th from San Francisco on the good ship "Mariposa," commanded by Captain Haywood. There was nothing to mar the pleasure of our trip, except that my old friend, Frank Moran, was taken sick, aboard, with an attack of paralysis. Previous to my leaving San Francisco, I appeared in a bout with Mr. James Corbett. It was simply friendly.

After a sail of six days we stopped at Honolulu, Sandwich Islands, long enough to give an exhibition and to enable the steamer to coal up. I found the people of Honolulu very kind and cordial. There was a little colony composed entirely of Americans.

While in Honolulu, Queen Isabelle, sister of King Kalakaua, called on me at our hotel. She referred with sorrow to the fact that her brother was dead, and told me had he been alive he would have been only too pleased to have called on me and entertained me to the best of his ability. We talked on various subjects, and I found her a most entertaining and interesting person. We spoke of America at great length, and she seemed to greatly admire our Republic.

We left Honolulu, and after a day's sail, stood off from Tintula, where we delivered the mail which was
taken with some passengers on a steamer that had sailed out to take them off. We did not stay there any length of time.

At the Samoa Islands I saw the harbor where the American and German warships were destroyed by one of the worst hurricanes ever known. The natives there exhibited great curiosity to see me, and made exclamations which I was given to understand meant something like "Great Chief."

We next left for Auckland, Australia, where we remained some few hours, but did not come to anchor. We landed about July 20th at Sydney, New South Wales, where we were met by a tug to take me off. Duncan B. Harrison, my partner, was aboard the tug with a number of Australian sporting men who had come to welcome me, but I refused to leave the ship as I did not want to leave my friend, Frank Moran, who was sick. We left the steamer the next morning, and were tendered a banquet by a great many friends in Sydney.

Remaining in Sydney a week, rehearsing, we prepared for our opening and made our debut there at her Majesty's theater, which is considered the best equipped and most beautiful theater in Australia. We stopped at the Australian Hotel, which is regarded as the best in the city.

From Sydney, New South Wales, we went to Melbourne, Victoria, a ride of 19 hours by rail. We stopped at the White Hart Hotel, and played for three weeks at the Grand Opera House. After leaving Melbourne, we stopped at the principal cities throughout Australia: Ballarat, three nights; Bendigo, two nights; Adelaide, three nights; Cathlenain, one night; Maryboro, one night; Stahl, one night; and in all, we showed about six and one half weeks. I did not give myself up to much pleasure in Australia. I went sightseeing on different occasions, visiting with my friend, Mr. Mactier, at Adelaide. We drove around the city and over the mountains, visiting the "Eagle on the hill," and the Falls.

During my stay in Australia, I met all the principal officials and men of note, among them Governor Hopeton, of Melbourne, Victoria. I had some general conversation with the latter, comparing my country and his. He is well informed, and he treated me very kindly. At Melbourne I was introduced to the members of the Parliament which was then in session. They stopped at the same hotel with us - the White Hart - corner of Burke and Spring Streets. As my readers probably all know, members are elected there by ballot, under the Australian system, which system is being generally adopted in the United States. I met and was introduced to Governor Jersey, of Sydney, at the race track, Melbourne, where we both witnessed the races. I have seen quite a number of horse races in this country, but I never saw any like those they have in Australia. They race distances of from one to three miles. No time is recorded, and racing, on the whole, tends to kill a horse rather than increase his speed. Hurdle racing is very popular there. They have a crude system of betting, very inferior to ours, and the English system of bookmaking.

In Melbourne I met the "Evangeline" Company and part of the "County Fair" Company. The railroad facilities of Australia I found no better than those of England, and altogether very inferior to our American railroads.

The Australian sporting paper, *The Referee*, voiced opinion in that country in the following:

> "Next Monday the 'Alameda' will once more set sail, a moving link between the two great continents of Australia and America. On board this splendid vessel, homeward bound, goes the renowned pugilist, John L. Sullivan, the hurricane comet of the fistic firmament. John has not made the barrels of money it was expected he would coin here in Australia, but, on the whole, private advices inform me, he has not done so badly.
>
> "I saw plenty of Sullivan while here in our city of Sydney; I certainly saw nothing that anyone of the most sensitive moral

organization could cavil at. He was free with his coin to those with whom he was acquainted, and the only time I saw his sympathies appealed to he gave, and gave liberally, to help a woman in hard circumstances. If he had landed in Australia on a knocking-out expedition, traveling from city to city with a boxing show, as he did in Great Britain and America, he would have made a little fortune, and would have been the idol of the sporting community. The fact of the matter is simply this: The populace had heard for years past of Sullivan, the man of magical quickness and terrible dexterity with the gloves. They had longed to see him in action; for of all the boxing people alive, none are so enthusiastic as the populace of Australia. Should Sullivan ever come this way again, and come in his true guise, with his grand physique in perfect trim, his brawny muscles braced for action and gloves on his hands, with an offer pasted on his portmanteau to 'stop any man in the country in four rounds,' then I venture to predict that he will not find halls big enough to accommodate his patrons. He has been marching through a hostile country, to a certain extent; and here, where Jackson, and Slavin, and Goddard are looked upon as being invincible, Sullivan has been regarded as the only man on earth who has a chance of lowering one or all of them."

We returned from Australia on the steamship "Alameda," under Captain Mose; leaving October 3rd, and arriving in San Francisco October 26, 1891. I remained in San Francisco some time arranging a company, and opened in Sacramento on my trip eastward. We showed all through the West, British Columbia, and Manitoba.

I then made a new contract with Mr. Harrison, appearing in Philadelphia for a week, in Brooklyn a week, and closing in Boston at the Howard Athenaeum on the 4th of June, 1892, the attendance being very large.

As the narration of my reminiscences now brings me back again to my native place, and very near to the rounding out of that portion of the career with which my name has been most connected, that of a boxer and pugilist, I feel in a position to give some expressions of opinion based on experience.

Of all the men with whom I have boxed, sparred, and fought, I consider Ryan, Kilrain, Slade, and Flood the gamest group. Of the genuine gameness of these men, in my opinion, there can be no doubt. Ryan stood up and fought me like a man, did not resort to any trickery or petty dirtiness, but fought from the start, and he was in the ring for the same purpose that I was, namely to demonstrate which was the superior man. Ryan has pluck, so has Kilrain, so have Slade and Flood. Others may differ from me in this opinion, but I really think I ought to know about the men, as I have faced and beaten them all.

Kilrain fought for all he was worth in my last battle with him, and stood his punishment gamely. Slade and Flood did the same. To show Slade's gameness, when I knocked him through the ropes in our glove fight, in New York City, he fell quite a distance, struck heavily, but got up and came back on the stage unassisted, and attempted to go right on and fight. Most persons, fighting under the same circumstances, would require assistance, and the chances are they would have quit rather than go back. Slade had the disadvantage that all big men have that I have met with - the bigger they are the more heavily they fall.

Very different from my encounters with these men was my fight with Mitchell. As the last round of that memorable fight will show, and is recorded, the last 39 minutes passed without a blow being struck, for the very simple reason that I was unable to catch him or get within striking distance. It was simply run, run, run, he in the lead and I not as good as a close second.

Repeatedly in that last round I asked him to let us have one decent round, to all of which he paid no attention, but went on with his talk, telling me that I could not catch him in a month. A spectator remarked that the fight had already lasted three hours, to which Mitchell replied very sarcastically, "I will make it last six hours before he catches me."

His whole game was to avoid me, not to fight me. Eugene Field gives the following cleverly humorous take-off on a fight between Mitchell and myself:

> "We fully expect to have the opportunity of laying before our readers, some time next September, an accurate report of the meeting between John L. Sullivan and Charlie Mitchell, beginning in this wise:
>
> "First Round. When the bell tapped both men scored evenly and got away, Mitchell securing a distinct lead from the start, which he steadily increased.
>
> "Second Round. Mitchell continues in good form. At the end of the seventh mile he threw off his shoes, and after that he traveled somewhat lighter and freer. Sullivan appeared to be losing wind, but his friends think he may overtake his competitor in the woods near the Alabama line along toward morning.
>
> "Third Round. Sullivan has just made a tremendous spurt of six miles. Mitchell is out of sight, and pools sell five to one in his favor.
>
> "Fourth Round. Mitchell has just stubbed his toe on the projecting root of a cypress. First blood for Mitchell.
>
> "Fifth Round. Slavin and Ryan, who have been acting as Mitchell's seconds, fell off their bicycles near the end of the 73rd mile completely exhausted. Mitchell, apparently as fresh

THE OPENING ROUND OF THE FIGHT.

as when he started, is still forging ahead. Sullivan is said to be laid up at a farmhouse, near Bayou Catouche, under the care of a chiropodist.

"Later. The race has been awarded to Mitchell, who is still running. Sullivan is severely punished about the feet, and may lose several toes," etc., etc.

Very different from this style of fighting was the style of the men I have mentioned, and I must add Joe Goss, for he was surely as game a man as ever breathed, and was also as true a friend as I ever had, or any man could have. One instance of his honesty was brought out by his refusing to accept $4,500 in cold cash, from parties whom I do not care to mention, who wanted him to drug me before the Ryan fight in 1882. He was offered this money by a certain clique to fix me, and, needless to say, he proved true blue to me as a friend.

Another thing I will mention about Mitchell: he gets credit, according to one of the best sporting papers in the country, namely the *Clipper*, for knocking me down in Madison Square Garden. While that is correct in one sense, I will repeat that in the position that I was in no man ever breathed who could avoid it, standing as I was with my feet close together; and, practically, I was "set down." For instance, if a man is standing with his feet close together and his opponent punches him in the stomach, his natural tendency is to double up; but he struck me somewhat higher, and the actual effect was that instead of falling backwards and being knocked down in the manner generally understood by being knocked down, I went down all in a lump, somewhat after the style of going to sit in a chair.

When I started out boxing, I felt within myself, as I do now, that I could knock out any man living. I could always beat a man's guard down, and when boxing for a contest I never attempt to spar for an opening, but I go right in to box, and win from the start. I do not believe in sparring to feel the other man out. The other man is second to me at every stage of the fight; I go in to win from the very first second, and I never stop until I have won. Win I must, and win I will, at every stage of the game.

I never had stage fright in my life; do not know what it is, and do not suppose I could understand it if somebody would try to explain it to me. Another thing I will say: I never have been hit hard enough by anybody to feel it during the fight. I have never felt a man's blow in my life.

I was the first one to demonstrate, under Marquis of Queensbury rules, that I could knock a man out of time in less than four rounds, which means, in actual fighting time, 12 minutes. In my career I have knocked out not less than one hundred men. Some of the encounters I remember, while others of little importance I have forgotten. Had I never started boxing, I question very much if there would ever have been any such attempt made. I have demonstrated my superiority as a boxer over every man living that I have ever met.

In attempting to knock men out in four rounds, the idea of which is original with me, I have been handicapped from the fact that the majority of audiences before which I have appeared have always been with my opponent. I have been supposed to possess such wonderful strength of hitting power, that unless I knocked the man dead, the audiences, especially in cases of local pride, have thought that my opponent was a wonderful man to even dare to put up his hands in front of me.

Any man of reason will readily understand, for it must be admitted that a referee is only human, every referee is more or less influenced by the feeling of the audience, and, being handicapped as I have been in the majority of my boxing matches, I have had to demonstrate beyond all possible doubt, my superiority over my opponents. I knocked out 59 men during my eight-months tour.

Tug Wilson was the first man who ever succeeded in staying before me for four rounds, and he only did that by floor crawling, hugging, and avoiding me in every way possible. He dropped twenty-eight times. After he succeeded, several others attempted to do the same thing; some of them have been successful. His actions, as well as those who have succeeded, are in direct violation of Marquis of Queensbury rules, but referees in those instances have never decided strictly according to the rules. Although I have known that the referees were wrong, and did not allow me full justice in a number of instances, I have never urged their doing their duty, and allowing me credit for all such fouls and infractions of the rules; but have allowed all my opponents leniency of which they took advantage. I have always taken into consideration the fact that people who had paid their money to see me boxing or fighting, are entitled to some consideration for their money, and instead of claiming all that has been due me, I have gone right on to give the audience their money's worth by defeating my opponent, despite the fact that I was handicapped by the repeated violations of the rules.

There are a thousand and one ways in which a man can violate the rules without doing so openly; not only that, but there are many instances that I might quote and have actually seen, where men have preferred to lose on a foul rather than be beaten fairly. Whenever I have boxed with men who have resorted to all the trickery and sharp practices which they or their friends could invent, the match has lasted longer than where the men have come up manfully and fought me.

The length of the match has always depended upon the amount of trickery my opponent could resort to and his sprinting abilities. Some made it last longer than others. Now, in the face of such matches the general public give the man who makes the longest fight the credit of being the best boxer or fighter; whereas such should not be the case by any means, for where one man stands up manfully and fights, and does his best to win and is consequently knocked out in short order, the other man does not attempt to win but attempts to make the fight last as long as possible, depending upon police interference and hoping to make a draw, and knowing that the public will give him credit for having made a long fight.

CHAPTER TWELVE
RULES OF THE RING

I have been asked a great many times what rules I prefer to fight under, and what I thought of the merits of the different rules of fighting. Now, I will say, for reasons which I will give, that I consider the Marquis of Queensbury rules the best for everybody, for under those rules each man has an even chance. The London Prize-Ring rules, of course, have been taken as the only ones for years back, but times and circumstances are continually changing.

I object to the London Prize-Ring rules, in the first place as being against the laws of all English-speaking countries; and in breaking the law of the land a man always lays himself liable to fine or imprisonment, and sometimes both. I have found, from my experience, that breaking these particular laws has been very expensive to me, for in all the fights that I have been in under the London Prize-Ring rules, I have not only lost money, but have also had the care and worriment incidental to arrests, trials, and penalties. It has always cost me more money to get out of my fights tinder those rules than I have ever gained from them. Again, I have never seen a fight under the London Prize-Ring rules but what those present were of a rougher character than I have seen under the Marquis of Queensbury rules; and wherever the rowdy element predominates, there is always sure to be trouble, both for the fighters and the audience. The London Prize-Ring rules require that the ring shall be made on turf, with eight stakes and ropes. The ring being pitched in the open air allows everybody to see the ring and fighters without any cost of admission; and, consequently, the audience is made up of a class of people who cannot afford to pay, and would not pay any reasonable amount to witness the contest. Where such an audience assembles there will always be found a certain class of dishonest men practicing their nefarious work, whereas, under the Marquis of Queensbury rules, the contest usually takes place in a hall of some description under police supervision, and the price of admission is put purposely high so as to exclude the rowdy element, and a gentleman can see the contest, feeling sure that he will not be robbed of any of his valuables or in any way be interfered with.

Under the Marquis of Queensbury rules the manly art of self-defense, of which I am considered an authority, is conducted for the benefit of gentlemen, not rowdies. Fighting, under the Marquis of Queensbury rules before gentlemen, is a pleasure; to the other element it becomes a brawl.

There are hundreds of ways in fighting under the London Prize-Ring rules, whereby the best man can lose, or at least not win, through trickery. In my descriptions of my various fights, I believe I have illustrated how several of these tricks are done. Under the Marquis of Queensbury rules no clinching is allowed, no wrestling, and the superiority of the contestants is judged by the actions of their hands, and not by kicking, nor biting, nor gouging.

Under the London Prize-Ring rules, all the mean tactics can sometimes be used right under the eyes of the referee without his seeing them. Contests last too long to demonstrate which is the superior man, and the length of time occupied does not depend on the superiority of the man as a fighter or boxer, but the contemptible trickery possessed. There are hundreds of instances where men fighting under the London Prize-Ring rules, and knowing that they were inferior to their opponent, have resorted to trickery, so as to lose the fight on a foul rather than to be beaten fairly, according to the rules. Fighting and boxing under the Marquis of Queensbury rules are conducted for the purpose of not only determining which is the superior man, but also for the benefit and education of its gentlemanly patrons. Gentlemen and business men of all vocations cannot afford to give up the time to witness fighting under the London Prize-Ring rules, for the reason that it takes too long in the first place, and in the second place it is against the law, and every spectator, as well as each participant, is amenable to the law.

Fighting under the Marquis of Queensbury rules is of such a nature that the superiority of the men can be demonstrated, to the satisfaction of everybody, in a reasonable length of time, and without obliging the audience to witness any unnecessary brutality and evidences of rowdyism. Fighting or boxing under these rules with gloves demonstrates to everybody's satisfaction which is the superior man, and never leaves either participant marked or maimed for life, as under the London rules. Any two gentlemen can compete in a contest under the Marquis of Queensbury rules with ordinary-sized gloves, and demonstrate which is the more skilful of the two, without feeling that afterwards they will have to appear among their friends with discolored optics, or marked faces. These rules recommend themselves to all gentlemanly boxers.

Another great objection to the London Prize-Ring rules, is, that public opinion is opposed to anyone fighting under them. There is not one man in a hundred who does not like to see a contest for points and science where neither participant is liable to become injured. I can win under any rules, but I don't want to break the law, nor go to the trouble and expense which always comes after fighting under the London Prize-Ring rules. I can demonstrate with gloves as well as with bare knuckles my superiority as a fighter; either way suits me. But I don't feel as though I ought to disregard public opinion and patrons of boxing matches.

Summing up my reasons, I will state that the Marquis of Queensbury rules are the best, for under these rules a man can demonstrate his superiority without fear of the law, without showing unnecessary brutality, either to himself or his opponent, without the great expense incidental to fighting under the London Prize-Ring rules, and also with better advantage to himself. The London Prize-Ring rules allow too much leeway for the rowdy element to indulge in their practices. Such mean tricks as spiking, biting, gouging, concealing snuff in one's mouth to blind an opponent; strangling, butting with the head, falling down without being struck, scratching with nails, kicking, falling on an antagonist with the knees, the using of stones or resin, and the hundred other tricks that are impossible under the Marquis of Queensbury rules, are under the others practiced almost openly.

In almost all boxing or fighting contests, the rules are more or less broken, but the extent to which they can be broken depends solely upon the referee. The judgment in his case must be relied on solely. A great many resort to all means for claiming a fight for their man, and on all grounds - some trivial and some of them worthy ones. I do not believe in deciding a contest on any trivial breaking of the rules, but it is impossible sometimes to tell whether it is intentional or not. Again, where a large number of spectators have assembled, and gone to the expense and trouble of attending a contest, it is not to be expected that a referee will decide a fight on technicalities, unless the rules be so grossly broken as to be plain to everybody present. People pay their money to see, and are never satisfied with any decisions the referee can give, but always want to decide for themselves which is the better man, and, as a rule, they want to see it fought to the end. They can hardly be blamed for so wanting.

My experience with referees has been that they have all endeavored to be as impartial as possible, and have decided as fairly as they possibly could under the circumstances. We are all human, and it is only fair to allow that a referee can be guided by an audience in his feelings and decisions, as any man would be under the same circumstances. There is no trouble in securing referees or seconds for fighting or boxing under the Marquis of Queensbury rules, as fighting under these rules is not illegal. A contest conducted under such management, and decided by such men, is always open and above board.

One thing for which I find fault with the London Prize-Ring rules is that, instead of a fight, it sometimes turns into a sprinting match, as Mitchell turned it with me in France.

There have been in England three notable codes or "Rules of the Ring," for the ordering of pugilistic contests. The first were known as

"Broughton's Rules." They governed all prizefights in England for nearly a century, till the adoption of the code known commonly as the "London Prize-Ring Rules."

The "Marquis of Queensbury Rules" provide for regular rounds of three minutes instead of the former system of ending a round when one of the contestants came to the ground. The London Ring rules are still followed in England, but never, it may be depended on, when the contest is intended to be fair and above board.

Jack Broughton

Broughton was the first man who made regular rules for modern boxing. Up to his time a prizefight was a rough-and-tumble scrimmage, in which the men might choke each other, wrestle, butt with the head, trip, and strike a man on his knees. "Broughton's Rules" were "produced for the better regulation of the amphitheatre, approved by the gentlemen, and agreed to by the pugilists, August, 1743." They continued in force till "The New Rules of the Ring" were adopted in 1838.

BROUGHTON'S RULES

1. That a square yard be chalked in the middle of the stage, from which the men shall begin the fight; and every fresh set-to, after a fall or being parted from the rails, each second is to bring his man to the side of the square and place him opposite the other.
2. After a fall, if the second does not bring his man to the side of the square within the space of half a minute, he shall be deemed a beaten man.
3. That no person shall be upon the stage except principals and seconds.
4. That no man be deemed beaten unless he fails coming up to the line in the limited time, or that his own second declares him beaten.
5. The winning man to have two thirds of the money.
6. The principals to choose two umpires who shall choose a referee.
7. That no boxer is to hit his adversary when he is down, or seize him by the ham, the breeches, or any part below the waist; a man on his knees to be reckoned down.

RULES OF THE LONDON PRIZE RING

1. The ring shall be made on turf, and shall be four-and-twenty feet

square, formed of eight stakes and ropes, the latter extending in double lines, the uppermost line being four feet from the ground, and the lower two feet from the ground. In the center of the ring a mark be formed, to be termed a scratch.

2. Each man shall be attended to the ring by two seconds and a bottle-holder. The combatants, on shaking hands, shall retire until the seconds of each have tossed for choice of position, which adjusted, the winner shall choose his corner according to the state of the wind or sun, and conduct his man thereto; the loser taking the opposite diagonal corner.

3. Each man shall be provided with a handkerchief of a color suitable to his own fancy, and the seconds shall entwine these handkerchiefs at the upper end of one of the center stakes. These handkerchiefs shall be called "Colors," and the winner of the battle at its conclusion shall be entitled to their possession as the trophy of victory.

4. The two umpires shall be chosen by the seconds or backers to watch the progress of the battle, and take exception to any breach of the rules hereafter stated. A referee shall be chosen by the umpires, unless otherwise agreed on, to whom all disputes shall be referred; and the decision of this referee, whatever it may be, shall be final and strictly binding on all parties, whether as to the matter in dispute or the issue of the battle. The referee shall be provided with a watch for the purpose of calling time; the call of that referee only to be attended to, and no other person whatever shall interfere in calling time. The referee shall withhold all opinion till appealed to by the umpires, and the umpires strictly abide by his decision without dispute.

5. On the men being stripped it shall be the duty of the seconds to examine their drawers, and if any objection arises as to insertion of improper substances therein, they shall appeal to their umpires, who, with the concurrence of the referee, shall direct what alterations shall be made.

6. The spikes in the fighting boots shall be confined to three in number, which shall not exceed three eighths of an inch from the sole of the boot, and shall not be less than one eighth of an inch broad at the point; two to be placed in the broadest part of the sole and one in the heel; and in the event of a man wearing any other spikes, either in the toes or elsewhere, he shall be compelled either to remove them or provide other boots properly spiked, the penalty for refusal to be a loss of the stakes.

7. Both men being ready, each shall be conducted to that side of the scratch next his corner previously chosen; and the seconds on the one side, and the men on the other, having shaken hands, the former shall immediately leave the ring, and there remain until the round be finished, on no pretense whatever approaching their principals during the

round, without permission from the referee. The penalty to be the loss of the battle to the offending parties.

8. At the conclusion of the round when one or both of the men shall be down, the seconds shall step into the ring and carry or conduct their principals to his corner, there affording him the necessary assistance, and no person whatever be permitted to interfere in his duty.

9. On the expiration of 30 seconds the referee appointed shall cry "Time," upon which each man shall rise from the knee of his second and walk to his own side of the scratch unaided; the seconds immediately leaving the ring. The penalty for either of them remaining eight seconds after the call of time to lie the loss of the battle to his principal; and either man failing to be at the scratch within eight seconds shall be deemed to have lost the battle.

10. On no consideration whatever shall any person except the seconds or the referee be permitted to enter the ring during the battle; nor till it shall have been concluded; and in the event of such unfair practice, or the ropes or stakes being disturbed or removed, it shall be in the power of the referee to award the victory to that man who, in his honest opinion, shall have the best of the contest.

11. The seconds shall not interfere, advise or direct the adversary of their principal, and shall refrain from all offensive and irritating expressions, in all respects conducting themselves with order and decorum, and confine themselves to the diligent and careful discharge of their duties to their principals.

12. In picking up their men, should the seconds willfully injure the antagonist of their principal, the latter shall be deemed to have forfeited the battle on the decision of the referee.

13. It shall be a fair "stand up fight," and if either man shall willfully throw himself down without receiving a blow, whether blows shall have previously been exchanged or not, he shall be deemed to have lost the battle; but this rule shall not apply to a man who in a close slips down from the grasp of his opponent to avoid punishment, or from obvious accident or weakness.

14. Butting with the head shall be deemed foul, and the party resorting to this practice shall be deemed to have lost the battle.

15. A blow struck when a man is thrown or down shall be deemed foul. A man with one knee and one hand on the ground, or with both knees on the ground, shall be deemed down; and a blow given in either of these positions shall be considered foul, providing always that, when in such position, the man so down shall not himself strike, or attempt to strike.

16. A blow struck below the waistband shall be deemed foul, and in a close, seizing an antagonist below the waist, by the thigh or otherwise, shall be deemed foul.

17. All attempts to inflict injury by gouging, or tearing the flesh with the fingers or nails, and biting shall be deemed foul.
18. Kicking, or deliberately falling on an antagonist with the knees or otherwise when down, shall be deemed foul.
19. All bets shall be paid as the battle money after a fight is awarded.
20. The referee and umpires shall take their positions in front of the center stake, outside the ropes.
21. Due notice shall be given by the stakeholder of the day and place where the battle money is to be given up, and he be exonerated from all responsibility upon obeying the direction of the referee; all parties be strictly bound by these rules; and in future, all articles of agreement for a contest be entered into with a strict and willing adherence to the letter and spirit of these rules.
22. In the event of magisterial or other interference, or in case of darkness coming on, the referee (or stakeholder in case no referee has been chosen) shall have the power to name the time and place for the next meeting, if possible on the same day, or as soon after as may be. In naming the second or third place the nearest spot shall be selected to the original place of fighting where there is a chance of its being fought out.
23. Should the fight not be decided on the day all bets shall be drawn, unless the fight shall be resumed the same week, between Sunday and Sunday, in which case the referee's duties shall continue and the bets shall stand and he decided by the event. The battle money shall remain in the hands of the stake-holder until fairly won or lost by a fight, unless a draw be mutually agreed upon, or, in case of a postponement, one of the principals shall be absent, when the man in the ring shall be awarded the stakes.
24. Any pugilist voluntarily quitting the ring previous to the deliberate judgment of the referee being obtained shall be deemed to have lost the fight.
25. On an objection being made by the seconds or umpire the men shall retire to their corners, and there remain until the decision of the appointed authorities shall be obtained; if pronounced "foul" the battle shall be at an end; but if "fair," "time" shall be called by the party appointed, and the man absent from the scratch in eight seconds after shall be deemed to have lost the fight. The decision in all cases to be given promptly and irrevocably, for which purpose the umpires and the referee should be invariably close together.
26. If a man leaves the ring, either to escape punishment or for any other purpose, without the permission of the referee, unless he is involuntarily forced out, shall forfeit the battle.
27. The use of hard substances, such as stones, or sticks, or of resin in

the hand during the battle, shall be deemed foul, and on the requisition of the seconds of either man the accused shall open his hands for the examination of the referee.

28. Hugging on the ropes shall be deemed foul. A man held by the neck against the stakes, or upon or against the ropes, shall be considered down, and all interference with him in that position shall be foul. If a man in any way makes use of the ropes or stakes to aid him in squeezing his adversary, he shall be deemed the loser of the battle; and if a man in a close reaches the ground with his knees, his adversary shall immediately loose him or lose the battle.

29. All glove or room fights be as nearly as possible in conformity with the foregoing rules.

MARQUIS OF QUEENSBURY RULES

1. To be a fair stand-up boxing match in a 24 foot ring, or as near that size as practicable.
2. No wrestling or hugging allowed.
3. The rounds to be of three minutes duration, and one-minute time between rounds.
4. If either man fall, through weakness or otherwise, he must get up unassisted; 10 seconds to be allowed him to do so, the other man meanwhile to return to his corner, and when the fallen man is on his legs the round is to be resumed and continued until the three minutes have expired. If one man fails to come to the scratch in the 10 seconds allowed, it shall be in the power of the referee to give his award in favor of the other man.
5. A man hanging on the ropes in a helpless state, with his toes off the ground, shall be considered down.
6. No seconds or any other person to be allowed in the ring during the rounds.
7. Should the contest be stopped by any unavoidable interference, the referee to name time and place, as soon as possible, for finishing the contest; so that the match must be won and lost, unless the backers of both men agree to draw the stakes.
8. The gloves to be fair-sized boxing gloves of the best quality, and new.
9. Should a glove burst, or come off, it must be replaced to the referee's satisfaction.
10. A man on one knee is considered down, and if struck is entitled to the stakes.
11. No shoes or boots with springs allowed.
12. The contest in all other respects to be governed by the revised rules of the London Prize Ring.

As to the popular interest in boxing I can speak with substantial knowledge, about half a million dollars having come to me in the way of prizes and earnings during my varied career.

How successful boxers are treated is humorously told in the columns of a New York newspaper. It is entitled "A Boston Scene."

"'Who is this well-dressed man with the sealskin overcoat, hat, and gloves? He carries a gold-headed cane and is followed by a bulldog in a scarlet blanket. Do you know him?'

"'Oh, yes, that is Sullivan, the pugilist. Fine man, hard hitter. Very popular. Always surrounded by a crowd of admiring friends, as you see him now. He is very well off; was given a benefit not long ago that netted him a sum of $12,000. He has also been presented with a valuable belt studded with diamonds.'

"'Indeed, he is very fortunate.'

"'Oh yes, a very fortunate fellow, ranks high in his profession, you see. Why, when he played in the Boston Theatre in this city with Lester and Allen's Minstrels, posing as statuary with William Muldoon, he was presented by his many friends with a statue of himself, his exact height and size, in boxing attitude, composed entirely of white carnations with red carnations for the belt. It was a magnificent piece of work and took over 14,000 flowers to make it.

"'And would you believe it, the chair on which Sullivan sat, during the intervals of his fight with Ryan at New Orleans, was snatched from the hands of Mr. John Murphy after the battle was over, and in a moment was broken up, and almost every one present had secured a splinter to be preserved as a memento of the best battle ever fought.

"'In England, too, he was very popular. The members of the Pelican Club, one of the most aristocratic clubs in England, made him an honorary member of their club and presented him with a Pelican scarf-pin and gold waistcoat buttons to match.'

"'Who is that white-headed weary-looking old man, close behind the pugilist and his friends? Poor man, he seems thinly clad for this wintry weather. Do you know him?'

"'Oh, yes, that is old Faithful, a country clergyman. Very learned man, they say. Been a preacher of the gospel all his life, but poor as a rat. He had a benefit, too, the other night.'

"'Oh, indeed! Did it net him much?'

"'I don't think it did; you see, it was a sort of surprise party. His parishioners called upon him in a body, ate up everything there was in the house, and left him presents to the amount of 60 cents.'"

CHAPTER THIRTEEN
TRAINING AND DIVERSE TOPICS

Now, as regards my mode of training, I have ideas of my own which I give for the benefit of my readers:

To begin with, I sleep in a good, airy, well-ventilated room. I do not believe in having a trainer sleep in the same bed with the person training. My reasons are that a man can sleep better alone and will not be obliged to inhale the breath of the other man.

I begin to condition myself by taking a dose of physic, which I prepare myself, and which consists of about 50 cents' worth each of zinnia, salts, manna, black stick licorice. I put all these ingredients into two quarts of water and boil the liquid down to one quart, allowing the mixture to simmer for an hour and a half or two hours. I then strain the liquid off into a bottle that holds merely a quart and cork it up, leaving it in a cool place. In the night, before retiring, I take a goblet full of this medicine. It acts the next day, during which time I merely sit around doing nothing of any importance. Two nights after my first dose, I take three quarters of a glass of the physic. This acts in the same manner as my first dose, and the following day I rest and pass the time as I did on the day after my first dose. On the second night after my second dose I take half a glass of my physic with similar results. I take no more of this physic, but on the following Saturday night I take a dose of good liver pills, which I have made for me in any drug store.

After this I am ready for work. I rise between six and seven o'clock in the morning, rinse my mouth, clean my teeth with a good dentifrice, take a sponge bath with salt water, and am rubbed perfectly dry with coarse towels. I then exercise with light dumbbells a few minutes, put on my clothes, go and loiter on the road for an hour or read the morning papers. Any light exercise I take before breakfast is simply for the purpose of getting up an appetite. Anything like a sweat at this time would be entirely out of place. At eight o'clock I have my breakfast, which consists of mutton-chops or a small piece of steak, stale bread, and two small cups of tea. The meat must be very lean.

After breakfast I sit around until about 10 o'clock, and then put on my sweater, which weighs from two and a half to three pounds, and a belt long enough to go around me and seven inches wide. This I wear outside of my sweater, as it helps to take the fat off the stomach. Having dressed myself, I go on a long walk for the day, consisting of six or seven miles out and the same number back, the distance to be covered as quickly as possible, and the last mile or two should be made on a dead run in. Having returned to my training quarters, I lie down on a couch, and my trainers cover me with heavy blankets and loosen my shoes. There I remain for a short time letting the perspiration come out, when I rise, undress myself and let my trainers rub me thoroughly dry. I then lie back on the couch again, when a second course of perspiration comes out. All this time I am covered with heavy blankets. When I rise a second time, my trainers rub me thoroughly dry again, and this operation is repeated two or three times or until I cease to perspire. I then go to a shower bath that I have arranged for me. If I am near the ocean or any other salt water, I use that in my shower, if not, I put sea salt into the water I use, making it equally good. I stand under this shower off and on for the space of 10 or 15 minutes, when I am rubbed dry with towels, I then lie on an oak plank that I have arranged for the purpose and am given a good hand rubbing, after which I dress in light material, but warmly enough not to take cold.

Between one and two o'clock I have my dinner, which consists of roast mutton or roast beef very well done, stale bread, and sometimes Bass' ale. I do not limit myself as to the quantity of meat, but I eat no vegetables except tender celery, asparagus, and once in a while one or two potatoes. A man can eat plenty of celery. Sometimes I eat three or four bunches a day. It is good for wind and good for the nerves.

Dinner being over, I go out and walk around or read the papers or a book. In some cases I smoke one nice cigar after dinner, but it is my belief that smoking, especially if it be immoderate, is injurious, and tends to shorten the breath.

The afternoon exercises begin with a swim at four o'clock. If I am near salt water, I prefer salt-water bathing, but if not, I bathe in fresh water. This little swim does not occupy more than 10 minutes. When it is over, I return to my training quarters, fight the football, throw a 10-pound ball backwards and forwards to my trainers at a distance of 15 or 20 feet; use dumbbells, weighing not less than two pounds nor more than four pounds each, and jump rope - all of which exercises last from one and a half to two hours, and sometimes longer. After I have gone through these exercises, I am perspiring as freely as I was after my long morning walk, so I am obliged to go through the same ordeal - the same rubbing with towels and hand-rubbing with a liniment I use, and which I find softens the muscles and hardens the skin at the same time.

This being done, I put on my evening clothes and partake of my supper between six and seven. This meal is, as a rule, with the addition of a little applesauce or a baked apple, exactly the counterpart of my breakfast. Once in a while, it is varied with Irish or Scotch oatmeal, well cooked with milk. After supper, I stroll around or amuse myself by playing billiards, pool, or cards, or with some other pastime or sport, until 10 o'clock, or until Morpheus has taken possession of my weary body. I keep on my feet as much as possible, so that my limbs will not get stiff or my power of free movement become in any way impeded. In undressing for the night, I always remove every article of clothing I wear during the day. I keep the windows of my sleeping room a little down from the top. The last thing I do before going to bed is to handle a pair of light dumbbells. The work is increased or diminished according to my condition. My bed covering is always put well over me, and is enough to keep me comfortable and nothing more.

During training, all hot baths or bed sweats must be carefully avoided, as they are debilitating in the extreme. The perspiration that may be induced in ordinary exercise is all that is required. Stimulants are carefully avoided, with the single exception of ale at dinner. Only a moderate quantity of salt in meats is allowable, and just enough water is permitted to quench the thirst. At the same time, every care must be taken that a man does not suffer for the want of it. Plenty of time must be taken in which to eat meals, and the stomach must not be overloaded.

Now this same work, that I have explained, is gone through every day for the space of about eight weeks, the length of time depending altogether upon how long it takes a man to get himself in condition. In justice to trainers let it be said that there are no two trainers of men who will pursue the same means or instructions or will have the same ideas, yet each one of them believes his mode of training to be the best. For this reason methods will always vary. There is always room for improvement no matter how great or how small it may be.

Some years ago, the trainer's ambition was to bring the largest-statured man to the least possible weight, and have him look like a human greyhound when he toed the scratch. This was not only the case when the match was at a stipulated weight, but even when fighting catch-weight. The old style of training tended to weaken a man.

It is needless for me to say that I consider my mode of exercise to be the easiest and the best. It keeps the body and muscles of young men as well as middle-aged ones in condition, without any injury resulting therefrom.

Of course this or any other mode of exercising has to be taught to every individual who wishes to become an athlete in any kind of sport. I wish to show my readers how easy it is, through exercise, for a man to get himself in condition. I will illustrate: There is a particular friend of mine, named Edward Murphy, who is instructor in the Young Men's Gymnasium in Cincinnati. He has a class of pupils in physical culture. At one time he weighed no less than 249 pounds, stripped, the effect of not having done any exercising for eight years. Now, through continually teaching exercises to his pupils in the different classes, which include business men in all branches, he is in as fine condition as a man can possibly be, and all through the routine of daily work that he goes through with pupils. At the writing of this book he weighs 204 pounds stripped, and is a magnificent specimen of manhood.

I have always been more than cautious as regards my food. For several days previous to my meeting Ryan at Mississippi City I did all my own cooking so as to prevent any possible doctoring or poisoning by outside parties. I do not believe in training by what is known as the old style. My method is original with me. I never attempt to put up heavy dumbbells in practice or training for I do not think they do any good. In fact, I think they hurt a man for boxing or fighting as they tend to bind his muscles, in a great many instances causing him to be what is known as shoulder bound or muscle bound.

I have always reasoned that I know when I feel well better than anybody can tell me, and I know what suits my stomach better than any one else knows. There is such a thing as a man overworking himself and becoming stale. That I provide against by light amusements such as card playing, billiard or pool playing or any other little amusement during training. Smoking, of course, I consider injurious, for it affects one's wind, but I do not think a few cigars a day do any serious harm except in particular cases.

When out of training I smoke a great deal, perhaps too much, but in training I am very careful in this matter. I drink no coffee while training. I consider dumbbells of from two to four pounds heavy enough for practice. Jumping the rope I consider one of the best practices possible in my training, for it brings into exercise the legs and arms at the same time and improves my wind wonderfully. I go on the principle throughout that I know what makes me feel well better than anybody can tell me, and all through my training I act and work on my own ideas, without regard to anybody else's. I have been advised and had suggested to me, on different occasions, various exercises, but after giving them a trial I find that my own way suits me best and brings about the best results.

Out of training or when not preparing for a fight or contest I take things as easy as possible. I eat and sleep whenever I feel so disposed; I usually rise about nine or ten o'clock in the morning, eat a light breakfast, sometimes a lunch in midday, and have dinner towards evening. My food consists entirely of whatever strikes my fancy. I smoke as many cigars as I feel like smoking, attend theaters and shows whenever I wish. In fact, I give my system its whole leeway.

By doing this I find that when I start to train I have some superfluous flesh to train off, and then curb myself accordingly. My whole existence and manner of living is guided by nature and nature only. Some athletes pride themselves on being in condition always, but this I do not approve of, for I reason that a man continually in training keeps nature up to its highest tension and without any relaxing he soon becomes mechanical and more like a steel spring than nature's own. Such a condition soon causes a man's system to break down, especially as all through life his mode of living is contrary to nature's laws. This matter of training and conditioning one's self is an all-important one. To train properly requires a considerable amount of will power. It is actually hard work; in fact, training is the hardest kind of work. The training and preparing for all my contests have always been 10 times harder than my fighting. In old times preparing for a fight required months and months of training; that is, that was the idea of the old-time pugilists. They sometimes trained as long as six months before the fight; this I do not believe in. From six to ten weeks I consider sufficient time to train any man; that is, for boxing or fighting; I would not give my opinion for rowing or any other athletic sport, because I do not know enough about them.

I think the most important things to be considered in training are, to get off as much fat as possible, to remove whatever water there is in the system, to harden the muscles of the body so as to increase the amount of endurance, to increase the "wind," and improve the breathing powers. As I have said before, every athlete has his own idea, the same as I have mine, and to improve my condition I have always felt that all that I wanted while training was regular living, sleeping, and habits, coupled with plenty of hard work in walking, running, jumping, and occasionally a little boxing. I do not box or spar much while in training; that I do not consider necessary. I consider punching the bag from 20 to 30 minutes as fast as I can possibly do it, the very best exercise for improving or exercising my hitting powers. I usually, in fact, always, if possible, rig and punch the bag to suit myself. To build it I want a good firm ceiling, strong and heavy enough so as to give the bag a good rebounding force, and hang the bag so that it will come on a level with my eyes, the ceiling to be from four to four and one half feet higher than the bag. Formerly a large heavy sandbag was used, but I do not approve of that as much as I do the common football or the Rugby ball. The heavy bag is all right to show how hard a man can hit, but I can hit hard enough without using any heavy bag to show it, and I use the little football, so as to give me plenty of practice for quickness; punching the bag as I do keeps me thoroughly active from the time I start. My first move in punching the bag is with my left hand; I punch it so that it hits the ceiling, rebounding towards me, and keep meeting it with my left and right hands alternately, walking around the floor and around the bag something after the way a cooper walks around a barrel. A man to punch the bag properly should not stand in any one spot by any means; I punch it so as to keep it going in all directions. I meet and chase it the same as I would an opponent in the ring. The idea in keeping it thoroughly on the rebound is to give me plenty of practice and keep me moving as fast as I possibly can. One of the best ways to punch it is with the left hand, say 15 or 20 times in succession, then either swinging the right hand or meeting it with a right-hand shoulder blow and catching it with the left on its return. Some men punch the bag very awkwardly, and while they are capable of dealing a very heavy blow, I have seen some miss it seven times out of ten. The most essential part, in my opinion, is to punch it so as to keep it moving in a circle. This brings into play not only the arms and wind but also the legs.

My one golden rule in conditioning myself is to disregard my weight altogether; that is, I do not care how much I weigh as long as I feel strong and my wind is good. Reducing weight by any means, whether by sweating, physicking, or any other method, if excessive, is very injurious. When a man feels within himself that he is in first-rate shape, and knows what he is capable of doing, he is a better judge than his trainer or adviser, no matter how much they know or how much practice they may have had in that line of work. Nervous force is the one great essential in a man's condition, and if a man is trained down or weakened through loss by too severe training or reducing, he is without the factor necessary to good condition.

I am always particular about not overworking myself, for that brings on exhaustion, which is hurtful, not to say dangerous.

I usually stop work three days before a fight, and then all the exercise required is moderate walking, with plenty of rubbing down, both with hands and towels. As soon as I stop work, I take castor oil in a little gin. The reason it is given in gin is that I can't take castor oil without vomiting. The oil makes me feel cool and refreshed. Then, until the day of the fight, I eat just enough to satisfy my appetite. A man who drinks should not expect to be a fighter, that is, if he drinks to excess. Drinking makes a man fat.

Training is terrible work. It is the hardest thing a man can do. When he gets through his 12 miles, about 12 or half-past 12, he naturally feels pretty dry inside, but he can get nothing to drink at all.

The more pleasant view of it was given by the late John Morrissey.

"You can form no idea," he said, "of the glorious feeling that a man experiences when he gets himself in perfect condition. Everything in the world looks different to him from what it does when his system is clogged up with bile and he is carrying a quantity of flesh that is only a burden to him. It is almost impossible to get a man, when in such a condition, into bad humor. He feels like a young colt, and wants to kick up his heels and have a good time with everybody and everything he meets."

If the man of business would only take a mild course of training every year or two he would find in the renewed energy and youthful feeling received from training splendid returns for his time and labor.

On the 17th of May, 1892, I underwent, for the first time in my life, a thorough physical examination at the hands of Dr. George F. Shrady, one of America's most eminent physicians, at his residence in New York. The result was very gratifying to my friends.

After looking over my frame with a great deal of care and thoroughness, the examination requiring one hour, Dr. Shrady said:

"In all my life I have never seen such a magnificent specimen of muscular development, and, indeed, I do not think that another such man is living today. You are in perfect health, Mr. Sullivan. Your heart, liver, stomach, lungs, and other organs are all performing their work properly. You are physically sound, and with some of the superfluous flesh in the abdomen region removed, your powers of endurance would be remarkable."

The examination was the result of my curiosity to know my exact physical condition. Ever since I was matched against Jim Corbett various alleged authorities throughout the country have been predicting my fistic downfall on the ground that I could never get well enough to fight again with the old-time vim which has marked all of my struggles in the ring.

During the examination the doctor looked over the muscles of my shoulders and neck and marveled at their size and suppleness. Then he felt my arms and soon ran across the spot on the bone of the left forearm, which had to be mended after it was broken on Patsy Cardiff's head. The doctor examined it critically, as he did the tendons in the arm.

"That must have been a pretty bad break," he said.

"Indeed, it was," I answered, "but one of the tendons troubled me more than the break; still, it's all right now. Don't you think so?"

"It's just as good as it ever was," replied Dr. Shrady.

The muscles of the back and arms next claimed the examiner's attention. Dr. Shrady explained to me where my tremendous hitting power came from.

"Your muscles are in excellent condition and they are the very best kind of muscles," he said. "They are long and flexible, just my ideal of what an athlete should have. The best muscle is never hard."

"These are perfect sledgehammers," exclaimed the physician, as he held my arms up with his little ones.

"Well, Mr. Sullivan," said Dr. Shrady, surveying me from his chair, "I pity Mr. Corbett or any other man who fights you. What sort of a man is Corbett?"

"He is taller than I am," I answered, "and weighs about 200 pounds, I should judge. He is quick and clever. I can beat him though," I added.

Up to this time nothing had been said of my legs. I looked at them and so did Dr. Shrady.

"They say my legs are too small for my body. What do you think?" I asked.

"My opinion is that they are plenty big enough," came the answer, after the limbs had been carefully inspected.

"That's what I think. I never in my life saw a man with big legs, who amounted to much in the boxing line," I replied, "these legs have served me very well, and I'm perfectly satisfied with them."

A recent writer says, "Standing before an audience in fighting costume, Sullivan suggests to the mind of the student of history the massive form and brawn of Spartacus as he stood among the Roman gladiators appealing to them to strike for their liberty.

"The term 'athlete' was applied in Greece only to those who contended in the public games for prizes, exclusive of musical and other contests where bodily strength was not needed. It was not applied to what we call amateurs, or those who exercised without the incentive of a prize. The 'athletes' were the distinct forerunners of the trained righting men who became a professional class in Greece.

"In the classic literature from which all our culture and particularly our purely aesthetic culture is drawn, the pugilist receives a greater meed of praise than the musician."

Another writer says, "We cannot condemn the cultivation of the physical powers, and Greece has as much instruction for our puny age in this regard as in the loftier and nobler realms of literature and art. Thousands of ministers, editors, and professors, whose brains have sapped the life forces of their bodies, might look with commendable envy upon this physical giant."

"John L. Sullivan, of Boston," says a Garden City writer, "came to our city like an ancient hero, and received the welcome which of old was accorded to the illustrious heroes when they were greeted back in triumph to Athens or to Rome.

"In the days of Caesar, the famous men were the runners, wrestlers, and fighters. Had John L. Sullivan lived in the days of ancient Rome, his perfection of physical power and great fighting qualities would have entitled him to a high rank as a man of the people."

"Boxing," says O'Reilly, "is the only art of attack and defense which we have as an unbroken inheritance from the ancients. When Pollux obtained the boxing victory at the Pythian games, he wore gloves or leathern bandages filled with lead and iron. When Sullivan defeats his man, he uses soft gloves filled with curled hair. This is the change of time and judgment. The latter is the better test."

Another writer says:

"The boxing exhibitions with their more serious arena of the prize ring are all that we have left of the gladiatorial shows of the ancients. There is something to be said in favor of a profession, the training for which requires so temperate and healthful a diet and discipline of man's physical being. There are few who have seen rival champions of the ring enter the arena for a decisive trial of skill and endurance, without admiring the bright complexion, clear eyes, the splendid muscle, and flesh, smooth and hard as marble, and the other characteristics which testify to the body and its members having been brought to the most perfect physical condition. Yankee Sullivan never attained to the supremacy which gave him the reputation of being the 'best man of either hemisphere,' without devoting months to the most temperate care and severest discipline of his forces. For months before achieving his great victory at New Orleans, no alcoholic drink passed his lips, his diet was guarded as carefully as that of the child of royal birth and kingly future, while all the best known means to the finest muscular development - dumbbells, sand bags, walking, and running - were used in his behalf with a prison-like rigidity."

Boxing was a favorite amusement of Englishmen for centuries; it is even said to have had such distinguished patrons as King Alfred and Richard III. But the golden age of pugilism, as a profession in England, commenced with the accession of the House of Hanover; then men calling themselves professors publicly announced their intention of giving lessons in "the noble art of self-defense." One professor challenged another to combat in the most bombastic language. In 1726, one Ned Sutton, who announces himself as "pipemaker from Gravesend, and professor of the noble science of defense," sneers at another professor, whom he calls "the extolled Mr. Figg," for having by "sleeveless pretense," shirked a combat with him, "which I take," says the pipemaker and professor, "to be occasioned through fear of his having that glory eclipsed by me, wherewith the eyes of all spectators have been so much dazzled." He further assures the said Figg, that if he can muster courage enough to fight with him, he (Figg) "will have the advantage of being overcome by a hero indeed!" Figg had an amphitheatre in Oxford Road, wherein fights were held, and a larger one was erected in the same locality in 1742 for one Broughton, the funds being subscribed by some eighty noblemen and gentlemen. The pugilistic encounters that took place here were patronized by many of the nobility. Towards the end of the last century fights were patronized by princes of the blood royal, and the Prince of Wales, afterwards George IV, was present at one at Brighton, in which one of the combatants was killed. When the allied sovereigns and their generals came over to England in 1814, Lord Lowther treated them to a series of boxing matches in his drawing room, which were so highly relished that they were repeated a few days afterwards. One of the pugilists,

172 • JOHN L. SULLIVAN

called Jackson, became quite a hero, and made enormous sums by giving lessons to young noblemen, among whom was Lord Byron. In 1817,
the Czar Nicholas, of Russia, witnessed a prizefight at Coombe Warren.

"We are the Romans of the modern world," says the distinguished
"Autocrat of the Breakfast Table," speaking of Americans, "the great
assimilating people. Conflicts and conquests are, of course, necessary
accidents with us, as with our prototypes. And so we come to their style
of weapon. . . . The race that shortens its weapons lengthens its bound-
aries."

"What business," continues Dr. Holmes, "had Sarmatia to be fighting
for liberty with a 15-foot pole between her and the breasts of her ene-
mies? If she had but come to close quarters, there might have been a
chance for her."

The brute strength to knock down an ox with a blow of the fist has
been credited to various men, among whom were the Venetian who challenged England in the time of the first fighter, Tom Figg; Bill Neat, who
was downed by the lively Tom Spring, and Hurst, the "Staleybridge
Infant," who was demolished by Mace. It will be noticed that in such
instances the men representing brute force have been overcome by
smaller and lighter men.

Richard Coeur de Lion, who could kill an ox with a blow of his fist, is
credited with saying he delighted to look upon a man. "He should have
taken a good square glance at John L. Sullivan, the champion pugilist of
the world," says a newspaper, "and he would have felt that delight to the
full. For such a man of muscle turns up but once in a lifetime. It is said
that when Sullivan returns from his visit to San Francisco to Boston, he is
going to close his public career by felling an ox with one blow on the
Boston stage. This reminds one of Hercules and the Cretan bull, and is
worthy of a son of classical Boston."

"How about the ox story?" was asked of him. "I never heard of it until
I read it in the papers. I am not a brute, and would not attempt such a
thing. People misrepresent me in such matters as that. In fact they misrepresent all pugilists. Boxing is one of the best athletic exercises a man
can take."

I have done much to elevate and bring boxing before the public to a
degree that had not been known for a number of years, previous to my
ascending this ladder of fame. As the profession stands today, barring no
athletic sport in any branch, it is conceded by all good judges of athletics
to be the finest exercise, developing the body, mind and brain; and so all
professionals, like myself, are strong and healthy. Of course, there are
persons, I am willing to admit, in this profession, that have made wrecks
of themselves through over-indulgence in the flowing bowl, which is more
or less suggested by friends partaking of their hospitality.

Being a public man and making my living off the general public, I have to stand public criticism. All public men of the 19th century have to bear any criticism that the press may wish to publish about them. I, as one of those public individuals, have been thoroughly discussed and quarreled about in the press. I have stood it for the past 33 years without the slightest apprehension or forgetting my place in this public life.

Many of our greatest statesmen and diplomats have recognized the fact that boxing is superior as an exercise for general health to any other form of exercise known, including wrestling, running, rowing, and dumb-bell exercise. Roscoe Conkling, ex-senator, and Ex-Secretary Chandler were both good boxers and judges of boxing bouts. As for Conkling, I looked for him at all my exhibitions which took place in New York and I do not think he ever missed one.

I saw by the paper the other day that Ex-Governor Flower of New York State had taken up boxing as a means of conditioning himself. Ex-Secretary Blaine, I understand, has been going through about this same treatment, and indeed many other public men who wish to keep themselves in a condition to endure the severe strain put upon their system in political life, especially during a campaign.

As to injuries, I don't think that a man can be seriously hurt with a boxing glove, unless he has heart disease. I do not know of any man killed in the prize ring by actual fighting (though there have been cases where they have died from over-exertion or heart disease), but the most cases occur through neglect after fighting. In returning from the ring, through carelessness and other causes, they take cold and abuse themselves. The change being so sudden, from actual training, it brings on colds and other things causing death, but in my opinion, few, if any, men have ever died from actual fighting or from its direct effects. No two men in my opinion enter the ring in modern times with the intention of killing each other. Of course they all feel as I do, that is, to best their man, but never in my whole career have I ever entered the ring wishing or in any way trying to disfigure my man. I always attempt to demonstrate my superiority over every man I meet, but I never yet have intended to maim or injure anyone. Various criticisms are made on a man fighting, each and every spectator having a different view and probably different opinions as to how a man should fight, but a man fighting in the same position as I have been in a great many times, thinks and sees a thousand things at the same time.

"It is surprising how I like a man after I have fought with him," is what Lord Lytton makes the sturdy old French officer say after his encounter with the brave young lover in "The Lady of Lyons."

The history of the prize ring gives many and remarkable able examples of this sentiment, showing that professional encounters are not carried on like street brawls, with any feeling of personal animosity. In many cases there could not be any animosity. Heenan and Sayers, for instance, had lived on separate continents, and had never met until they shook hands in the ring, as required by the rules. After the fight, they sparred and traveled together, as some whom I have vanquished have done with me. The records of the champions are also full of such cases as that in which Tom Hyer paid liberally to secure the release of his former antagonist, Yankee Sullivan.

"The generosity of John L. is well known," says a friend. "He has been as open-hearted in disbursing his riches as his punches. Wealth and blows he has showered on friends and foes."

In a Cleveland paper, when Holden and White were imprisoned for fighting, was printed the following:

"A letter received from Frank White before going to press states that John Sullivan, Billy Madden, and Bob Farrell traveled 110 miles out of their way to visit him and Holden and hand them the proceeds of the Cleveland show. 'That,' says Frank 'is what I call a friend indeed.'"

Leaving out such cases as the spiking done by Mitchell and Kilrain under the London Prize-Ring rules, it is a fact that boxers when doing their utmost to down each other have been known to utter a polite "Excuse me," on accidentally stepping on an opponent's foot or doing something at variance with the rules.

In regard to my match with Corbett the following has been published:

> "The agony is over, and the great champion of the world is matched at last. He is to meet James Corbett before the Olympic Club of New Orleans, for a purse of $25,000 and a stake of $20,000. The contest is to decide the heavyweight championship of the world, and will take place on the 7th of September, 1892.
>
> "This battle will be one in which the whole world will be interested, and will no doubt be one of the most exciting and interesting contests ever witnessed in America. 'Dandy Jim,' or 'Pompadour Jim,' as he is sometimes called, is also called one of the most scientific boxers in the business, and is as shifty as they are made and very quick on his feet.
>
> "While Corbett's friends are boasting of his ring generalship and science, it must be borne in mind that John L. knows something of the art himself, and is one of the quickest big men in the ring on his feet.
>
> "'Do you ever think of those famous Sullivan rushes?' was asked of Corbett, recently.
>
> "Corbett laughed heartily, shrugged his shoulders, and replied:
>
> "'Well, I should say I do, but then I do not permit them to

worry me. As I said at the outset, I know that I have a big task before me, but I do not propose to permit myself to be frightened by any of the marvelous tales I hear about John L.'

"Corbett was then asked about that famous story with reference to his father's strenuous objection to his entering the prize ring, and especially against a colored man, and also whether it was true that he was at one time a bank clerk. These queries seemed to carry him back to his earlier days, and his eyes fairly sparkled as he related the story:

"'To commence with, I will answer your last question first. It is true that I am an "ex-bank clerk." I was employed for many years in the Nevada Bank, of San Francisco, which I entered at the age of 13 years. Now, as to father, he naturally objected to prize-fighting, and when it was finally announced that I was to meet Peter Jackson, well, to put it mildly, he fairly went crazy with anger, and vowed that if I dared attempt to do such a thing he would have me arrested. I knew that the old gentleman thought a great deal of his boy, even though he was a prize-fighter, and I thought I knew how to get around it. So I took my good old father off to one side, and said: "I have signed an agreement to meet Jackson. True, he is a colored man and I appreciate your feeling. Now, however, that I have signed the agreement I cannot get out of the fight without disgracing myself and losing the friendship of my friends as well as their money. If you do not permit me to meet him in San Francisco, I shall go with him to Australia and fight him there. Now you would not want me to go away off in a strange country where I would not get fair play, would you?"

"'There is no need of relating the remainder of the story. I was not arrested, and for the first time I will confess, though I was of age, I had to get my father's consent to do the work I did in the ring with Peter Jackson.'"

"Corbett informed Mr. Al Smith and myself in New York, a short time ago," said Hugh Coyle in a letter dated February 17, 1892, "that he was the very first to enter the gates at five o'clock in the afternoon in the Mechanics Pavilion at San Francisco to witness the fight between John L. Sullivan and George Robinson, at which time he was a bank clerk.

"To avoid the crush the doors were advertised to be opened at five in the afternoon and Corbett was the first man to pass the doorkeeper. Such a crush - nothing probably ever before or since has been like it. More money taken in than at any similar event since, and if the pavilion could have held the clamorous crowd, over $100,000 would have been the receipts. Cable lines two and three blocks away were stopped from running by the surging crowd of humanity which filled the streets in every direction. Billy Muldoon was the guest of Al Smith on that eventful night, and I can see him now at the main entrance with a hundred others, including a large force of the police, trying with his great brawny arms to keep the crowd back without avail.

"Corbett says he got his first lesson in practical and professional pugilism that evening, but when it comes to knocking out three men, I mean fighters, in a night, that job had better be left to the boss, John L. It is useless for any other to attempt it, except they have in front of them, as you so aptly termed it, 'stiffs.'"

Having given so much as to Corbett in connection with our projected contest I may say for myself that I never let myself think of a contest till I get into the ring. I can sleep till within a minute of the time to enter. I never lost a pound worrying over anything; I guess all my nerves are in my muscles. In my time, though, I have seen good game men worry themselves into losing their heads, and they lost their fights.

In this connection, I must claim it as one of the best effects of boxing exercises, that they serve to unite the powers of the nerves and muscles, giving a quick command over both, and enabling the possessor "to look danger in the eye." No other exercise compares with it in this result. The faculty of thinking and acting at the same time is what has made one or two men, that I might name, kings of baseball, but this power is called for at closer quarters in boxing. Here may be found the answer to the question which is often asked me:

"Have you any particular plan of action before you go into the contest?"

My reply might be similar to that which Admiral Farragut made to a Boston gentleman with whom he dined in my native city. As it has not been published before I give it here.

"The fact is," answered the Admiral, "I had a plan before I entered Mobile Bay, as I have before undertaking anything; but a good American fighter is always quick enough to make a new plan in an emergency, and go on to win on that."

As to a boxing contest, a man may enter it with a general plan of campaign, but he must be ready to change it, if necessary, every minute. From this point of view I may say that a man fights as much with his head as with his hands, especially with such a "shifty" boxer as Mr. Corbett is reputed to be.

As I kissed the "Blarney Stone" during my tour in Ireland, it may be that I now have a weakness for giving my antagonist too much credit; and I will only say that, while I have complete confidence as to the outcome, I am conscious that the victory over him, especially as it is for the largest sum ever involved in a ring battle, will be not unworthy to round out 'a career that has covered three continents and a hundred competitors.

And now, as I sit calmly at my training quarters at a spot where Long

Island seems to reach out in friendship to the Old World, with the new haven that promises to bring it so much nearer, and as I watch the placid waters of Shinnecock and Peconic Bays that have been made to shake hands in a new found harmony, I resolve that after this, my last battle, I shall no longer remain in a position where, in the words of Byron, "A man must prove his fame four times a year." Just before me stands the colossal form of Hercules that so long adorned the old fighting ship, "Ohio," and as I look on him, I am reminded that I, too, have accomplished my "tasks," and that like him I should take the skin of the lion I captured - my reputation as a boxer - and put it over my shoulders hereafter only as a mantle of protection and peace.

I do not wish to be understood, however, as retiring from my position as an exponent of the science of boxing with the gloves. In various places through this volume will be found the testimony of others as to what I have done towards encouraging a substitution of scientific contests with gloves for the finish fights with bare knuckles. Having been often asked my opinion as to the most suitable gloves for boxing, I will reply here that I have used all kinds and makes, but in the past few years only those made by A. G. Spaulding & Brothers, which I have found to be the best. A boxing glove that they are now making under my instructions, which they call "The Sullivan Glove - California Style," I can recommend to anybody as the best that is made.

My own opinion is that such glove contests as I have referred to, under fitting conditions, will arouse the interest of classes who have sacrificed the benefits of boxing, as an exercise, on account of prejudice caused by the work of bared fists in the old-fashioned prize fighting.

ADDENDUM

THE FALL OF JOHN L. SULLIVAN

Sullivan's autobiography is notable for terminating just prior to his bout with James J. Corbett. The book ends on an optimistic note, with Sullivan preparing for his upcoming fight with the self-assurance that it would be yet another victory for the "Boston Strong Boy." History, however, has proven otherwise. On September 7, 1892, in a stunning upset, Sullivan lost to Corbett in the 21st round.

The following account of the fight is taken from the book, The Roosevelt that I Know: Ten Years of Boxing with the President--and Other Memories of Famous Fighting Men *by Michael Joseph Donovan. Although no complete account of the bout exists in John L. Sullivan's own words, this ringside account by one of Corbett's seconds represents a reasonably fair and appreciative view of this defining moment in Sullivan's career.*

Both men stepped briskly to the center of the ring. Sullivan slapped his left hand on his thigh several times, chopped with his left and then swung his right. Corbett skipped away and avoided the rush easily.

Again Sullivan rushed and Corbett sidestepped, jumping aside as lively as a cricket. Sullivan kept trying to get within hitting distance of Jim, but the latter was too elusive.

The second round was a repetition of the first, Sullivan rushing and Corbett avoiding him easily.

In the third round John started with a rush and Corbett sidestepped, swinging his left like lightning to Sullivan's nose as he did so. The blood spurted from John L.'s nose like a crimson fountain. It was the first blow Corbett had landed, but it was a telling one.

Corbett jabbed John L. at will on the nose and jaw for the rest of the round.

Sullivan seemed all at sea and unable to guard, and when he returned to his corner he was in a most dilapidated condition, his face, arms and chest being covered with blood.

When Corbett returned to his corner he said to me, "Old man, you're right," meaning I had been right when I told him how John L. would fight.

I advised Corbett to punch Sullivan in the stomach for the next couple of rounds, which would have finished him, but, to my surprise, he jumped around like a grasshopper through the fourth, fifth and sixth rounds, allowing Sullivan to recover to some extent from the blows he had received in the third round, although he was still bleeding profusely.

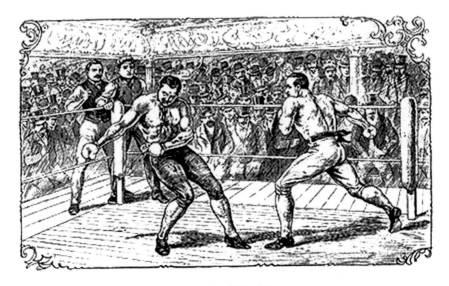

When he came to his corner I said to him:

"Jim, don't you see he's recovering? Go in close to him. He can't hit you."

When the next round, the seventh, opened, he walked right up to Sullivan, and as John L. drew up his left to chop it down on Corbett 's guard, Jim sunk his right and left into his opponent's body several times, causing him to double up like a jack-knife with agony. These blows were the result of the training I had given him at the New York Athletic Club the first time he came to New York.

I shouted: "Now is your chance, Jim, finish him."

Delaney, however, called out: "Look out for his right, Jim! Look out for his right!" This stopped Corbett, who in reality had nothing to fear from the now crippled and helpless Sullivan.

Instead of going in and finishing his man, Corbett started a series of feints which took him about 10 seconds. Sullivan recovered somewhat in the meantime, but was very weak when he reached his corner.

I again urged Corbett to go in and finish him. Sullivan was all in and couldn't hurt him.

Sullivan came up for the eighth round puffing and weak from loss of blood. He was so weak he could hardly raise his arms.

In spite of this Corbett still pursued his hopping tactics, jumping away from John L.'s rushes and stabbing him occasionally with a straight left.

Sullivan was getting weaker and weaker from his own exertions, and in the 14th round Jim hit him twice on the nose in rapid succession.

It was pitiful to see John's unavailing efforts to raise his guard. Blood was streaming from his nose in torrents, but he was game.

"That was a good one, Jim," he said, speaking for the first time during the fight.

"Here's a better one," Corbett replied savagely, and stepping in close planted several hard blows on John's mouth and jaws.

Although I, of course, wanted to see Corbett win, I felt very sorry for poor John L., for he was in a pitiable condition.

About the 16th round Sullivan made a desperate effort to reach Corbett. The latter, however, would skip away like a dancing master. It was more like a game of tag than a fight. Sullivan became furious and rushed at Corbett like a bull, trying to strike him with his body, his arms being so tired he could not lift them. Sullivan ran up against the ropes, which shook him up fearfully. As he bounded back he caught sight of Corbett and rushed at him again, chasing Jim around the ring. He caught him in a corner and swung his right. Corbett dodged, but was disconcerted; then he sidestepped and John crashed against the ropes again. Then the gong sounded.

It made me mad to see poor John L. floundering around the ring absolutely helpless, and when Corbett returned to his corner I said to him: "What's the matter with you, Jim? Don't you see he's helpless? Why don't you get it over and finish him?"

As Corbett left his corner I said to him:

"He can't hit hard enough to dent a pound of butter."

Poor John must have realized that he couldn't win, for in the next round he rushed at Corbett with his arms down and his chin stuck out, inviting a knockout. He would not quit, but wanted to be knocked out and have the thing over.

During the 18th, 19th and 20th rounds I kept begging Corbett to finish him. He replied: "I will pretty soon," but kept up his dancing and dodging tactics.

In the 21st round, however, he rushed as soon as the gong rang. He met Sullivan in the latter 's corner, where he stood flat-footed, too weak to raise his guard. Corbett feinted and swung his right to Sullivan's jaw. John fell to his knees, but with a determined effort slowly raised himself to his feet. Crash! went Corbett 's right and left against his jaw. Sullivan fell forward, his face and chest hitting the floor. He made an effort to rise. It was useless.

John L. rolled over on his right side and was counted out.

The house was as still as death.

John L. Sullivan, the people's idol, had been beaten.

Charley Johnson, Jack McAuliffe and the other seconds picked up poor Sullivan and carried him to his corner. There they put him down on the small, yellow kitchen chair he had sat in between the rounds. John was gone - not knocked out, but so exhausted that he could neither move nor think.

As the seconds worked over him with ammonia at his nostrils and pieces of ice on his head and at the back of his neck he began to come back a little. The moment life stirred in him he tried to get up on his feet. Johnson and McAuliffe pushed him back, fearing that he was trying to attack Corbett. But John could not be stopped. He was hardly more than half conscious when he made a great effort. I can see him now, his eyes dazed and half closed, throwing back two or three strong men with one sweep of his big right arm.

Then he got up and stood for a moment, swaying from side to side. He paid no attention to Corbett. There was something else on his mind. Dazed as he was by the punishment he had undergone, there was still one idea that he had to express. His knees bent under him as he tottered across the battlefield. On he went until he stumbled against the ropes on the other side. He raised his left hand and ran it along the top rope until it struck a post. He patted the post a few times, then held up his right hand. The cheering and applauding stopped instantly. The house was as still as the stars shining down on us from the black sky.

"Gentlemen," said Sullivan, his voice still thick and weak, "gentlemen, I have nothing at all to say. All I have to say is that I came into the ring once too often - and if I had to get licked, I'm glad I was licked by an

American. I remain your warm and personal friend, John L. Sullivan."

There was many a good, strong man with tears in his eyes as those simple words were uttered. Here was the man who had stood for 12 years the acknowledged physical king of the human race. In one brief battle his kingdom was swept away from him, but he took his defeat like a man. There was no whining, no excuse, no begging for another chance.

In defeat as well as in the hour of triumph, John L. stood head and shoulders above all the rest. He was on the level when he was up and he was on the level when he was down. It will be many years before another champion stands as close to the hearts of the people as did honest, brave John L. Sullivan.

The following articles attempt to close out the story of John L. Sullivan. Where possible, Sullivan's own words and writings were used along with articles that significantly quoted him.

SULLIVAN'S SORROWFUL RETURN

The Ex-Champion Gets to Town, But Doesn't Care to Talk

The New York Times
September 12, 1892

NEW YORK, September 11. - John L. Sullivan, the former idol of the fistic fraternity, arrived here yesterday from the scene of his Waterloo. He was accompanied by his backers, Charley Johnston and James Wakely, and the trio looked like mourners at a funeral. Sullivan's nose was peeled, his eyes were slightly discolored, and his left jaw showed the effects of Corbett's right-hand blows.

As the ex-champion left the train in the Grand Central Station, it was evident that he had been drowning his sorrow. His eyes were swollen, his face sported a stubby beard of several days' growth, and his gait was very unsteady. The members of the Sullivan party were travel-stained, and from their action it

was plain to be seen that they did not care for personal appearances. They were sore at heart, weak in mind, and weaker still in pockets. Friends of the Boston "slugger" say that his backers will have to sell whiskey for years to come to make up their losses. As Sullivan walked from the car somebody shouted:

"There's the big fellow!"

Sullivan tried to smile, but he could not. Several of his friends grabbed him by the hand and whispered words of encouragement, but Sullivan paid but little attention to them. He pushed his way through the crowd, and in a few minutes was in the Vanderbilt Hotel. Rooms where engaged, and the party went upstairs to compare notes and at the same time to sample the wet goods.

"I don't care to talk of this fight," said Sullivan. "I was whipped, and that's all there is to it. Corbett's a good feller, and I'd rather see him win than some foreigner. I've got no excuses to make. Corbett did me up, and that's all there's to it. No, I won't accept his offer to buy a box for my benefit and pay $1,000 for it. He may need all the money he's got. If he wants to go there, let him pay the price as anybody else. His offer's a kind one, though, and he deserves a lot of credit. I guess I'll get along without his money, though. I'm quite a hustler when I start out to make money."

Sullivan's friends say that he will start at once to rehearse "The Man from Boston." In spite of the fact that the man from Boston was hammered all over the ring by the youth from San Francisco, it is thought that Sullivan will make money out of his new play. Luckily he arranged his route and made his contracts before he faced Corbett. One edition, however, will supply the demand of the ex-champion's book, *Reminiscences of a Nineteenth Century Gladiator*.

THE SULLIVAN BENEFIT IN NEW YORK

St. John Daily Sun
September 20, 1892

NEW YORK, September 18. - John L. Sullivan came home last evening. Seven or eight thousand of his friends paid for the pleasure of cheering his name, and met in Madison Square Garden to receive him.

Outside on the sidewalk, small crowds stood about in the electric, and a number of tattered but energetic men offered photographs of Sullivan for 10 cents. One with rusty clothing and a rusty voice called out in touching tones: "Give John L. credit for what he has done."

Around the top of the new fangled garden, there runs an immense gallery. This was packed full of genuine Sullivan worshippers. The seats up there were cheapest, so they had to take them, but they peered longingly down through the blinding electric light at the big ring, and when the time came they cheered and yelled as effectively as though all that painful distance between them and this great man was eliminated.

The galleries under the big topmost ones were all crowded, sow ere the long rows of boxes and the long stretches of seats piled up over each other from Madison to Fourth Avenue. Two or three thousand men walked about the floor. Seven or eight thousand men at least were there, and any man, no matter how great his services to the public, might have been proud of such an outpouring.

Sullivan, as every man knows, was to appear with Corbett, who beat him in New Orleans, and the idea of the meeting was to tell the big fellow that his defeat had, if possible, endeared him to his countrymen more than ever, at the same time making up to him for the money he did not get from the New Orleans fight.

After Jack Sheridan, Jim Travee, Jack Fallon, the Brooklyn strong boy, Tom Green, Jack Burke, George Woods, Johnny Stuart and Jack Skelly, who failed to win a dowry for his bride by using up a remarkable young colored man named Dixon, had done all they could to make the time pass pleasantly, there appeared Jack McAuliffe.

Johnnie Dunn of Brooklyn was the happy man who introduced McAuliffe and who was to have the honor of doing the same for Sullivan and Corbett. The fighting which McAuliffe did was not serious tonight. He simply showed in the language which he speaks that that he could make a monkey out of any ordinary man of his size, and that was all that was wanted by the crowd.

As McAuliffe left the stage there was noble applause for him and he bowed his head meekly as one who is not at all set up by the knowledge. He deserves what he gets, but as he dropped down into the crowd, the applause, which was begun for him, swelled into such a roar as no man but one ever called forth in an American fighting crowd.

Sullivan was coming out after a struggle, in the course of which he good-naturedly crushed a number of his admirers against each other, he appeared in the ring alone. A big leather strap held up his trunks and a bright green shirt without sleeves reminded his Irish friends that he was still faithful to old principles.

At first he looked around the crowd slowly with a troubled look on his face.

It had been a hard thing for him to face all those men himself for the first time a beaten man.

He tried to look defiant but it was natural and there was no need.

For a second or two the crowd remained quiet to have a look at him then such cheers of pure affection and admiration burst out as no man could mistake. Even Sullivan was satisfied. He knew every man yelling in that crowd was sorry he was beaten and that every one looked on him as the great Sullivan still. All that time several thousand men were shouting "speech." They were gratified in due time.

Meanwhile Corbett had entered the ring from another corner.

His belt was encircled by an American flag. His shirt was white, but his stockings were bright green.

When Corbett entered the ring, he and Sullivan shook hands very solemnly.

It was a fine dramatic incident. The cheers had warmed Sullivan's heart. He smiled quite serenely under the little stubby moustache which he is now raising for stage purposes and almost jerked Mr. Corbett off his feet.

Still the crowd was shouting for a speech. Corbett sat down, Sullivan folded his arms and his voice went out over the crowd with the old familiar deep bellowing sound.

Here is Sullivan's speech just as he delivered it. He had to wait for three cheers to be given as soon as he had began, and he was often interrupted in the course of his remarks, but everyone heard what he had to say. The stage has a fine voice in John L. Sullivan at any rate.

"Ladies and gentlemen: I thank you one and all very kindly for this hearty reception, a dearer reception on account of my defeat. I have nothing to say but to bestow good honors upon the present champion. I hope he will continue in the right path. He has a noble record. He being an American, I want to see him hold it. I have no excuses to make upon my defeat. I was defeated, and every defeated man that makes excuses makes the mistake of his life. Therefore I have none."

As soon as he could be heard, Mr. Dunn introduced Corbett, and Sullivan for the first time in his life had another man in the ring with him introduced as the champion of the world. He was getting a number of new experiences.

The introduction of Corbett seemed at best, however, mere formality. It would have been hard to convince even the calm Sullivan admirers at that time that he was not the only great man in the place. When he got a chance Corbett made his speech.

After these speeches came a friendly bout at boxing between the two fighters. A good many men do not know Sullivan had predicted that he would attempt at the end of the bout to land one of his old time blows on Corbett, and, by knocking the lighter man down, try to gain prestige. He had no idea of breaking faith. Sullivan, as far as honesty goes, is a good model for any man to follow. He boxed along, solemnly swinging his big arms aimlessly around, landing on Corbett with his hands open, and receiving friendly blows of the latter cheerfully.

An anxious admirer far up in the air yelled out, "Now is the time for hunk, John," meaning that Sullivan should take revenge. Sullivan smiled kindly in the direction of the advisor but neglected that advice. Another man shouted, "Give him your right," and again Sullivan only smiled. The hurricane of old time had decided to play the role of spring breeze and did it to perfection.

They boxed three short rounds and the great Sullivan benefit was over.

It is probable that Sullivan will get as much as $5,000 for himself, and perhaps he will get more.

The best part of the show, which was valuable as a demonstration of the loyalty of which all classes of men are capable, came when Sullivan in his friendly bout with the man who beat him out of the ring. There was a rush of men towards him which was irresistible. Men were knocked down, chairs turned over and smashed, and policemen joining in the rush forgot to abuse anyone. Dozens of men, who in calm moments would fight if anyone accused them of sentiment, crowded around the big fellow, patting him on the back and showering the most affectionate language upon him.

SULLIVAN TALKS OUT
Says He Was Foully Dealt With At New Orleans

Chicago Daily
December 26, 1892

NEW YORK, December 25. - John L. Sullivan, ex-champion of the world, arrived from Washington today and immediately went to the Vanderbilt Hotel. The ex-champion did not appear to be at his best. In fact, he looked much dejected and appeared to have been celebrating Christmas in an old-fashioned way. His eyes were dull and heavy, his face unshaven, and his general appearance that of a man not altogether pleased with himself. He seemed as if he were staggering under a load of trouble. No one would have taken him for the bold defender of the world's heavyweight championship of several months ago.

Many persons who saw Sullivan enter the hotel thought that this unhappy mood was due to the sudden attack of illness he had in Washington Saturday morning. They imagined that he was still ill and worrying over the statement of Dr. R. A. Neale that he was suffering from fatty degeneration of the heart, and was liable to drop dead at any moment.

But there was something more heavy than fat around John L.'s heart, and it soon came to the surface. He had carried it there for many long days and nights, too long, he said, and he was determined that others should know of it as well as himself.

Sullivan declared for the first time since his fight with Corbett at New Orleans that he attributed his defeat to something else than his conqueror's fistic ability. He told a reporter that he was at liberty to publish his reasons for believing that he was not fairly treated by the men in whom he had utmost confidence at the time, but who he has since discovered played him false. He asked for the present to withhold the names of the accused for particular reasons.

Foully Treated in New Orleans

Sullivan said, taking a locket from his watch-charm: "See that locket? Well, I open it and show you my mother's hair. I swear by that bit of hair I was foully treated in New Orleans when I fought Corbett. He never defeated me - no, never. I wasn't John L. Sullivan that night. After the first two rounds I couldn't see Corbett. I didn't know where he was. I was in a trance.

"That leg," continued Sullivan, pointing to his left, "has never been the same since I fought in New Orleans, and the other is a little better. Corbett didn't knock me out. He knocked me down, but I couldn't get up. My leg would not hold my body. They were powerless and had evidently been doctored. I was treated badly - yes, shamefully.

"One man who pretended to be my friend and backer I have found out to have been an enemy in disguise. He is responsible for my defeat. He was supposed to have had a part of my stake. As God is my judge, that man did not have a cent bet on me. He backed me with money belonging to another man while he posed as my financial ally. The same man once tried to hit me with a mallet. I have never done a man a wrong turn in my life and never will. I have always acted fairly and squarely with everybody, and for being honest I was rewarded by being thrown down. It is a fact and I can prove it.

"One of the funny features of my match with Corbett was the Californian's backing. It is funny how that stake was made up, and funny how certain people acted in the matter. The combination in New Orleans at the time of the Olympic Club's carnival was McAuliffe, Dixon, and Sullivan. I was the biggest favorite of the three and was beaten for the benefit of gamblers.

Sullivan Men Backed Corbett

"It is strange how many people knew I was going to win several days before the fight backed Corbett. They were all smart people who backed the Californian. They were gamblers and people who generally knew they were going to get a big run for their money.

"Well, you can say for me that I will be champion of the world again. Corbett can't beat me. I will fight him once more. I can get lots of backing for another meeting with the man who got the championship from me. I won't have to go to sporting men to get the money, either. There are half a dozen businessmen who will back me for any amount against Corbett. They know I wasn't right when I fought him in New Orleans, not withstanding all reports to the contrary. I am just as strong as I ever was in my life, with the exception of my legs. I admit that I cannot fight as fast as I used to, but I can fight well enough to beat Corbett.

"I intend to fight Corbett after my theatrical engagements are over. I will go to Hot Springs and train there for two months. I will boil all the bad stuff out of my system, harden my muscles, and be as fit to fight for the championship almost as well as ever in my life.

"I would like to say a word about my training for my fight with Corbett. I wanted a glass of ale with my meals but was denied that pleasure. I like a glass of ale after eating and it made me sick to go without it. Frequently at mealtime I didn't care whether I ate or not. I had no appetite. As I could not get ale, I stole bottles of lager and drank them in a farmhouse."

Sullivan made the above statement in the presence of a friend, who advised him not to talk for publication, as it might injure him. Sullivan replied: "It can't do me any harm. I know what I am talking about."

A PUPIL OF ANANIAS

John L. Sullivan Has a Few Words to Say About Mr. Corbett

New York Times
February 21, 1893

CHICAGO, February 20. - John L. Sullivan paid his respects to James Corbett here today. The ex-champion says:

"During the past week there have been published several statements as coming from Mr. Corbett which no gentleman with a spark of manhood could bear without reply. These statements I would rather refute in a more personal manner, and I promise the public that our first meeting will prove fully as memorable as our last.

"No man ever yet called me a coward and escaped punishment. I fought all corners for 11 years, and this is the single exception where a man has the audacity to state that in all my battles I have ever taken an unfair advantage or played a dishonorable part.

"Before the Milwaukee Press Club, Corbett stated that my fight with Ryan was 'fixed,' and also that I had arranged with him to give a 'fake' exhibition in the four-round glove contest in that city. At first I gave no attention to these statements, thinking that his silly head had been befuddled by beer - he seldom buys anything more extravagant. I now have come to believe that he is a pupil of Ananais, the father of liars. I can prove by several reliable witnesses that the day of my exhibition with Corbett in San Francisco he came to my room in the Baldwin Hotel and begged that I would not knock him out. He then claims that at New Orleans I made a plea to him in the ring that he would take no unfair advantage. This I brand as a lie."

Mitchell, in Mr. Sullivan's opinion, has proved that he is afraid of no man, even if he didn't always fight fair.

"I do not wish to be understood to be against Corbett," he added, "in the fight with Mitchell, for my sympathy is with the American. However, should the former be defeated, there is a probability that I shall again appear in the ring, and I sincerely believe that I have a good chance to regain my lost championship.

"If Corbett thinks he is a better man than myself, I will give him the benefit of meeting me in a small room, and if I do not make him cry 'Murder!' he may never expect to hear from me again.

"There is another would-be champion that I will settle with at our first meeting, and that is Goddard. He will never 'bluff' me as he has Corbett, and if we ever meet, the public may rest assured that a free exhibition will result. I am not looking for trouble, but it greatly disturbs me when I think that, having worked 11 years to bring pugilism to the present high standard, such apes as these will thrust their greatness upon the public.

JOHN L. SULLIVAN'S WORD
Thinks Corbett Will Leave the Ring a Badly-Beaten Man

By John L. Sullivan

New York Times
March 1, 1893

So far as Corbett is concerned, I have no ill will toward him because he defeated me, for that was my own fault. The only objection I have to Corbett is that he is not on the "level." He is a man without a country, and no one knows today whether he is an Irishman, and Englishman, or an American. I am not alone in the opinion I express of Corbett. Every man interested in ring sports will eventually join the ranks of the majority who have already formed like opinions to that I have just presented - that Corbett will not last long, and that in the history of the ring he does not figure as he might have figured had he carried himself differently.

You know, all the world knows, that I have no use for Mitchell personally, but I venture the assertion that he will be the popular favorite, the money favorite, in his coming meeting with Corbett. Corbett knows this; every man who knows anything about ring matters know it, and the majority openly, and the remainder secretly, hope to see Mitchell win.

Do you think he can win?

Frankly, I do, unless Mitchell's physical condition is worse than I understand it to be. I do not think so because I am talking about Corbett. Don't misunderstand me, for I will give you my reasons for so thinking. It is admitted, to begin with, that Corbett is taller and longer in the reach, and that he will not mix matters unless driven unto a corner. He did not knock me out at New Orleans; I simply fell from exhaustion in the 21st round. True, he hit me almost at will, but of all of the blows he delivered not one was sufficiently hard to knock out an ordinary man. You will recollect that I have also met Mitchell, and am therefore in a position to gauge the punishing abilities of the two men.

Mitchell is twice as hard a hitter as Corbett, every bit as quick, far more cunning and tricky, and, to put it mildly, equally as good a boxer. In addition, Mitchell is "game" to the core. There is no suspicion of a yellow streak in his composition. He will, to use a common expression, "fight at the drop of a hat," and he cares very little whether he is in his own crowd or somebody else's. As I said, if his physical condition is good and he is fit, as he undoubtedly will be if he can get there, Corbett will leave the ring a badly beaten man.

JOHN L. SULLIVAN "BROKE"
Ex-Champion Prizefighter, Who Made a Million, Acknowledged Plight on Witness Stand

New York Times
December 21, 1899

Figures prove that during the 12 years he was champion heavyweight pugilist of the world John L. Sullivan earned more than a million dollars, and yet yesterday the ex-prizefighter declared, under oath, in Part IV of the City Court that he is "broke." The Anheuser-Busch Brewing Company was the plaintiff against him in a suit to recover $1,600 for beer supplied by them for the saloon Sullivan conducted until recently at 608 Sixth Avenue. The case was called on the one-hour short-cause calendar, but, as it was not over within the required time, it was put at the foot of the long-term calendar and the plaintiff paid the $30 costs.

The news that the old champion was to be on the stand brought many visitors to the court. Sullivan gave the brewing company his notes for the beer they delivered, but did not take tem up on time, and not long since closed the saloon and moved to another saloon on Broadway.

"It's all because I have always been on the level with everybody that I'm here," Sullivan explained as he sat in court waiting to be called. "I though they were on the level with me, too, but they put the place on the bum, and I got the worst of it. That's the way these guys always treat the old champ, see!"

Sullivan's lawyer asked if any of the jurors knew the defendant. Most of them smiled, but none of them acknowledged an acquaintanceship with the old gladiator. Sullivan sat uneasily in the witness chair and eyed every one fiercely. He was asked if he had signed last July the notes offered in evidence, and in answer he shouted out so savagely that Justice Hascall and the jury were startled.

"Now, look here, them's the notes I signed, but not in July. I signed them in August. That's them; they're all right, all right. Meyer, the agent of the brewing company, told me and me partner, Gorman, he was glad we were going to sell his beer, and he promised to make a lot of improvements in the place. Well, the kept jollying us along all right, but they made no improvements."

Sullivan was asked by the opposing counsel if he had held a chattel mortgage on the fixtures of the saloon, and was about to answer when his counsel objected to the question. The old pugilist made several attempts to answer in spite of his counsel, but was shut off. His counsel said he did not want his client to be trapped into making irrelevant statements, but when Justice Hascall looked at the burly form of the witness he remarked: "I don't believe the witness needs any protection from the Court." Sullivan and almost every one else in court smiled at this sally.

The examination of Sullivan ended then, and the case was transferred to the long-term calendar.

JOHN L. SULLIVAN'S BUSY DAY
Unsuccessful Effort to Obtain a Pardon for a Murderer

New York Times
April 11, 1900

John L. Sullivan spent yesterday in a vain attempt to see Assistant District Attorney McIntyre. He arrived at a saloon opposite the Criminal Court Building early yesterday morning in a cab with a sleepy driver and a tried-looking horse. Going inside he saluted the bartender with a resounding thump on the back.

"Set up the best in the house for everybody," he said, "and send for Abe Levy, the lawyer."

The drinks were set out and consumed, and Levy appeared a few moments later.

"See here, Abe," said Sullivan, "I want you to introduce me to Johnny McIntyre. I want to ask him to pardon me friend Eddie Wise, who was convicted for murderin' a man named Beasley on 28th Street. He'll be executed soon if I don't get him off. He's a dead game sport, and I want to get him off."

The lawyer explained that the District Attorney had no power to pardon a murderer, and refused to introduce Sullivan to him. He escaped from the saloon before the ex-champion pugilist had fully grasped his meaning.

Sullivan spent the rest of the day in the saloon sending messengers for all the Assistant District Attorneys in turn. All of them declined the invitation, however, saying that it would be beneath their dignity to enter a saloon. Meanwhile the sleepy cabman slumbered peacefully in the sunlight outside the saloon, and Sullivan ordered drinks inside and hurled a variety of compliments at District Attorneys, individually and collectively. At five o'clock the cabman awoke and looked at his watch.

"Say, boss," he shouted to the ex-pugilist, who appeared in the doorway of the saloon, "you've had this cab for 22 hours now. We ought to be getting' a move on."

"All right," said the ex-champion. "Drive me home. I can see that there ain't no consideration for a public man in this town."

JOHN L. SULLIVAN BANKRUPT
Ex-Champion Files a Petition in Order to Prevent Arrest by a Creditor in Boston

New York Times
November 29, 1902

John L. Sullivan, the ex-champion pugilist, filed a petition in bankruptcy here yesterday, in order that he might go to Boston and appear there in a show without being arrested at the instance of a creditor - J. H. Lewis of 417 Washington Street, Boston - on five notes amounting to $450.

James F. Mack, attorney for Mr. Sullivan, said that Sullivan was under contract to appear in Boston on December 8th and had been threatened with arrest if he went there. An effort had been made to settle the claim by paying $150 cash, but the offer was refused, and the only course left was to file a petition in bankruptcy. Sullivan does not remember anything about contracting the debt, but a judgment for it has been obtained against him in Boston.

The liabilities mentioned in the schedules are only $2,658, and his assets consist of wearing apparel valued at $60, which is exempt. The creditors are J. H. Lewis, $450, Anheuser-Busch Brewing Association, $1,500, contracted in 1899 on notes disputed, Charles H. Stevens of 955 Park Avenue, $150, disputed note, contracted in 1899, and Julius Palm & Co. of 669 Sixth Avenue, $558, contracted in 19000 with his partner, J. J. Carroll, for liquors when they had a saloon.

Sullivan gave his residence as the Vanderbilt Hotel, corner of Lexington Avenue and 42nd Street. He can obtain a certified copy of the order of adjudication in bankruptcy at the Clerk's office of the United States District Court here, take it with him to Boston, and prevent arrest there. Sullivan did not present his petition in person.

SULLIVAN SPENT A FORTUNE
Record of the Swift Pace the Old Champion Has Gone With His Money

The Saturday Budget
January 10, 1903

John L. Sullivan says he's "flat broke" again. This is John's annual statement, and it is generally truthful. The other day Sullivan startled the small boys of Boston by throwing glittering coins about the streets. But that is nothing new, for the big fellow has been separating himself from gold ever since he won the heavyweight championship from Paddy Ryan more than 20 years ago. John has been receiving $300 a week as a monologue artist, but in his own language "that ain't enough to buy beer." Probably no pugilist has had as much money as Sullivan, who, with all his faults, has always been charitable. Few have asked a favor of him and been refused.

Always an Attraction

Always an attraction on the stage, John L. can keep the wolf away from the door as long as he cares to work in that line, but he sometimes grows tired of the calcium and wants to cut loose with the boys. Then it is that he empties his pockets and goes "broke." How much money has John L. Sullivan allowed to pass through his fingers in 20 years? This is a question that John himself cannot answer with accuracy, but it is safe to say that $1,000,000 is not far out of the way. Sullivan has toured the world, he has had countless benefits, has engaged in the saloon business various times, has been an actor and a vaudeville artist and has had other sources from which to squeeze the almighty dollar when times were hard, too. Pugilistic historians who are strong on statistics have hunted through the records and have succeeded in accounting for $785,000 which John has pocketed. Here are the figures:

LIST OF THE EARNINGS

May 16, 1881 - John Flood $750
Fenruary 7, 1882 - Paddy Ryan $5,000
July 17, 1882 - "Tug" Wilson $18,000
May 14, 1883 - Charley Mitchell $8,000
August 6, 1883 - Herbet Slade, the Maori $14,000
Tour of the country under Pat Sheedy's management $500,000
June 30, 1884 - Failed to meet Mitchell, money split $5,000
November 10, 1884 - John M. Laflin $12,000
November 17, 1884 - Alf. Greenfield $12,000
January 19, 1885 - Paddy Ryan $13,000
June 13, 1885 - Jack Burke...$8,600
August 29, 1885 - Dominick McCaffrey $11,000
November 13, 1885 - Paddy Ryan $5,000
January 18, 1887 Patsy Cardiff $5,000
December 9, 1887 - Jake Kilrain $15,000
During 1890 - Theatrical tour $25,000
During 1891 - Australian tour $10,000
August 21, 1896 - Tom Sharkey $2,000
Benefits at different times $10,000

Total, about $785,000

John Would Buy Coal

Somebody showed this table of earnings to the big fellow the other day, and asked him if it was correct. John's reply was:

"If I had that coin now I'd make some of them guys that's rich look sick. I'd buy all the coal in sight, give it to the poor people, and then get a good load aboard simply for joy. You can bet that when John had it he was a good fellow. Then everybody shook him by the hand, and said:

"John, yer kin kick 'em all!"

"But now, when Sullivan is 'broke,' yer hear them all askin' What did he do with it? Well, Sullivan spent it and had a good time. But he never took a dollar that didn't belong to him, and was always your truly, John L. Sullivan, ever on the level!"

JOHN L. SULLIVAN SEES ROOSEVELT
Tells Taft He Has Him "Skinned a Block" for Weight

New York Times
May 9, 1907

WASHINGTON, May 8. - John L. Sullivan, ex-pugilist, had an interesting chat with President Roosevelt today, covering various subjects. Sullivan said that he had seen the president at several bouts in New York, and called his particular attention to a fight with Mitchell, the English heavyweight, in 1883, when Sullivan knocked him over the ropes.

Although it was noon, Sullivan wore a Tuxedo coat, low-cut white waistcoat, and a large diamond. Etiquette abroad requires evening clothes for a daylight call on royalty, and the ex-champion was asked if he was trying to introduce this custom.

"Now, son, none of your kidding," he protested. "I don't know much about kings, except shaking hands once with King Ed when he was Prince of Wales. He was a good sport - take it from me. These glad rags are for my turn at the matinee, see?"

Sullivan met Secretary Taft at the doors of the Executive offices, and put in a good word for clemency for a friend [his nephew] who is serving a sentence on Governor's Island.

"Guess I got you skinned a block," remarked Sullivan to the Secretary in talking about their respective weights. John L. said he weighed 335

pounds, while Secretary Taft remarked that his weight was only 283, and that the best he ever did was to tip the beam at 330.

As he was leaving the White House Sullivan paid his compliments to big men, saying, among other things"

"That man Taft is what I call a man, too. The president is a great man, It takes big fellows a long time to get started, but when they are going they go some."

JOHN L. SULLIVAN'S NEPHEW PARDONED
President Makes Condition That He Re-Enlist for Four Years

New York Times
May 17, 1907

WASHINGTON, May 16. - President Roosevelt has granted a conditional pardon to John L. Lennon, a nephew of John L. Sullivan, serving a sentence at Governor's Island for alleged desertion from the Marin Corps while in Cuba. The president makes the condition that Lennon re-enlist and serve the full term of four years.

Sullivan recently saw the president and argued that his relative did not intend to desert, but had merely overstayed his leave of absence three days.

JOHN L. SULLIVAN'S VIEWS ON THE BIG FIGHT
Ex-Champion Talks About Upcoming
Jeffries Versus Johnson Battle

By John L. Sullivan

New York Times
May 1, 1910

The fight which is to be held at Emeryville, California, on Independence Day between James J. Jeffries, representing the white race, and Jack Johnson, who now stands sponsor for the fighting qualities of the black man, is, to my mind, going to be one of the greatest battles, if not the very greatest, in all ring history.

When I phrased it as I did - that the contest is really between representatives of two races rather than between two individuals regardless of race questions, I felt certain that many would undoubtedly share my opinion. Nor can I, after having given the matter a great deal of thought, see it in any other light.

From what I can gather it seems to be the universal impression over here that the fight is a race question, and if I am not mistaken, that is the aspect it is assuming in America. I know that when Stanley Ketchel fought

Johnson all the Negroes in the South absolutely refused to work and tied up the steamboats, and the colored firemen refused to run on the trains in several of the Southern states.

I myself feel sorry the match was ever made. I am not biased, but I do believe that the Negroes should fight in a class by themselves. Many times during my career I was urged by outsiders to throw reason to the winds and fight a black man. But I always refused.

Now, as to the fight itself. To my mind it all depends on Jeffries' condition. Jeffries should win if he stands in the ring with the same degree of strength and skill that characterized his fighting before he retired. If he does not touch that form then Johnson has his chance.

I was about the same age when I fought Corbett that Jeffries will be when he fights Johnson. I am well aware - from experience - that the wheels of Nature are not made to roll backward. Everything presses onward: an impetuous current bears all toward the breaking point; and the man who undertakes to break the contract of human nature has a job on his hands which he cannot fill.

When a man goes out of business for some years and then suddenly re-enters it and assumes great responsibilities the odds are against him. There are a lot of ways in which Jeffries has put himself in the shade, and these give Johnson a chance.

There is the matter of properly timing or judging a blow, and such a great deal may turn on such a little slip. If a great rifle shot puts his weapon aside and then some years later goes again to the range, he may still know all about the game and he may still know all about the rules, but his eye cannot be as well trained. Such misjudgment will mean a great deal in the result. The same thing applies to boxing.

When I was training for my fight with Corbett, people used to flock to the gymnasium and see me pull the heavy weights around and watch the muscles stand out during the various exercises. Then they would rush away and say, "I've seen enough. My money goes up on Sullivan."

I thought they were right. But when I stepped into the ring I found that, although the muscle was there, the machinery inside had given out.

You cannot straighten an engine out with a little oil. If it is impaired or bent it has got to be set right, and how are we to know the inner workings of our anatomy? In my case nature simply asserted itself. I fell, as one might say, from sheer exhaustion. No one has ever known of me traveling around the world telling how it happened or what I should have done if I had another chance. There is a cause for everything, and I knew and know the cause of my defeat at Corbett's hands.

Jeffries has a very great difficulty to contend with, and that is having been out of the ring for so long a time. Now comes the big question: Does Jeffries realize this difficulty?

Of course we shall all like to see the white man win, but wishes can never fill a sack. Should the Negro win there is not a white man in the world who could throw up his hat and dance with glee. Yet Jeffries cannot sail as he would, but must sail as the winds blow. Jeffries cannot depend upon any man, upon any friend; he must face the issue squarely - the matter of getting into first-class condition.

Experience, as my friends all know, has been my great and only teacher, and I realize that the world is getting wiser all the time. When I see the men and I know the company they keep and have kept, what they are doing and what they have done, I shall be able to tell just what they are. I know well that what is stamped one cent will never be worth one dollar.

CORBETT'S UNPLEASANT REMARKS TO FORMER CHAMPION NOW FORGOTTEN
Muldoon Acts Part of Peacemaker and Harmony Now Prevails

By John L. Sullivan

New York Times
June 26, 1910

Well, this has probably been one of the pleasantest days of my life, not only because I am here to see what I think is going to be the greatest fight of modern times, but because the atmosphere of good feeling and harmony that was created today by our old friends out at Jeffries' camp has done more to make me feel my old self than anything that has happened to me in relation to my old athletic friends for many years.

I was on my way in from Johnson's quarters this morning when I was met by a friend in an automobile who had been out searching for me. The minute he espied me he burst out with, "Hurry up, John! I want you to go out to Jeffries' camp and see what has happened." For a moment I was rather nonplussed, as it occurred to me that something had befallen the former champion. My mind was soon disabused as to this, however, when I was told that the negotiations which had been working toward a reconciliation between my old friends and myself had come to a head, and that my old antagonist, Jim Corbett, had especially sent for me.

That was mighty good to hear, because Jim and I have not been on

friendly terms for some time back, but I never was very bitter toward him, and in the light of what transpired today I don't think he could have been very bitterly disposed toward me.

When I arrived at Mona Springs the first person I saw belonging to the Jeffries party was Corbett, who was standing across the road as I drove up in the automobile and stopped in front of Jeffries' house. As soon as he saw me he came toward us with hand outstretched.

I think I must have flushed all over my body, and I seemed to feel a little bit embarrassed, so that I did not get my hand out as quickly as I might, but Corbett is a little more active than I am, and probably that accounts for his quicker motion. However, it was a hearty handclasp, and we stood and looked at each other for some time. Muldoon, the dear old trouble-chaser, who had been working this up ever since he arrived, came up alongside and beamed and beamed.

Jim said to me, "Well, John, old boy, I am glad to see you again."

I think I said, "Jim, old boy, I am glad to see you, too." I say I think I said that because my mind was so full of so many good things to say that I am somewhat muddled as to my exact words. The feeling was there, all right, and, after all, that is all that was necessary.

After our little greeting, Corbett said, "John, the big fellow would like to meet you."

I replied, "He wouldn't like it any more than I would like to meet him. Where is he?"

"He is just being rubbed down after his morning session," said Corbett. "He is over in the rubbing room."

"I will go right over there," I replied, and Corbett, Muldoon, and Choynski accompanied me to the bathing house, which is across the road from Jeffries' house, about 200 feet.

I came up on Jeffries as he lay on the wooden rubbing board, and, looking up, he saw me coming through the door. I think that if anything had been between the two arms as they shot out - "Jeff's" right and mine - something would have been jolted. I was never gladder to see a man in all my life.

I think I was the first to speak. I said, "Well, old fellow, you look fit to fight for your country."

He replied, "That is what I am going to do, John, on the Fourth of July. How are you?"

"Pretty good, Jeff. I need not ask how you are. Anybody with half an eye can see that," I retorted.

After these few preliminaries, "Jeff" had his rub finished, and then he, Muldoon, Corbett, Choynski, and myself went over some old-time stuff. I think it did our hearts good.

There is nothing so peaceful and gratifying to a lot of athletes whether they have been champions or are still champions than to talk over the old times. As fast as one would get through with a little story about where he or we figured, another of us was ready with one that popped into our minds. Good old Joe Choynski was so happy over the whole morning's work that I think he hugged all of us. I know I saw him hugging Corbett. Joe is a good old scout, the salt of the earth.

Before I left Moana Springs we had several pictures taken. One group that I am very anxious to see the print of is Jeffries and I in the center with hands clasped and Muldoon, Corbett, Choynski, Farmer Burns, Sam Berger, and "Jeff's" brother Jack flanking us. I have already ordered a frame for this, and it's going to be one of my precious possessions.

THE BOSTON STRONG BOY

Interview conducted in 1911 by Jerome Power
Via the Library of Congress Records

"Shake the hand that shook the hand of John L. Sullivan!"

I offer my hand thus, through the medium of printer's Ink. John L. Sullivan, former heavyweight champion of the world, was 53 years old when I interviewed him, as a young newspaper reporter, in the summer of 1911 while he was stopping at the Claypool Hotel in Indianapolis, Indiana. He shook my hand on that occasion. Without meaning in the least to hurt me, he gave my carpals such a sardining that they still ache at the memory, after all these years. He was that strong, even at 53.

"Come on up, my boy!" he boomed over the telephone, when I called him from the lobby. Then, at the entrance to his room, came the handshake. He took my card, waved me to a chair near a table and walked over to the double window, where the morning sunlight streamed through the curtains.

I took a good look at him and saw what seemed like an unusually big Irish policeman, off duty in plain clothes. That was the first impression. Further inspection, however, showed me more - a great deal more. To tell the truth, he did not look as big as my knowledge of his ring exploits had led me to expect. He was tall, but his great shoulders and the paunch which he had developed at 53 prevented this from being apparent at first glance. He weighed, I should judge, well over 200 pounds, but having seen him walk across the room, on the balls of his feet, with all the lightness and grace of a cat, I had trouble in convincing myself that even this was true.

He had a well-shaped head - not the "bullet" type of many pugilists - and dark hair which was turning gray. He carried this head at a proud angle which gave emphasis to his prominent jaw. His face was somewhat florid, so that even without knowing who he was, on would have said: "Here is a man who has been a hard drinker." He had a fine mustache in the old tradition. Starting below his nostrils this mustache, a few shades grayer than his hair, extended in leisurely fashion over his lip and all the way across his face on both sides. The under edges were a trifle ragged and the curl at the ends was upward. He had a custom of snorting sometimes, as he was about to say something, after which he would stroke his mustache, first on one side, then on the other. I got the idea that this stroking business acted as a sedative on him.

He wore a wing collar around his bull neck. During the interview he told me that he had these made to order, since the largest stock size was much too small for him. His shoulders were broad, without being in any sense square. They sloped beautifully into arms which seemed not unusually long or heavy. The hands were large and powerful, as I had received recent evidence. He sported a blue tie, bow fashion, with a conservative white figure, but his suit, while of good cut and material, did not set well upon him. The knees of his trousers bagged and the whole could have stood pressing. He had a fancy vest of flowered material and a heavy watch chain, prominent across the front.

John L. Sullivan's eyes, to my mind, were his most remarkable physical characteristic. They were the rare type which change color according to emotion. I decided at first that they were blue and rather mild, then a little later, as we talked, that they were steel gray and hard. Once or twice I could have sworn that they turned black and shot sparks of red fire, as he became vehement about this or that point.

In repose his features were rather pleasant - just a trifle on the stern side, perhaps. But when anger stirred him, he could assume the most ferocious scowl I have ever seen on a human. I began to understand why some of the men he fought were beaten even before he hit them.

He talked with a perceptible, but not pronounced, brogue. When he became excited, however, this brogue grow thicker. He made small errors in grammar, which stamped him as a man of little education, but remembering how brief his education really was, one had to admit that he talked remarkably well.

"Mr. Sullivan -", I began.

"Let me see," he rumbled, glancing again at my card, "You have an Irish name. Call me John L. I give you permission."

No king, making a ruling from the throne, ever spoke with greater, more sincere majesty. Believe me, I needed permission to take such a liberty with the old warrior. I told him that I had been sent up by my paper to learn what he had to say about fighting, in a most general way and along the lines which might seem good to him. He asked me to draw my chair up to the table. He would stand, he said, as he could think better on his feet.

"Well, there's nothing to fighting," he opened up, "Just come out fast from your corner, hit the other fellow as hard as you can and hit him first. That's all there is to fighting."

He laughed, then at once grew serious.

"What I should like to talk about is something else. Whiskey! There's the only fighter that ever really licked old John L. Jim Corbett, according to the record, knocked me out in New Orleans in 1892, but he only gave the finishing touches to what whiskey had already done to me. If I had met Jim Corbett before whiskey got me I'd have killed him. I stopped drinking long ago, but of course, too late. Too late for old John L., but not too late for millions of boys who are starting out to follow the same road. I desire to use the years of life which remain to me to warn these boys, to turn them back. John L. Sullivan, champion of the world, could not lick whiskey. What gives any one of them the notion that he can."

I didn't wish to hear anything about temperance, but the famous scowl was in evidence and the red sparks about which I was telling you gleamed in the dark eyes. You would think twice about trying to stop John L. Sullivan, no matter what he was doing. I listened, therefore, while for the next 20 minutes, without a break, he paced up and down the room talking about whiskey. He talked with eloquence, too. Billy Sunday could have gotten ideas. He snorted and stroked his mustache. Once a small chair got in his way. He kicked it absently, without seeming to use much force, but the chair flew end over end all the way across the large room. When the torrent of words ended, I put my cards on the table.

"John L.," I said with truth, "you have given me a talk about whiskey which I shall never forget, but if I go back to my city editor with nothing else, he will throw my story into the ash-can and me, too, I expect. He wants you to talk about fighting. After all, you were the fighting champion, not the temperance champion."

He sighed and sat down, then looked at me with a quick smile. His mood had changed.

"I'm just an old man now," he resumed, "and what I have to say about fighting has all been, said - thousand times or more, I guess. Mostly, I said it with my dukes (fists). I leave talking to these present day fighters. Jim Corbett is one of the best talkers that ever lived."

"I thought you and Jim made it up years ago," I ventured. I referred to the feud, well known in sporting circles, between these two great champions. For a long while John L. could not forgive Corbett for taking the championship from him. In New York mutual friends at last got them together and forced them to shake hands. Corbett was willing enough, but John L., even though admitting freely that the pompadoured speed merchant had beaten him fairly, could never quite forgive him.

"Oh, of course," he roared, slapping his knee, "Jim and I are great friends now. I still say, though, that if I had met him before whiskey got

me, I'd have put him away like I did the others. I'm trying to give you now the real inside story of that fight in New Orleans. Tell your city editor, damn him, that whiskey has more to do with fighting than he imagines."

"Who gave you the toughest fight of your career?" I asked.

"Well, that's a question! Most of them were plenty tough. Jake Kilrain was one of the hardest to lick. Charley Mitchell, the Englishman, gave me a lot of trouble, too, but in a different way. By talking to me all the time in the ring, from the first bell, he got my goat. He threw more insults in my direction than blows. When I took out after him, he ran. He did not dare to stand up and slug with me and that is why I had trouble in licking him."

"Yes, Charley Mitchell had the reputation of being a bad actor, all right," I agreed, "but should we expect too much of Englishmen?"

"Well, no, not as a rule. But I have known a few who were strictly on the up and up. One in particular."

"Who was that?"

"Why, King Edward VII," said John L. "He was a real fellow. Common as an old shoe. We got well acquainted when I was across the pond. He made me forget that I was taking to royalty."

"Yes, if some of the things they say you said to him are true," I laughed, "that must have been the case."

"Oh, none of that stuff is true. I always remembered that I was an American, and never slobbered in the dirt to him or any other king. On the other hand,[I?] treated King Edward with the full respect due his station at all times. This seemed to get on his nerves a little, because he told me, in exactly these words, to forget that he was royalty and to treat him just like he was one of the boys. After that, I did as he asked. I suppose all those newspaper yarns which try to make a chump out of me started on that account."

"How about that story which tells about you killing a horse with on blow of your fist?"

"That's another one, That never did happen. I always liked horses and I swear on the cross that I never killed one, with my fist on any other way.

"In fact," he continued, look at a gold watch almost as large as an alarm clock, "most of the real harm I ever did in this world was done to just one man - yours truly, John L. Sullivan. I make no secret of that. Even the fellows I pounded in the ring were all right again after a few days - [crowing?] fresh challenges at me as if nothing had ever happened to them. Today, many second-rate fighters make more money than I made when I was champion of the world. Fighters new seem to think of nothing buy money. I thought first of the fact that I was champion of the world and I was always ready to prove that I was, any time, any place, against any contender. I fought in barns, on barges and in the back rooms of [saloons?]. The gate, as they say, was a secondary consideration. I would bet heavily on myself and, of course, always won until Jim Corbett beat me for the championship. That time I lost my shirt. Thousands of my friends all over the country, who thought I was unbeatable, I guess, lost their shirts, too. That is the thing which made me so sore about this fight."

"Yes," I hastened to agree, "the old-timers cannot understand, even today, how you came to lose. But I have never heard any man question your honesty."

"Well, I have traveled a long, hard road," he went on - and the eyes were blue and mild again - "but I have been honest all the way. I toured this country from one end to the other, offering $50 to any man who could stay on his feet for three rounds in the ring with me. Nobody ever collected, but don't think they didn't try! Can you imagine the champion of the world doing that today?"

I couldn't and said so frankly. Then, judging the interview to be at an end, I started to leave. He walked with me to the door.

"I realize," he concluded, "that it is hard for me to say anything new about fighting. I never had a great deal to say, even when I was champion of the world, because, as you have said, I was a fighting champion, not a talking champion. I give you permission to write anything about me you please, within reasonable limits. My fighting days are all over and what's printed now makes little difference to me. If you can get some of the things I have said about whiskey past that city editor of yours, so much the better. If he wants a story about fighting, he'll have to pay some attention to whiskey, because I say to you again, that in spite of the record, whiskey is the only fighter who ever licked John L. Sullivan, champion of the world!"

JOHN L. SULLIVAN TO RETIRE
Thinks the Man Who Reads
the Comic and Sporting Pages is Happiest

New York Times
June 27, 1911

RICHMOND, VA., June 26. - At the close of a week's engagement with a local theater in vaudeville just finished, John L. Sullivan announced his intention of retiring from the stage and public life.

"I am through with the game," said Sullivan. "Since 1880 I have been more or less before the public. I do not advise any young man to go into the pugilistic arena for show or financial reasons, but I advise every young man to go into physical training. This will help him to meet the battle of life.

"I have no grouch against the world nor an inhabitant thereof. Follow the man who reads comic and sporting pages of the papers, and you will find that he has a happy household and is fully satisfied with life."

JOHN L. SULLIVAN FARMING
He's Resting, Though Doing Chores
and Building a Stone Bungalow

New York Times
July 17, 1911

WEST ABINGTON, MASS., July 16. - John L. Sullivan, former champion heavyweight pugilist, is enjoying life upon the farm here doing the hundred odd chores that makes the life of the farmer what it is.

"No Muldoon farm for me," says Mr. Sullivan.

"I have had a hard season on the stage and now I want to rusticate. But I am always glad to see my old friends.

"I am really interested in that farm of mine. It's a good farm, and I'm going to make it first-class for a Summer place."

This is the way that John L. rests:

He sees to the cutting of the hay on his 70-acre farm.

He buys farming tools and orders the milk and meat.

He goes over the survey of his private island, a body of land entirely surrounded by the waters of Mill Meadows Brook.

He reviews plans for the tearing down of the old brick house and barn.

He goes over plans for a stone bungalow.

JOHN L. SULLIVAN OPENS
CAMPAIGN AGAINST DRINK
John Barleycorn Was the Only Champion
Who Ever Knocked Him

The Stanstead Journal
August 15, 1915

John L. Sullivan, the noted ex-prizefighter, made his bow as a public lecturer on temperance at Asbury Park, New Jersey, the other night. With an old reputation as a great consumer of liquor, the stalwart ex-pugilist attracted a large audience, among whom were many gaily attired women.

With a few gestures, but with a good deal of force, Sullivan said:

"Ladies and gentlemen and my friends, now you know I could never be but one person, and that is John L. Sullivan as he is at all times.

"My friends, on the fifth day of March, 1905, I took my last drink of liquor. If I had not stopped drinking at that time I wouldn't be here talking to you. Now I do not come before you as a crusader, but just to talk to you and ask this of you who drink - to stop drinking, because temperance is common

sense.

"In all my experiences I have found the man that is always going to leave liquor alone always takes it. Doubtless there are such men that do leave it alone, because there must be exceptions to all rules, but I used to think I could take it or leave it alone, and that belief hung to me for many years.

"But by the bitterness of experience suffered by myself, I found out I must leave it alone. Strong, healthy parents gave me a strong, healthy body and more or less resolution of spirit.

"I thank God I can say without boasting that it takes considerable degree of resolution for a young man to work himself to the championship of the world in any line of endeavor, but it was my resolution and spirit that carried all antagonists before me.

"But they were no use at all when I faced old John Barleycorn. Now, why I speak to the young men in regard to the liquor question is this: Everybody more or less, says to themselves they can take a glass of beer or two and be done, but let me tell you, my friends, as soon as you start drinking you are bound to rub elbows with a run hound and become smudged.

"The rum hound is a familiar sort of human being. His favorite saying is: 'Come let us have another.' That is where the money runs out, and as the money runs out they take the door mat from the bar room door.

Why He Took a Tumble

"I want to speak particularly to the young man who is trying to break into the game. He will say: 'I know men that drink every day. They are wonderfully prosperous and healthy.' I say to the young man, 'If you want

to be prosperous and healthy, do not drink at all.' Take the young ballplay-
ers. They are a stamp of men who do not drink any liquor. I was a money-
making machine, and my success depended upon my spirit and ability to
hang fast.

"In all my career in the prize ring I never was knocked down. It was
said Charlie Mitchell knocked me down. That is not true. I slipped, and
was up and at it again in a second. I had managers and trainers because
of my superior skill. Naturally it was for their benefit to keep me in the best
physical shape so that I could fulfill my best effort, because if John L.
played out their meal ticket was gone. But they were generally unsuccessful when they tried to stop me. They were afraid of me.

"But booze wasn't afraid of John L. Sullivan. It was a long time before
I began to realize there could be but one finish. So I took a tumble to
myself.

Learned From Experience

"But I want to tell you if God had not given me a good constitution, I
wouldn't have held championship but a very short while.

"Now I want to tell you something from the book of experience of
John L. Sullivan. The booze has more ways of hitting you than you have
of dodging, no matter how successful an individual you may be.

"It will steal and cheat him of activity and the muscular development
he has got, the activity of his brain, the muscles of his organs. It will dead-
en him so that he becomes useless at the age of 40. Instead of being a
young man and living to be 80, he dies in the neighborhood of 45.

"It is evident that all men have their plans made out before them.
They have their destiny in their own hands. It is so with the young man
when he starts the booze habit. He corrodes his stomach or brain. His finish will be a drunkard's grave of the Potter's field. The booze question
today is in the mouths, the ears, and the hearts of every individual of this
country.

"I have met all classes of people in the north, east, and west, and I
am telling you the truth when I say that today, if they were to take a vote,
there is no question in my mind there would be 28 to 30 states that would
vote prohibition."

JOHN L. SULLIVAN, 59, DIES SUDDENLY
FOR TEN YEARS DOMINATED SPORTING CIRCLES

*Said to Have Made Two Millions in Fighting and Spent One in Drinks
For Himself and Admirers - Last Years Spent Fighting For Prohibition -
Defeated By Corbett*

Rome New York Daily Sentinel
February 2, 1918

ABINGTON, MASS., February 2. - John L. Sullivan, formerly the heavyweight champion of the United States, died at his home here today. Sullivan, who was 59 years of age, had lived on a farm here for the last 10 years. He was taken ill with heart trouble three weeks ago, but his health quickly improved and he went to Boston yesterday. This morning he arose as usual and planned another visit to the city, but during the forenoon had an attack of the old trouble, from which he failed to rally. He died at noon. Sullivan's wife died some months ago.

Ten Years American Champion

John Laurence Sullivan was one of the most picturesque characters in the history of prizefighting. For more than 10 years, from the time he defeated Paddy Ryan in 1882, in a bare-knuckle fight under the London Prize Ring Rules, until he was defeated by James J. Corbett, in 1892, his personality and methods of fighting completely dominated sporting circles in the United States. Sullivan was the last champion of the United States under the London Prize Ring Rules. It was largely through his achievements that the championship title was made a prize of great monetary value. In the early days of his career, $1,000 a side was looked on  as a great sum. He received only $53 for the fight that made him a national character in fisticuffs and won him the right to challenge Paddy Ryan for the championship.

His friends ranged all the way from the ordinary 'fight fan' to many men of social and financial distinction in the United States, and it is said he was on chumming terms with the late King Edward VII of England.

He began his fighting career soon after he was 17, when as the "Boston Strong Boy" he took part in amateur boxing contests in several cities in Massachusetts.

His Fight With Paddy Ryan

After his nine-round fight with Paddy Ryan, on the strip of greensward on the Gulf of Mexico, the word "knockout" was manufactured by Billy Madden, Sullivan's trainer, to describe the effect of his blows when properly delivered.

His hardest fight was with Jake Kilrain. It was fought near New Orleans and lasted for 75 rounds. That was the last championship contest in the United States to be fought with bare knuckles, under the old rules.

That fight practically decided the uselessness of trying to beat Sullivan by combating him in his own sledgehammer style. A 39-round fight with Charley Mitchell, a wary and skillful boxer, seemed to show fighting managers that the great John L. might be vulnerable to a man who could box well and stay with him long enough to wear him down. The opportunity to try this method on the champion fell to James J. Corbett. The purse was the largest ever put up in a ring battle up to that time. The purse was $25,000 and the stakes $20,000.

Fighting Spirit to the End

Sullivan's old fighting spirit remained with him to the end. The first fainting spell left him unconscious for 10 minutes, and when he rallied, George M. Bush, a friend who lived with him, was applying ice bags to his head. Bush told the former champion to keep quiet, that he had sent for a doctor.

"I don't want any doctor," John L. said. "I've listened to a lot of them in my life, and I know I am all right and can doctor myself."

He protested when Dr. Rann, who had been summoned by Bush, told him he had better go to bed for a couple of hours. When Dr. Rann left, Sullivan beckoned Bush.

"Is the bathroom warm, George?" he asked.

"Yes."

"Well that's fine. I want to take a bath."

Ten minutes later he was dead.

William Kelley, a 15-year-old boy, who had been adopted by Sullivan, and Bush, his faithful friend, were with him when he passed away.

ROOSEVELT LAUDS SULLIVAN
Eulogizes Late Pugilist, but Cannot Attend Funeral

New York Times
February 5, 1918

OYSTER BAY, N.Y., February 4. - Colonel Theodore Roosevelt will not be able to attend and act as pallbearer at the funeral of his old friend, John L. Sullivan, which will be held in Boston Wednesday morning.

"I had a genuine regard for my old friend, John L. Sullivan," the Colonel said today. "He was an old and valued friend, and I mourn his death."

MEMORIAL SERVICE FOR DEAD GLADIATOR
Colonel Roosevelt Unable to Attend

Hartford Courant
February 5, 1918

BOSTON, February 4. - An almost unbroken line of men, women, and children today and tonight passed before the bier of John L. Sullivan, the last of the old guard of heavyweight pugilists. In full dress, the body of the dead champion lay in the darkened parlor at the home of his sister, Mrs. Annie E. Lennon, in the Roxbury district.

Meanwhile, final arrangements were made for the funeral, which will be held from St. Paul's Church, Roxbury, Wednesday morning. The Reverend Peter C. Quinn will officiate at the funeral services. Hundreds of men prominent in the sporting world, representatives of temperance societies, and others from far and wide sent word that they would be present.

Regret was expressed at the Lennon home tonight when word was received from Colonel Theodore Roosevelt that he would be unable to attend the funeral of his old friend because of a speaking engagement in Springfield Wednesday.

It was hoped that the Reverend William A. Sunday, the evangelist, who declared that John L. won his greatest battle when he "gave booze the knockout," would attend the funeral. Jake Kilrain, the pugilist who battled 72 rounds with Sullivan in the old days, is also expected to be here.

Mace Finnerty, one of Sullivan's old cronies, told at the Lennon home today of how John L. prepared for the 72-round bout with Kilrain at Richburg, Mississippi. Finnerty said that Sullivan had been ill for several weeks with typhoid fever when he received the challenge. Undaunted by his condition, the "Boston Strong Boy," hobbling on crutches, went to Canada to sign the agreement for the bout. Later, on reaching his training quarters, Sullivan was able to get about with a cane. Finally, his legs became stronger, but he was not in prime condition when he entered the ring at Richburg. Nevertheless, he went 72 rounds, and was acclaimed the victor.

Contrary to popular impression, Sullivan did not leave much of an estate. Although he hade received a fortune in the ring and later in theatrical ventures, his friends said today that the veteran's estate consisted only of his farm at Abingdon and a few securities.

CORBETT AT SULLIVAN BIER
Conqueror of John L. Pays Last Tribute to Great Fighter

New York Times
February 6, 1918

BOSTON, February 5. - Hundreds of the younger generation of Boston who had known John L. Sullivan only as the hero of innumerable legends will be able to tell their offspring in the future that they had gazed upon the famous champion of the prize ring, whose funeral is to be held here tomorrow morning. All day and evening, notwithstanding the bitterest weather of the winter, a stream of persons passed through the Crescent, on which the home of Sullivan's sister, Mrs. Annie Lennon, is situated, and where, in a coffin broad as a bed, the huge frame of the mighty fighter lay as if asleep. There were those who lingered in sadness. Conspicuous among them was James J. Corbett,

the man who wrested the American championship from Sullivan at New Orleans in 1892.

Corbett will be on of the pallbearers. Many other figures of national prominence in sport will attend the funeral tomorrow. Jake Kilrain, defeated by Sullivan at Richburg, Mississippi, in 1880, in the last and one of the greatest fights conducted according to London Prize Ring Rules, will come from Woburn to pay final tribute to his conqueror.

William Muldoon, the veteran trainer, will be an active pallbearer. The others are local men, friends of the champion and of his near relatives, who now include only his sister, her husband, and their eight children. William Kelly, a boy recently adopted by Sullivan, will be the only other close mourner. Sullivan will be buried beside his second wife in Calvary Cemetery. Requiem high mass will be celebrated at 10 A.M. in St. Paul's Church, Roxbury, by the pastor, the Reverend Peter C. Quinn. The church can hold only about 2,000, but the members of the family opposed the idea of a more public funeral.

The honorary pallbearers will be James M. Curley, now ex-mayor of Boston, Corbett and Muldoon, Police Captain James P. Sullivan, Daniel J. McHogarty, Clarence W. Rowley, John Mahoney, and Fire Chief William J. Gaffey.

The ushers are Henry Blackwell, John J. Mitchell, United States Marshal Daniel J. Sullivan, Lewis R. Sullivan, William L. Hogarty, Jack Sheehan, the boxing referee, Gerould Savage, Miah J. Murray, and John I. Taylor, former president of the Boston American League Baseball Club.

Telegrams regretting inability to be present were received by Mrs. Lennon today from Theodore Roosevelt, James E. Madden, the turfman, Jim O'Rourke, Charlie Comiskey, veteran baseball man, and hundreds of others.

JOHN L. SULLIVAN BURIED

Many Pay Tribute to One-Time Champion
at Services in Boston

New York Times
February 7, 1918

BOSTON, February 6. - The body of John L. Sullivan, one-time heavyweight champion, was laid at rest beside that of his wife in Old Calvary Cemetery, Forest Hills, today, after a service held in the parish church in the Roxbury district, where his early days were spent. Crowds lined the streets near the church and the church itself was filled to overflowing with friends, old and young, of the ring celebrity.

A handful of veterans of the sporting world, companions of Sullivan in his pugilistic career, and men prominent in city and State affairs, were in the gathering at the church, but the funeral was largely a neighborhood affair, made up of residents of the district, their wives and children.

Jake Kilrain, principal in one of Sullivan's, most celebrated battles, served as an usher, as did Jack Sheehan, a referee; Daniel Dwyer, of Chicopee, a former sparring partner of Sullivan, with a few others of note in prize ring circles, but aside from this group, there was little to suggest the prominence of the former pugilist in the sporting world.

PHYSICAL EXAMINATION
OF JOHN L. SULLIVAN

That the exponents of the science of boxing with gloves are capable of gaining attention from the scientific and cultured, as well as sporting people, may be judged from the interest which has been shown in the physical examination of myself by that notable specialist, Dr. Dudley A. Sargent. The facts here contained have never before been given to the world.

John L. Sullivan

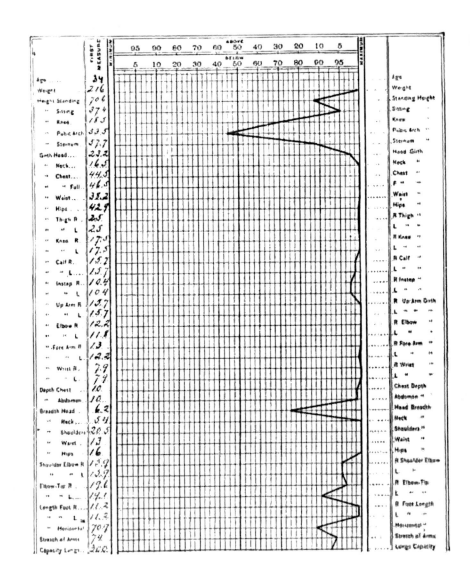

	FIRST MEASURE		ABOVE 95 90 80 70 60 50 40 30 20 10 5 / BELOW 5 10 20 30 40 50 60 70 80 90 95		
Age	34				Age
Weight	216				Weight
Height Standing	70 6				Standing Height
" Sitting	37 4				Sitting
" Knee	18 5				Knee
" Pubic Arch	33.5				Pubic Arch
" Sternum	57.7				Sternum
Girth Head	23.2				Head Girth
" Neck	16.5				Neck "
" Chest	44.5				Chest "
" " Full	46.5				F " "
" Waist	38.2				Waist "
" Hips	42.9				Hips "
" Thigh R	25				R Thigh "
" " L	25				L " "
" Knee R	17.5				R Knee "
" " L	17.5				L " "
" Calf R	15.2				R Calf "
" " L	15.7				L " "
" Instep R	10.4				R Instep "
" " L	10.4				L " "
" Up Arm R	13.7				R Up Arm Girth
" " L	15.7				L " " "
" Elbow R	12.2				R Elbow "
" " L	11.8				L " "
" Fore Arm R	13				R Fore Arm "
" " L	12.2				L " "
" Wrist R	7.9				R Wrist "
" " L	7.4				L " "
Depth Chest	10				Chest Depth
" Abdomen	10				Abdomen "
Breadth Head	6.2				Head Breadth
" Neck	5 4				Neck "
" Shoulders	20 5				Shoulders "
" Waist	13				Waist "
" Hips	16				Hips "
Shoulder Elbow R	13.9				R Shoulder Elbow
" " L	13.9				L " "
Elbow-Tip R	19.6				R Elbow-Tip
" " L	19.1				L " "
Length Foot R	11.2				R Foot Length
" " L	11.2				L " "
" Horizontal	70.7				Horizontal "
Stretch of Arms	74				Stretch of Arms
Capacity Lungs	360				Lungs Capacity

REPORT OF
DR. D. A. SARGENT'S EXAMINATION

ANTHROPOMETRICAL CHART AND PLATES; ALSO, SPECIAL MEA-
SUREMENTS OF JOHN L. SULLIVAN, TAKEN WHILE IN TRAINING
FOR THE CONTEST WITH JAMES CORBETT, SHOWING PHYSICAL
RECORD AND MUSCULAR DEVELOPMENT.

CAMBRIDGE, MASSACHUESETTS
August 16, 1892.

I have given John L. Sullivan a physical examination by the same
method that I have pursued during the past 15 years, in examining men,
women and children of various classes in the community. The chart by
which Sullivan's physical characteristics are shown was made from a
table based upon the measurements of several thousand students and
athletes, ranging in age from 17 to 30 years.

The chart is so constructed as to show the number of persons in a
community who surpass or fail to attain a certain size or degree of physical development, and may also be used to show the distribution of physical power as determined by actual tests of strength.

In this instance, I shall use the chart to show how Sullivan compares
physically with the student and athletic type, and comment at some length
upon his wide variation from the normal.

According to Sullivan's history, he is 34 years of age. Weighs 216
pounds without clothes, and is five feet ten and one-half inches in height
without shoes. This weight is considerably in excess of what it should be
for a man in good condition, of this stature, and is surpassed by less than
1% of the persons on my tables.

In height, standing, Sullivan surpasses 88% of all those examined,
arid in height, sitting, 95%. In the height of the lower leg, however, which
is represented on the chart by the height of knee, Sullivan surpasses but
70% of those examined, while in length of thigh as indicated by height of
pubic arch he only surpasses 45%.

This is the only measurement in which Sullivan is below the normal.
As the height of knee and length of thigh are the two factors that contribute the most in raising the total height above the average, it is safe to
assume that he would have been at least six feet two inches in total
height had his legs been as long proportionately as his body. His sitting
height is now 53.14% of his total height.

It is interesting to conjecture what the probable influence of this discrepancy has been upon Sullivan's ability as a boxer. Would two or three inches additional length of leg have added anything to his quickness, power or endurance?

I am of the opinion that other things being equal, increased length of thigh adds to a man's speed as a runner for distances from 50 to 600 yards, but quickness in starting, and the ability of rapidly changing one's position, through small spaces, in all directions, as is necessary in boxing, are more likely to be possessed by men of relatively short legs. Add to this advantage what is gained in mechanical power and endurance by the use of the short levers, and it will be seen that Sullivan's short thighs have probably added to, rather than detracted from, his efficiency as a boxer. As a general rule tall men have less endurance than men of the average stature. As increased height is due in most cases to increased length of leg, great stature, if accompanied with a relatively short body must be looked upon as indicative of constitutional weakness rather than constitutional strength.

All of Sullivan's girth measurements are unusually large, and most of them exceed the maximum. The girth of head is 23 and 2/10 inches, and surpasses in this respect 97.5% of all those examined.

A large head usually indicates a great amount of nervous energy, and when accompanied by a large neck is as much a sign of physical force as a large trunk and limbs.

In this case the neck is 16.5 inches in circumference and exceeds the largest measurement of this part taken by 7/10 of an inch. The natural chest is 44.5 inches in circumference and the inflated chest 46.5 inches, the former exceeds the maximum measurement on my tables 1.2 inch, and the latter one and 6/10 inches. Sullivan's circumference below the chest muscles, the ninth rib measurement so called, is 40.9 inches natural and 43.7 inches inflated. This measurement is not indicated on the chart, but I have come to regard it of more importance than the chest measurement as it does not include so many large muscles, and shows the actual mobility of the ribs in full, deep 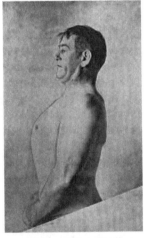 breathing. The abdominal method of respiration, practiced by Sullivan and other athletes, goes far to compensate for the small expansion shown by the difference in the measurements of the natural and inflated chest. The circumference of the waist is 38.2 inches, and just equals the largest measurement of this part on my tables. The hips are 42.9 inches in girth and are exceeded by the measurements of but one other person.

The thighs are each 25 inches in circumference, and are exceeded by only three other persons, the largest one having a thigh girth of 26.4 inches. The circumference of the knee is 17.5 inches, which surpasses the maximum on my tables by one inch. The above measurements of chest, waist, hips, thighs and knees may well be considered Sullivan's strong points, for, although in immediate effectiveness in his art, great size of arms, and shoulders may be of importance, it is difficult to see how these members could be of long-continued service without the large trunk, as a reservoir of vital action, and the powerful hips and thighs as a basis of support.

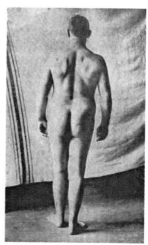

The calves, ankles and feet, though well developed, are not proportionately up to the other parts.

The calf is 15.7 inches in circumference, and surpasses over 98% of those examined, the maximum measurement of this part being 16.9 inches. The girth of the ankle which is not given in the chart is 9.6 inches, while the girth of instep is 10.4 inches. The largest measurement which I have of this part is 11.4 inches.

In the girth of the arms, elbow and wrist, Sullivan's measurements again go up into the region of the maximum. His girth of upper arm contracted, is 15.7 inches, right elbow 12.2, left elbow 11.8, right forearm 13 inches, left forearm 12.2 inches, while both wrists are 7.9 inches. It is interesting to note that Sullivan's upper arm is exactly the same girth as that credited to John C. Heenan. The left forearm has been fractured, and the favoring this member has received, undoubtedly accounts for the difference in development of the two forearms. One of Sullivan's strongest points, is his great depth of chest, as shown by plate, representing a side view during extreme inflation. Although he is surpassed by one or two others, on my tables,

in this measurement, when his great breadth of chest is also taken into consideration, the antero-posterior diameter is rather remarkable. Where breadth, or depth of chest is in excess of the normal, great strength is usually associated with the greater breadth, while increased vital capacity or endurance is thought to accompany the greater depth.

All of Sullivan's breadth, except his breadth of head, surpass the maximum, his shoulders being 20.5 inches, waist 13 inches, and hips 16 inches. His shoulders are not quite so broad as they would be were the muscles in this region as well developed as those of the arms and chest, but while this development of the shoulders, would add to perfection of figure, from the artist's or sculptor's ideal, there is no doubt but what the antagonizing influ-

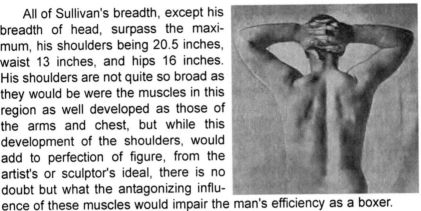

ence of these muscles would impair the man's efficiency as a boxer.

The length of the upper arm as indicated on the chart by the measurement from the shoulder to the elbow, is 15.9 inches. This exceeds 95% of those measured, but falls short of the maximum by nearly three inches. The length of the forearm, as shown by the measurement from the elbow to the tips of the fingers, is 19.6 inches on the right hand, and 19.1 inches on the left, the latter being shortened by the fractured forearm, to which I have previously alluded. This measurement also surpasses over 96% of those examined, though falling two inches short of the highest.

It is interesting to notice that the arms, though proportionately short for the girths, are not so for the sitting height, or as short comparatively as the legs. Length of forearm is an advantage to a boxer, though proportionate length of upper arm would detract from his physical power, and it would be interesting, could we determine whether the added strength of blow that can be delivered from close-set shoulders and short upper arms, would more than compensate for the longer reach of longer arms. Sullivan's stretch of arm is 74 inches, and is surpassed by over 6% of those examined, the maximum being 80 inches.

The length of foot is 11.2 inches, and is surpassed by 1% of those examined, the longest foot being 11.6 inches. This is equivalent to about 16% of the total height, which differs but little from the artist's ancient canon of proportions.

Sullivan's lung capacity is 300 cubic inches, and is surpassed by only 5%, the highest record, on my books, at the present time, being 400 cubic inches.

Before summing up the physical condition of this man, a comparison of some of the measurements before and while in training will be of service.

In so doing, I shall only give those parts, where a change of girths has taken place, due to the reduction of fat.

	June 2nd	August 13th	Difference
Weight	236 pounds	216 pounds	20 pounds
Girth of neck	17.1 inches	16.5 inches	.6 inches
Girth of chest	46.1 inches	44.5 inches	1.6 inches
Girth of chest inflated	48.4 inches	46.5 inches	1.9 inches
Girth of waist	42.1 inches	38.2 inches	3.9 inches
Girth of hips	46.1 inches	42.9 inches	3.2 inches
Girth of thighs	26.4 inches	25.0 inches	1.4 inches
Girth of calves	15.9 inches	15.7 inches	.6 inches

It will be observed by this table that in many persons fat makes up a considerable portion of what is measured as muscle, and it is only fair to say, that the tables, from which my charts are made, have been compiled from the measurements of men, at that age when fat does not usually encumber them.

We often read of 17-inch biceps, and 17-inch calves, but these proportions are more likely to be found on dime museum freaks than on well-developed athletes. As a matter of fact, nature has but little use for such limbs, and where they exist, they are apt to be accompanied by some constitutional defect, that renders them inefficient.

In the language of athletes, a good "big" man is better than a good "little" man, but where one thoroughly sound and well proportioned big man can be found, a hundred men of average size can be met with, who are better prepared, constitutionally, to stand the wear and tear of life, and contend with its successes and reverses.

It is this fact that makes Sullivan something of a phenomenon, for with his large limbs and powerful trunk he has inherited the vital machinery to operate them with all of the rapidity that characterizes men of smaller parts and less weight.

How rapid these movements are, may be judged by an actual test, made by Sullivan, with an electrical apparatus, specially devised by Dr. G. W. Fitz, of Cambridge, for taking and recording reaction time, and rate of speed. In this instance Sullivan was requested to strike at a bag suspended from the ceiling, upon seeing a given signal. When he first tried this experiment, in June, the time which elapsed between seeing the signal and striking out at the bag was .48 seconds, and the time which it took his fist to travel 40 centimeters (or 15.7 inches) was .08 seconds.

Two months later, after he had been in training a few weeks, the same experiment was repeated, and the time which elapsed between seeing the signal and striking out, was .43 seconds, and the speed of the blow, was 15.7 inches in .57 seconds.

At the present time, the apparatus has not been tried by a sufficient number of persons to obtain sufficient data for formulating any important conclusions, but one can form an approximate idea of the force and momentum of a blow struck by a man weighing 216 pounds with his fist moving at a velocity of about 20 miles an hour.

It is to be regretted that an actual test of Sullivan's physical strength could not have been made by the same method as that employed in taking the strength of those with whose measurements he has been compared. The rigorous exactions of training, rendered such a test inexpedient when the man was in condition to make them, and the tests made two months previous would not do him justice.

Therefore, in summing up our estimate of Sullivan's physical condition, we must judge him partly by his measurements - which may be termed his potential strength - and the way his system reacts under the trials of training. This routine consists of walking and running 10 to 20 miles a day, exercise with two-pound dumbbells for a half hour; playing handball against an expert for an hour or two, punching a striking bag for an hour, skipping rope from 500 to 1,000 times without stopping, and bathing and swimming for a half hour.

After six weeks of this daily drill, the stomach and nutritive system seem to be in the best condition of the vital apparatus. The heart's impulse was strong and regular and only rose from 80 to 120 beats a minute, after 200 jumps with the skipping rope, at the end of the forenoon's work. The respiration was a little hurried and somewhat labored, for a man in good condition, and I cannot help thinking that Sullivan's respiratory apparatus is his weak point vitally. By this assertion I do not mean that the lungs are diseased, or that they have a diminutive capacity, compared with other men of his proportions. But I mean that they are functionally weak, as compared with his other remarkable organs, and considering the amount of energy he is capable of expending in a very short time, and the amount of waste resulting from this increased activity, as well as the immediate consumption of fat, in the tissues, the question of how to relieve breathlessness after vigorous exertion is a matter that may concern him as he advances in years.

Sullivan's reaction time as tested by the instrument referred to, although reasonably quick, shows no evidence of irritability of the brain centers or nervous system.

The economical way he has of doing ordinary things and the apparently sluggish and indolent manner he assumes when not in active exercise might lead a stranger to assume that he was wanting in energy, and was just recovering from an attack of nervous prostration. But this is the way men of power conserve their energy for great physical or mental efforts. In fact it takes a great occasion to fully arouse them from their apparent stupor, as was the case with Daniel Webster and Patrick Henry.

It would be a valuable lesson for the American people to learn that, in order to generate and sustain an unusual display of energy they must follow their efforts with an unusual amount of rest.

In looking for the original source of Sullivan's remarkable physical power, we must ascribe it to a happy combination and balance of the several temperaments inherited from his ancestry, near and remote, and the motor apparatus inherited from his mother. This is apparent in the shape of the hips and thighs, the lines of the shoulders and chest, and in the ankles and wrists.

All men, though the product of two beings, are born of women; but that a woman, usually considered the weaker vessel physically, should be so able to impress her progeny with the strong points of her own physique as to enable him to meet all comers in a test of skill, strength, and endurance for a term of a dozen years, is, to my mind, the most valuable lesson of this man's life.

If the women of the land can learn from this man's physical development, how potent the influence of the mother is in fashioning and transmitting not only the refined and delicate parts of her organism, but also the brawn and sinew that conquers both opponents and environments and sustains the race, John L. Sullivan will have served to illustrate a very important fact.

D. A. SARGENT
HISTORY PAPER

AUGUST 13, 1892

Full Name: John L. Sullivan
Occupation: Boxer
Date of Birth: October I 5, 1858
Birthplace: Boston
Father's Racial Origin: Irish
Mother's Racial Origin: Irish
Occupation of Father: Laborer

If father is dead, of what did he die?

Pneumonia.

If mother is dead, of what did she die?

Rheumatism of the heart.

Which of your parents do you most resemble?

Mother.

Is your general health good?

Yes.

Have you always had good health?

Yes.

What hereditary disease, if any, is there in your family?

None.

Indicated diseases as you may have had:

Boils. Paralysis (threatened). Colds in Head or Throat. Rheumatism. Skin Eruptions.

Name any others that have left ill-effects.

None.

What injuries have you received?

Arm broken.

What surgical operation have you undergone?

Setting the above.

When did you first begin to practice athletics?

1878.

Were you naturally strong and active?

Always.

Did you surpass those of your own age, size, etc., in your own community in the practice of your specialties when you first began training?

Yes.

Were your father, mother, or grandparents noted in any way for their strength and endurance (state particulars)?

From what I have heard I should say so, particularly my mother.

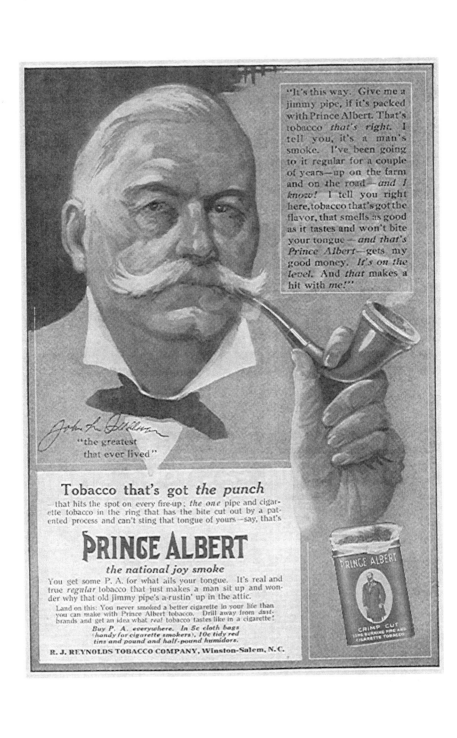

AVAILABLE NOW

Scientific Boxing: The Deluxe Edition
by James J. Corbett

In 1892, "Gentleman" James J. Corbett defeated John L. Sullivan to become the heavyweight champion of the world. Using his own "scientific boxing" techniques, Corbett delivered a blistering lesson to the previously unbeatable Sullivan, ending the fight with a knockout in the 21st round. With Corbett's win, a new era in boxing began.

Corbett is considered by many to be the "father of modern boxing" for being the first person to apply scientific principles to the art of pugilism. In *Scientific Boxing*, the creator of such boxing innovations as the "left hook" distills his scientific methodology into an accessible manual of boxing techniques. This classic book contains sections on fundamental boxing techniques, fouling techniques, and the various boxing rules of his time.

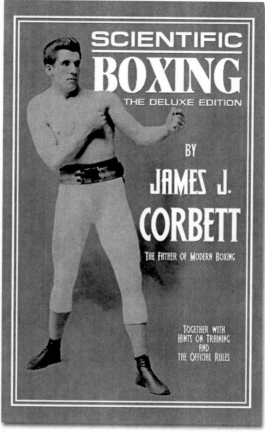

This deluxe edition of *Scientific Boxing* contains additional photos and an added account of the fight between Corbett and Sullivan.

ISBN 978-0-9737698-9-0
WWW.PROMETHEAN-PRESS.COM

ADDITIONAL TITLES IN THIS SERIES:

The Straight Left: How to Cultivate It by Jim Driscoll
The Text Book of Boxing by Jim Driscoll
Out-Fighting by Jim Driscoll
Ringcraft by Jim Driscoll
The Art of Boxing and Manual of Training by Billy Edwards

LaVergne, TN USA
05 November 2009
163167LV00009B/83/P